Human Nature, Class, and Ethnicity

Human Nature, Class, and Ethnicity

**Milton
M.
Gordon**

**New York
Oxford University Press
1978**

Library of Congress Cataloging in Publication Data

Gordon, Milton Myron, 1918-
    Human nature, class, and ethnicity.

    Includes index.
    1. Race relations.   2.   Social classes.   3.   Man.
I.   Title.
HT1521.G67   301.45' .1'042   77-8881
ISBN 0-19-502236-X
ISBN 0-19-502237-8 pbk.

To my *wife*,
Gesa—
worldclass violinist
and
worldclass human being

Acknowledgments

I wish to thank the following sources for permission to republish my articles and chapters listed below:

Harvard University Press, for "Toward A General Theory of Racial and Ethnic Group Relations," from Nathan Glazer and Daniel P. Moynihan (eds.), *Ethnicity: Theory and Experience* (Cambridge, Mass., Harvard University Press, 1975), pp. 84–110. Copyright © 1975 by the President and Fellows of Harvard College.

The University of Chicago Press, for "*Kitty Foyle* and the Concept of Class as Culture," *American Journal of Sociology*, Vol. 53, No. 3 (November 1947), pp. 210–17.

The American Sociological Association, for "A Qualification of The Marginal Man Theory," *American Sociological Review*, Vol. 6, No. 1 (February 1941), pp. 52–58. (This article was published under my original name, Milton M. Goldberg. I changed my name legally from Milton Myer Goldberg to Milton Myron Gordon in the fall of 1941.)

Daedalus, Journal of the American Academy of Arts and Sciences, for "Assimilation in America: Theory and Reality," *Daedalus* (Spring 1961). pp. 263–85.

Random House, Inc., for "Marginality and The Jewish Intellectual," in Peter I. Rose (ed.), *The Ghetto and Beyond: Essays on Jewish Life in America* (New York, Random House, 1969), pp. 477–91. Copyright © by Random House, Inc.

Morroe Berger, for "Social Structure and Goals in Group Relations," in Morroe Berger, Theodore Abel, and Charles H. Page (eds.), *Freedom and Control in Modern Society* (New York, D. Van Nostrand Company, Inc., 1954), pp. 141–57.

American Association of University Professors, for "Social Class and American Intellectuals," *American Association of University Professors Bulletin*, Vol. 40, No. 4 (Winter 1954–55), pp. 517–28.

Social Forces, for "The Concept of the Sub-Culture and Its Application," *Social Forces*, Vol. 26, No. 1 (October 1947), pp. 40–42. Copyright © The University of North Carolina Press.

Duke University Press, for Chapter 8 (slightly revised), "A System of Social Class Analysis," from *Social Class in American Sociology* by Milton M. Gordon (Durham, N. C., Duke University Press, 1958), pp. 234–56.

Oxford University Press for Chapter 2, "The Subsociety and The Subculture" (slightly revised), and Chapter 3, "The Nature of Assimilation" (abridged and slightly revised), from *Assimilation in American Life: The Role of Race, Religion, and National Origins* by Milton M. Gordon (New York, Oxford University Press, 1964). Copyright © 1964 by Oxford University Press, Inc.

Contents

Preface

Why is a sociologist writing about human nature? Perhaps I can borrow an answer from the literature of mountaineering by simply stating: "Because it is there." Not only, of course, is it there, but it is highly relevant to the understanding of human behavior. This I have tried to demonstrate in the first two essays in this book. The first of these essays was written especially for this collection and has never before been published. It is a long piece, divided into two parts: the first portion reviews the history of sociology from the perspective of the degree of attention given by major and representative sociologists to the question of human nature and psychological variables in their work; the second section presents my own theory of human nature, tries to provide some account of how and why I derived it, and exposits the reasons for my belief that sociologists must take human nature and psychological variables into serious account if their work is to be optimally fruitful. The second essay, which was written and published earlier, incorporates some attention to the subject of human nature in the development of a general theory of racial and ethnic group relations.

The other essays in this book comprise highlighted portions of the theoretical work I have been doing for a generation in the fields of racial and ethnic group relations and social stratification, and consist of articles published in various journals and collections and a few chapters or portions of chapters from my two previously published books, *Social Class in American Sociology* and *Assimilation in American Life*. The question naturally arises, then, as to whether my current salient concern with the subject of human nature represents an abrupt break with my previous work which was carried out within the standard sociological framework. My answer is definitely that it does not. Both sociological perspectives and psychological perspectives are necessary to provide a full and satisfactory account of human behavior. In fact, my book on assimilation, which explored in considerable depth the nature of pluralistic group life in America (and, by implication, in any multi-ethnic society) constituted a deliberate attempt to place the study of racial and ethnic group relations in a sociological framework which, I was convinced, had been largely ignored in the field's preoccupation with culturally and socially produced personality variables in the study of prejudice formation. The book's highly favorable reception and continued use and resonance justifies, I believe, that attempt. But science does not stand still. Neither, and this is simply the complement to my previous sentence, does the scientist's attempt to probe more and more deeply into the dynamics of his subject matter. This is the spirit in which my growing interest in the subject of human nature was conceived. It is for the sake of achieving a fuller understanding of social phenomena that I advocate the development of a serious concern for the nature of human nature by all social scientists, whether they call themselves sociologists, psychologists, anthropologists, political scientists, or historians. A general theory of human behavior will require the use of variables and data from all these disciplines and a willingness to cross traditional disciplinary boundaries in the search for convincing causal explanations of man's multi-faceted actions—actions which he variously undertakes with blithe unconcern for the historically and somewhat arbitrarily created lines which separate university departments in the social sciences which have him as their focus. In no way, then, do I consider myself to be a sociologist who is becoming doubtful of the value of the sociological perspective. I do regard myself, however, as a sociologist who is unwilling to stop at artificially constructed disciplinary fences when I feel that I need variables beyond those fences to help me in providing a fuller and more satisfactory account of the behavior of man. *Satis dictum*.

At several points in the development of my introductory essay on human nature, I asked for critical comment on selected issues, or bibliographical assistance, from several of my colleagues either at the University of Massachusetts or in the Five College area. In all cases, the response was gracious. I wish, therefore, to thank Charles Page, Randall Stokes, Richard Tessler, and Curt Tausky of the University of Massachusetts sociology department, Nancy Angrist Myers, Seymour Epstein, and Daniel Anderson of the University psychology department, and Cecelia Marie Kenyon of the Smith College government department for their comments or advice. If I have not always used their comments or bibliographical suggestions to maximum advantage, it is obviously my fault, not theirs. I should also like to say that it has been a pleasure to deal with James Anderson of the Oxford University Press. His enthusiasm for, and cordial reception to, the idea of this book provided me with the ideal publication ambience in which to work. The libraries of the University of Massachusetts and Amherst College were indispensable for my task. And finally, to the University of Massachusetts at Amherst, I am deeply grateful for the sabbatical semester which gave me the time to do the research for, and to write on, the subject of human nature, and in general to put this collection of essays together.

My thanks to my wife, Gesa Gordon, for just being herself are, I hope, adequately expressed on the dedication page.

Amherst, Massachusetts
August, 1977   *Milton M. Gordon*

part I

Human
Nature
&
Social Action

Human Nature & Sociology

Every sociological theory contains either explicitly or implicitly a theory of human nature. It cannot be otherwise. The discipline of sociology attempts to explain and predict human behavior, and though it does so from its traditional perspective of group life, social structure, institutions, norms, roles, and other interactive artifacts, the stubborn fact remains that these interactive constructs are themselves the crystallized results of behaviors of individuals who have performed actions in the past or are performing them in the present. The explanatory function, causal analysis, or call it what one will, demands, then, that the explanation of past behavior or prediction of future behavior call into play the specifics of particular motivations of actors under particular conditions, and this process, in turn, demands an implicit or explicit judgment about how much or how little, and in what ways, the human biological organism is subject to environmental influences at particular stages in his (or her) development. This is true whether we are concerned with the causes of crime and the treatment of criminals, the nature and dynamics of social stratification, the development and containment of racial and ethnic conflict, the workings of an industrial bureaucracy, the rise and fall of birth and death rates, the interactions of family members, or the causes and control of international warfare. In all of these research endeavors and the policy recommendations which emanate from the findings and discussion of particular studies, some conception of the basic nature of the human actor, ranging from extreme biological determinism (rare among sociologists) to extreme cultural determinism, is present, whether or not it is laid squarely and openly on the table for examination. Furthermore, the extrapolation of policy implications from research results will usually depend heavily on the assumptions about the nature of man which underlie the sociologist's recommendations. Thus the accuracy of these assumptions becomes an unavoidably crucial issue. I argue strongly, therefore, that the construction of a valid theory of human nature is indispensable to the sociological enterprise.

The logical necessity of constructing an accurate view of the nature of the human being inheres not only in sociology, of course, but in any science or discipline which aspires to deal with the mysteries and complexities of human behavior. Indeed, speculation about the nature of human nature dates back to the earliest writings on history, philosophy, religion, and government, and no doubt has always been a favorite parlor (or spatial equivalent) pastime of the average man without special intellectual training or particular inclination to offer his thoughts to the world on papyrus, parchment, or paper. In the more modern era of western civilization, the issue was joined, as is well known, by the contrasting views of the three most prominent political philosphers of the seventeenth and eighteenth centuries—the approach to and fruition of the Enlightenment period which ushered in the contemporary world: Thomas Hobbes, who conceived of man in an imagined state of nature prior to the rise of governmental institutions as "enemy to every [other] man" and summarily characterized human life in this stage as, in the famous phrase, "solitary, poor, nasty, brutish, and short;" Jean-Jacques Rousseau, who painted a glowing picture of a noble savage living idyllically, peacefully, and compassionately prior to the onset of corrupting civilization; and John Locke who, while taking an intermediate and sometimes ambivalent position on the condition of man in the state of nature, saw him at least as virtually infinitely malleable, representing that *tabula rasa* or blank slate upon which experience could write with an unfettered hand and easily lead into the paths of reason and reasonableness. Unsophisticated as the contexts and particulars of these presentations were in the light of modern behavioral science, it is interesting to note that in many ways they still represent modal positions competing for validation in a much more complex framework, none of them wholly without champions even in the arena of contemporary scientific discourse.

For those thinkers who came to call themselves sociologists (or who were later called so) in the nineteenth century, however, the question of the intrinsic nature of man tended to fade into the background, although it did not disappear entirely. For Auguste Comte, Henri Saint-Simon, Karl Marx, and Herbert Spencer, the salient issues revolved around society and its institutions, social and intellectual evolution, social structure, pressing questions of social reform or revolution, the relationships between state and society, and other macrocosmic matters whose resolution did not appear to call into play a close examination of the human psyche. There are at least two principal reasons for this relative preoccupation with the total societal enterprise. The intellectual currents of the Enlightenment and the breakup of feudal society which culminated in the French Revolution produced a series of vast social transformations and upheavals in nineteenth-century Europe which appeared to invite both analytical and prescriptive attention to the broader currents of rapid social change as they were set in motion by the presumably discernible laws or uniformities of society itself. Comte, who coined the term "sociology," and is traditionally considered to be the "father" of the discipline, had proclaimed the emergence of human thought from previous theological and metaphysical stages to a new scientific or "positive" stage in which society could at last be studied objectively without the hindering baggage of obfuscating preconceptions. And in his famous "hierarchy of the sciences," sociology stands at the top, and psychology is conspicuous by its absence. Although psychologistic concerns were present in the writings of the classical economists and the Utilitarian philosophers, and though even Spencer's work was not untouched by such concerns, the dominant mode of

5

nineteenth-century sociological thought as it confronted the multifarious and burgeoning problems of its own age was holistic, organismic, evolutionary, and prescriptive. It left little room for consideration of the nature of human nature.

The second reason for sociology's relative lack of concern with the individual and his native or developing psyche was both pragmatic and, at least on the surface, logical. If sociology really existed as a field of serious intellectual study, if it were not simply a neologized version of political philosophy or history or economics, it had to have, presumably, a subject matter of its own. The natural sciences clearly had their own specific subject areas; the preoccupations of a biologist did not, at least at that time, encroach upon those of a physicist, nor those of an astronomer on a chemist. In those disciplines that dealt with the behavior of man, the student of politics studied government and the state, the economist concerned himself with behavior in the market place, the psychologist had preempted the study of the individual. What was left for the sociologist, that Johnny-come-lately who now presumed to discern yet another hitherto uncharted star in the behavioral horizons? This was a question that was of particular concern to the second generation of sociological "fathers" who wrote in the last decade or so of the nineteenth century and the first quarter of the twentieth. "The trouble," stated Georg Simmel as late as 1917, "is that the science of society [read sociology], in contrast to other sciences that are well established, is in the unfortunate postion of still having to prove its right to exist."[1] Simmel found the basic subject matter of sociology in social interaction itself and attempted to construct a "pure sociology" of forms of social interaction that would deal with their nature and consequences.

However the definitive prescription for sociology's subject matter—one that has played a dominant and decisive role in the development of the subject throughout the twentieth century up to the present—had been written by Emile Durk-

[1]Kurt H. Wolff, ed. and trans., *The Sociology of George Simmel* (Glencoe, Ill., Free Press, 1950), p. 4 (from *Grundfragen der Soziologie*, 1917).

heim, the great French sociologist, as early as 1895. In his treatise, *The Rules of Sociological Method*, published in that year, Durkheim had delivered the dictum that the compelling function of the sociologist was to study what he called "social facts." Social facts were manifestations of group and collective life such as moral values, customs, laws, currents of thought and feeling, and social structures, all external to the individual and exercising a coercive restraint upon him, regardless of his individual will. Individual psychological states could not be used to explain these social collectivities, Durkheim declared, since the latter existed prior to the appearance of the particular individual on the scene. Sociology and psychology are two distinct disciplines since, "social facts do not differ from psychological facts in quality only: *they have a different substratum;* they evolve in a different milieu; and they depend on different conditions."[2]

The distinctive subject matter of sociology, then, according to Durkheim, consisted of social facts. And these social phenomena constituted not only the effects in a statement of causal relationships, but also the precipitating factors, as declared in his well-known methodological principle: "The determining cause of a social fact should be sought among the social facts preceding it and not among the states of the individual consciousness."[3] Two years later, Durkheim published his classic study, *Suicide*, in which rates of self-destruction for different collectivities at different time periods were quantitatively related to degrees and types of social cohesion presumed to be characteristic of these social groupings. It is not too much to say that, putting aside its relatively primitive, though pioneering, methodological techniques, this work became the prototype for much of twentieth century quantitative sociology, and that Durkheim's strictures on the subject matter of sociological investigation and sociological explanation carried the day even unto the

[2]Emile Durkheim, *The Rules of Sociological Method* (Glencoe, Ill., Free Press, 1938, copyright, The University of Chicago), p. xlix, in "Author's Preface to Second Edition." (Italics as in original.)
[3]*The Rules of Sociological Method*, p. 110. (Italicized in original.)

present. In effect, in the modern language of multivariate analysis, Durkheim laid down the principle that the function of the sociologist was to study sociological variables only and to use only sociological variables in both the cause and effect portions of generalizations about human behavior.

It is not my purpose in this essay to attempt to provide an exhaustive (and exhausting) account of the relationship of every major or prominent sociologist of the past or present to the issues of psychologistic concerns and a theory of human nature. The identification of major trends in each era constitutes my major goal in this portion of my paper, and this portion itself is a prelude which I hope will aid in transmitting a richer and more resonant understanding of my own efforts to justify the need for, and to construct, a theory of human nature which will be useful to sociologists. It may be said, however, that of the sociologists whose major work falls in the twentieth century, those who insisted on maintaining some focus on the individual human actor and on the need for including in the sociological discipline the subjective meaning of action for the actor, a stance which necessarily encapsulates attitudes and motivations, helped keep alive a necessary link between sociological analysis and the human being as a dynamic thinking and feeling element in the behavioral process. Of these, none was more eminent and influential than Max Weber, perhaps the greatest of the pioneer sociologists.

Weber's work was so vast in its scope, and he so studiously avoided any integrative summary or codification of it, that to attempt to interpret its significance for, and relevance to even my specialized concern in this paper poses problems of some magnitude. Nevertheless, it is indisputable that, at least in his methodological writings, Weber regarded the central task of sociology as the explanation of social action, and that the agents of such action were individuals for whom their respective actions had subjective meaning. The possibility, and thus the necessity, of *Verstehen*, or interpretive understanding, of the motives of human beings in social interaction served to differentiate the social from the natural

8

sciences: "We can accomplish [in sociology] something which is never attainable in the natural sciences, namely the subjective understanding of the action of the component individuals. The natural sciences on the other hand cannot do this, being limited to the formation of causal uniformities in objects and events and the explanation of individual facts by applying them."[4] And, furthermore, "for the subjective interpretation of action in sociological work . . . collectivities must be treated as *solely* the resultants and modes of organization of the particular acts of individual persons, since these alone can be treated as agents in a course of subjectively understandable action."[5]

Instances of social action are placed by Weber into four categories established by particular combinations of type of source, presence or non-presence of rationality, and type of goal. There is 1) *zweckrational* action, or rational action directed towards a goal which, in itself, contains cost-benefit calculation; 2) *wertrational* action, or action directed towards the achieving of a particular value; 3) affective or emotional action; and 4) traditional action, which has been induced by custom and habituation.[6] In this typology Weber clearly recognizes both cognitive and emotional factors in human action and also the role of cultural norms and conditioning and some of the ways in which these elements are combined in human behavior. It would be difficult to argue, however, that this categorization is exhaustive, particularly in its combination of categorizing elements, and since it merely categorizes, it gives us no quantitative estimate of the predominance or relative frequency of these types of action in human behavior.

In his substantive writings, Weber's insistence on the importance of understanding the subjective meaning of ac-

[4]Max Weber, *The Theory of Social and Economic Organization*, trans. A. M. Henderson and Talcott Parsons, ed. Talcott Parsons (Glencoe, Ill., Free Press, 1947, p. 103.

[5]*The Theory of Social and Economic Organization*, p. 101. (Italics as in original.)

[6]For a thorough discussion of Weber's typology of social action, see Talcott Parsons, *The Structure of Social Action* (New York, Free Press, 1949), pp. 640–58. (Original publication by McGraw-Hill, 1937).

tion for the individual actor is reflected in his concern for the role of values and ideas in influencing outcomes in various institutional areas, not least the economic. If we interpret his voluminous writings on the relationship between religious values and economic systems as a "debate with the ghost of Marx," then this consistency between his methodological strictures and his substantive concerns is quite apparent. Nevertheless, in Weber's vast corpus of substantive monographs on religion and society, the rise of rationalization and bureaucracy in Western economic and political life, the role and dimensions of social stratification, and the various relationships between power and economy, leadership, and authority, all of it buttressed with a stunning historical knowledge denied to most sociologists, it is the larger framework of sociological structures, collectivities, and institutions that take center stage, while the analysis of the individual actor and his motivations recedes into the background. Certainly we do not get a theory of human nature from Weber. And while his insistence on value neutrality insulated him from most pejorative comment, his essential pessimism stemming from his fear of the creativity and charisma stifling "iron cage" which he believed that increasing rationalization and bureaucratization would tend to build for man, whether under capitalism or socialism, appears to be firmly based on a conception of indigenous trends in societal evolution rather than on anything innate in the human psyche. And in this pessimism, it is interesting to note that, in the words of Lewis Coser, "[Weber's] message is thus fundamentally at variance with that of most of his nineteenth-century forebears. He is not a prophet of glad tidings to come but a harbinger of doom and disaster."[7]

In the first quarter of the twentieth century, however, there was one lone and magisterial figure who produced a sociological *magnum opus* which was both pessimistic in tone and psychologistically oriented in its projection of a

[7]Lewis A. Coser, *Masters of Sociological Thought* (New York, Harcourt Brace, 1971), pp. 233–34.

society which changed only in recurrent cycles and merely succeeded in reproducing the human follies of the past. This was Vilfredo Pareto, the Italian engineer and economist who turned to sociology in the latter portion of his life and produced the *Treatise on General Sociology*, a gargantuan work of almost 2000 pages and one million words, orignally published in 1916, and made available to English-speaking readers in a four volume translation which was retitled *The Mind and Society* and first published in the United States in 1935.[8]

Like Weber, Pareto essentially begins with an analysis of types of social action. The classification is simpler, however, since Pareto wishes to make only a basic distinction between logical and non-logical action. The former term applies to all action where means and ends are logically conjoined, not only in the mind of the actor but objectively—that is, to the knowledgeable observer. Thus a carpenter who uses appropriate tools and methods to construct a picket fence has engaged in logical action. Engineering and strictly economic phenomena would be typical loci of logical action among men. Non-logical action embraces all other types of human action where, very simply, the previous criteria are not present. Non-logical action is Pareto's analytical target in his treatise. And his principal thesis is that human beings are engaged in a constant either hypocritical or, more characteristically, self-deluding process of attempting to make their generally non-logical behavior appear to be logical. In other words, they attempt to "logicalize" (Pareto's term), or "rationalize" (using this term now in the psychological or psychoanalytical sense rather than in Weber's meaning) their behavior.

The elements which make up this system of analysis are given by Pareto the arbitrary appellations of "residues" and "derivations." The residues stand for certain constant "instincts" or "sentiments" in man, while the "derivations" are theories, explanations, ideologies, and faith systems pro-

---

[8]Vilfredo Pareto, *The Mind and Society*, 4 vols., ed. Arthur Livingston (New York, Harcourt Brace, 1935).

11

duced by the actor to justify his behavior, which in reality is based on the residues. There are six basic types of residues and these types have such esoteric (except for the last) names as I. Instinct for Combinations; II. Group-Persistences (Persistence of Aggregates); III. Need of Expressing Sentiments by External Acts (Activity, Self-Expression); IV. Residues Connected with Sociality; V. Integrity of the Individual and His Appurtenances; and VI. The Sex Residues. Each type is usually also broken down in various subtypes. Pareto illustrates them all in vivid detail, drawing upon examples from history, literature, and myth, although their conceptual definitions tend towards a certain vagueness and lack of precision. Their attempted translation into terms familiar in the current social-scientific vocabulary would take more space than is here available. Suffice it to say that they appear to reduce to certain basic cognitive processes and to certain emotional predispositions congruent with receptivity to social change, desire for group-formation, stability, and security, need for self-expression and for affective social relationships, need for well-being and self-integrity, expression of hierarchical tendencies, and so on. The classification of "derivations" is into four types (also augmented by breakdown into numerous subtypes), namely: I. Assertion; II. Authority; III. Accords with Sentiments or Principles; and IV. Verbal Proofs. The relationship between these appellations and the processes of rationalization and logicalization which they are alleged to typify are perhaps more readily apparent on initial inspection.

There is a certain amount of ambiguity surrounding the question of whether Pareto actually advanced an "instinct" based explanation of man,[9] an ambiguity produced by his own lack of conceptual clarity on the point and his evident haste to get on (with great relish) with the matter of illustrat-

[9]For instance, Joseph Lopreato takes the position that many of Pareto's residues are "basic values or mores, deeply learned and entrenched." See his "Introduction" to a volume of selections from the *Treatise*: Joseph Lopreato, *Vilfredo Pareto* (New York, Thomas Y. Crowell, 1965), particularly pp. 7–10.

ing the gap between the real and the self-advanced motivations in human behavior. There is no doubt that he uses the word "instinct" profusely in his discussion of the residues. However, the residues are evidently to be considered as being at one remove from the instincts and sentiments which they represent, as the following passage indicates: "The residues . . . must not be confused with the sentiments or instincts to which they correspond. . . . The residues are the manifestations of sentiments and instincts just as the rising of the mercury in a thermometer is a manifestation of the rise in temperature. Only elliptically and for the sake of brevity do we say that residues, along with appetites, interests, etc. . . . are the main factors in determining the social equilibrium."[10] And it is evident that he is not interested in providing an in-depth analysis of the origins of the psychological bases of human action, for early in his discussion he warns the reader that "Non-logical actions originate chiefly in definite psychic states, sentiments, subconscious feelings and the like. It is the province of psychology to investigate such psychic states. Here we start with them as data of fact, without going beyond that."[11] Moreover, he does not purport to enumerate a complete system of basic human instincts since only those that result in the constructed derivatives are to be subsumed under his concept of residues. Nevertheless, it is difficult to stray far from an "instinct" interpretation in the face of such a rock-like assertion as "The element a [that is, the residues] corresponds . . . to certain instincts of man . . . and it is probably because of its correspondence to instincts that it is virtually constant in social phenomena."[12]

At least a portion of the scheme of residues and derivations is then used by Pareto in the last quarter of the *Treatise* to help explain the cycles of change and stability in the larger society, particularly in the economic and political spheres. In

[10]*The Mind and Society*, p. 511 (numbered paragraph 875 in Pareto's preferred method of citation).
[11]*The Mind and Society*, p. 88 (par. 161).
[12]*The Mind and Society*, p. 501 (par. 850).

his famous theory of the "circulation of the elites," elites dominated by Class I residues (Instinct for Combinations) rule by cunning, innovations, and manipulation but are eventually overturned and replaced by a newly arising elite which is impelled much more powerfully by the Class II residues (of Group Persistences) and thus emphasizes the use of force, loyalty to group, physical courage, and zeal. Eventually, particularly if the channels of social mobility are blocked, they in turn are replaced by those typifying the first group of residues. In other words, Machiavelli's "lions" and "foxes" in a perpetual cycle of oscillation. It should be noted that Pareto here confronts himself with a fundamental inconsistency in his analytical scheme which he nowhere resolves. If the residues are, in fact, representative of "instincts," which he has hitherto designated as "constants" in human behavior, why should they differ in intensity and incidence for different groups, or for that matter, different individuals?

Inconsistencies aside, and granting the lack of depth and completeness in his psychological analysis, it is clear that Pareto presented to the world a not entirely implausible picture of man and society which was quite different from that embraced by most of his contemporary and antecedent sociologists—a social landscape in which the emotional predispositions of man, coupled with his indestructible capacity for self-delusion, do much more to produce social institutions and structures than the other way around. The conception of man is one which summons up the grim and chilling views of Hobbes and Machiavelli. The projection for society contains none of the optimism which was present in the work of many of the earlier sociologists who saw in their discipline either a means to, or a discernment of the improvement of the social order. In its totality it is a point of view which must be reckoned with, examined, and studied, whatever ultimate conclusion one may reach about it. The fact that Pareto's work, although it was received with enthusiasm when it first appeared in America by George Homans and was given careful attention by Talcott Parsons, has not played a significant role in the development of twentieth-century sociology thus far (in spite of a certain respectful consideration given to his more strictly societal analysis and his theory of elite circulation), has hindered the ability of the discipline to provide a fully rounded account of social action and its consequences and unduly restricted the spectrum of its analytical modes. Only in very recent years, as we shall see, has the ghost of Pareto begun to reappear, often unrecognized, but casting at least some light on the human condition in ways which may eventually affect sociology deeply enough to put his work in entirely new perspective.

Among the early American sociologists, psychic forces and instinctual tendencies were frequently recognized and alluded to but put into different frameworks depending on the writer's overall conception of society and its possibilities. Lester Ward, the first president of the American Sociological Society, believed that the feelings and emotions of individuals were the basic dynamic forces of society and thus "the social forces are . . . psychic, and hence sociology must have a psychologic base."[13] The combination of social (psychic) forces he enumerates reflects his essentially optimistic and anti-Spencerian view of the potentialities of human planning and collective action for producing a better society. In addition to a simple pleasure-seeking and pain-avoiding dynamism, a sexual drive, and a positive affective feeling for family members, man is also assigned a moral force "seeking the safe and good," an esthetic force "seeking the beautiful," and an intellectual force "seeking the useful and true."[14]

On the other hand, Ward's contemporary ideological antithesis, William Graham Sumner, vigorously exhorting successive cohorts of Yale students on the evils of governmental intervention into social affairs, proposed in his masterwork, *Folkways*, that the great variety of usages, customs, and mores found in different societies were based on man's utilitarian interests under differing life conditions which all

[13]Lester F. Ward, *Pure Sociology*, 2nd ed. (New York, Macmillan, 1911), p. 101.
[14]*Pure Sociology*, p. 261.

15

expressed "four great motives of human action," namely, "hunger, sex passion, vanity, and fear (of ghosts and spirits)."[15] An interesting and often unrecognized irony of intellectual history surrounding Sumner's work is that the total impact of *Folkways*, with its rich and abundant illustrations of man's variable behavior taken from history and contemporary ethnography, was, particularly in later decades, to serve as a widely used underpinning for doctrines of cultural relativity and cultural determinism—doctrines which led to inferences concerning political action quite at variance with Sumner's own.

Meanwhile, Charles Horton Cooley, the gentle sociological thinker of Ann Arbor, was putting on paper his own ruminations on "social organization" and "human nature and the social order."[16] Contrasting the fixity of instinctive behavior among the lower animals with the plasticity of behavior in the human species, and emphasizing the interactive nature of heredity and the learning environment among men, Cooley took what he regarded as a middle course and declared that man is endowed with certain "instinctive emotions" or "instinctive emotional dispositions," the "plainest" being anger, fear, maternal love, male and female sexual love, and self-assertion or power.[17] However, an instinctive emotion rarely or never constitutes a satisfactory explanation of human behavior by itself alone since "in human life it is not, in any considerable degree, a motive to specific behavior at all, but an impulse whose definite expression depends upon education and social situation."[18] In other words, man has hereditarily given emotional predispositions, but these are activated and take specific form only under particular en-

[15]William Graham Sumner, *Folkways* (Boston, Ginn, 1940, original publication, 1906), pp. 18–19.
[16]*Human Nature and the Social Order* appeared in 1902 and *Social Organization* in 1909, Charles Scribner's Sons, publishers. Both volumes are republished in a one volume edition, with an "Introduction" by Robert Cooley Angell, issued by The Free Press, Glencoe, Ill. in 1956.
[17]*Human Nature and the Social Order*, Free Press Edition, pp. 24–25.
[18]*Human Nature and the Social Order*, Free Press Edition, p. 27.

vironmental conditions which can, themselves, be humanly influenced. The emphasis in his discussion is on plasticity in human behavior and the possibility of controlling, taming, and transforming the more aggressive and self-assertive tendencies in man within the bosom of the family, the play group of children, and the neighborhood group—the famous "primary groups," as Cooley named them, and which he regarded as the civilizing agents of the social order. Also, in his equally well known concept of the "looking-glass self," Cooley described the way in which a concept of the self is developed through imagination of the way in which others regard us, thus again emphasizing the role of the social environment in personality development and expression.

One of the last noteworthy and influential listings of basic human motivations by earlier American sociologists was contributed by W. I. Thomas, the for a time University of Chicago-based researcher and teacher, whose writings span almost the first half the twentieth century, and whose subject matter was as diverse as the Polish peasant, the immigrant community, the social psychology of sex, primitive behavior, and the unadjusted girl. In 1917, Thomas declared that human behavior was reducible, at least at one level, to four fundamental "wishes:" the desire for new experience, the desire for mastery, the desire for recognition, and the desire for safety or security. Several years later, without explanation, in a new presentation of the "four wishes," the desire for mastery was omitted and in its place was inserted the desire for response which, in its exposition, appears to include both sexual love and maternal love, along with a miscellany of other types of positively affective social feelings. Thomas' later writings deemphasized the role of the four wishes, and used more prominently as an analytical tool the concept of the "definition of the situation," in which the actor's subjective interpretation of particular experiences was held to be of prime sociological interest.[19]

[19]See Edmund H. Volkart, ed., *Social Behavior and Personality: Contributions of W. I. Thomas to Theory and Social Research* (New York, Social Science Research Council, 1951), *passim.*

There remains to be dealt with, in a consideration of the work of the sociologists of this earlier period, from the point of view of a concept of human nature, the contributions of George Herbert Mead. Mead, in fact, was not a sociologist at all either by training or by disciplinary adherence. He was a philosopher with some interest in psychology, brought to the department of philosophy at the University of Chicago by his close friend, the eminent American pragmatist and educational reformer, John Dewey. At Chicago, he taught for many years a course in Social Psychology which attracted students from both psychology and sociology. Never a prolific publisher, he left no monograph which summed up his major conceptions in this area; however, faithful and admiring students used verbatim transcripts of his lectures to publish, after his death, the corpus of his social psychology course in the volume, *Mind, Self, and Society*.[20] Mead's work had a various but steady influence on later sociologists, and has in recent years, been acknowledged as the basis for an influential "school" of sociological and social psychological analysis known as "symbolic interactionism," a name assigned to it by its most prominent exponent, Herbert Blumer.[21]

Mead's principal thesis, shorn of some of its particularistic language, is that the self is formed through a process of interaction with others in which the developing child gradually learns to take the role of other significant persons in his field of life experience, imagining how they are reacting to himself and others, and thus enabling him to look upon himself as an object as well as a subject, and to carry on a continual dialogue with himself. In time, these conceptions of others coalesce into a "generalized other," which represents the general moral norms and expectations of the community. But the self, as it is formed by particular experiences, has an

[20]George H. Mead, *Mind, Self, and Society*, ed. Charles W. Morris (Chicago, University of Chicago Press, 1934).
[21]Herbert Blumer, *Symbolic Interactionism: Perspective and Method* (Englewood Cliffs, N.J., Prentice-Hall, 1969). See also, John P. Hewitt, *Self and Society: A Symbolic Interactionist Social Psychology* (Boston, Allyn and Bacon, 1976).

be called instinctual. In the field of anthropology, works like Ruth Benedict's *Patterns of Culture* and Margaret Mead's *Sex and Temperament in Three Primitive Societies*, both published in the middle thirties, provided portraits of wide cultural variation in over-all behavior for various pre-literate societies and emphasized the way in which these variant cultural configurations influenced individual behavior in the direction of conformity to the cultural mold.

Secondly, sociologists, as well as psychologists, anthropologists, and members of other academic disciplines dealing with man, were presumably responding, in greater or lesser degree, to the times in which they lived. An acute world-wide economic depression that lasted for virtually the entire decade of the thirties raised questions about the possibility of alternative, or at least modified, economic institutional arrangements to those of classical capitalism. The enthusiasm and transformations generated by the New Deal in America under its charismatic leader, Franklin Delano Roosevelt, together with the drastically new experience in economic arrangements taking place in the Soviet Union (while its political persecutions and excesses were kept out of the limelight), induced a social climate in which students of human behavior were receptive to the idea that man could create his own economic institutions and was not linked to any one system by innate biological traits. The emergence of ominous clouds in the sky of international relations occasioned by the rise of Facism and Nazism and the actual outbreak of hostilities in the Italian foray into Ethiopia and the Spanish civil war led many social scientists, brought up in a generation which had been strongly led to believe that World War I had been the "war to end all wars," to attempt to reassure both their audience and themselves that warfare was not an inevitable product of man's genes and could be avoided by reason and diplomatic resolution of differences in ideology and national interests. Sexual mores and patterns of marriage and divorce were undergoing change in the direction of greater permissiveness partly as the result of the spread into the popular mind of ideas from the writings of

21

such figures as Sigmund Freud (whose prescriptive conclusions were rather substantially misunderstood) and Havelock Ellis, and partly as a result of developing technologies as, for instance, the automobile and more effective methods of contraception. Behavioral changes in this area of life further pointed to the apparent plasticity and modifiability of man's most intimate actions. And, finally, there was the matter of racial and ethnic prejudice and discrimination. The United States of America was still living with the legacy of slavery in its Southern Jim Crow laws, its constant and omnipresent physical intimidation of Negroes in the Southern states, its relegation of black men and women everywhere to segregated inferior housing and jobs, and its widely spread belief that blacks were intellectually and emotionally inferior to whites as a result of racial genetic inheritance. Orientals were treated as an inferior people, particularly in the Western coastal states, and were legally discriminated against by various devices. Anti-Semitism was prevalent, if not in overt physical expression, still in numerous exclusionary and attitudinal manifestations, and immigration from southern and eastern Europe, generally, had only a few years before been severely restricted by federal legislation based implicity on theories of racial and ethnic superiority. And now the specter of racism as a nation's explicit and total commitment loomed in the rise to power in Germany of the Nazis and their anti-Semitic and pro-Aryan ideologies and policies. In this context, concerned American academicians looked to cultural determinism as a powerful and valid intellectual tool with which to combat the patently destructive ideas of racial purity and racial superiority.

Concerning the question of the relationship of the race issue to conceptions of human nature, two important points must here be made and strongly emphasized. In the first place, there is no necessary connection between a theory of the origins of *individual* human behavior and theories dealing with the behavior of *groups* designated with varying degrees of accuracy as "races," and as "ethnic groups." To put it somewhat more specifically, while a conception of human behavior favoring cultural determinism does militate against the idea of genetically based racial inequality, a view of human behavior which leans in the direction of biological determinism for individual behavior is also not in the least incompatible with the idea of racial equality. The point is that the two do not necessarily stand or fall together. To illustrate, a belief that intellectual potential is largely inherited on an individual basis, is quite compatible with the idea that such individual genetic potentialities are distributed on an equal basis among all so-called racial groups. Or, a hypothesis claiming the existence of an "aggressive instinct" would, normally, assume that such an instinct would be present in members of all groups, regardless of race or ethnicity. The failure to distinguish between theories that deal with individual behavior and those that concern the race question has led to some, from a logical point of view, unnecessary controversies and obfuscations, particularly in recent years.

My second point is that, in fact, the attack on racist doctrines which was mounted by the social scientists of the 1930s and later decades, using data and theoretical conceptions which emphasized cultural influences on behavior, together with their utilization of newer understandings in the field of genetics which entirely invalidated the idea that there were such entities as "pure races," succeeded beyond the shadow of a doubt in destroying the intellectual validity and respectability of the doctrine of the inequality of races and thus constructed a climate of scientific and intellectual opinion in America which constituted the basis for all future advances in American racial and ethnic relations. Books such as Ruth Benedict's *Race: Science and Politic*, Ashley Montagu's *Man's Most Dangerous Myth: The Fallacy of Race*, Donald Young's *American Minority Peoples*, Jacques Barzun's *Race: A Study in Modern Superstition*, Otto Klineberg's *Race Differences* (in which a noted social psychologist marshalled experimental studies to show that there were no proven race differences in mentality), E. Franklin Frazier's *The Negro in the United States*, R. M. MacIver's *The More Perfect Union*, and Gunnar Myrdal's *An American Dilemma*, among others, all contributed in various ways to building up a body of evidence and logic against racism which came to constitute the core of social science teaching absorbed by generations of college students in courses in sociology, psychology, anthropology, and history, and to become an indispensable part of the intellectual arsenal of opinion leaders and civic activists in the United States who were waging a major battle against racial prejudice and discrimination. It was in this area, in fact—the area of racial and ethnic relations—where the scientific orientation favoring cultural explanations of behavior achieved its greatest both theoretical and practical success, a success which, I believe, was entirely justified by the scientific evidence. This intellectual breakthrough was also aided, no doubt, in its ideological and emotional impact by the fact that the United States in World War II, along with its allies, fought and defeated an enemy whose major premise of existence and action was the idea of racial superiority, and who, under the fanatical leadership of Adolf Hitler, had brought this doctrine to its ultimate diabolical expression in the extermination of millions of Jews and other "non-Aryan" peoples who had been fatally stigmatized.

After the conclusion of World War II, and through the period of the 1950s, cultural determinism as a dominant *motif* in American sociology continued its reign. A. H. Hobbs, a University of Pennsylvania sociologist, published an attack on the doctrine as part of a pattern of charges that current sociology was infused with a set of unproven scientific and political assumptions leaning towards liberal or radical positions in such areas as economic systems, war and peace, and family life.[24] The accusation of neglect of biological and hereditary factors in human behavior figures prominently in his presentation. The book was dutifully and somewhat negatively reviewed and had no measurable impact on the discipline. Most textbook writers continued to emphasize cultural and social factors in the development of personality and be-

[24]*The Claims of Sociology: A Critique of Textbooks.*

havior, although hereditary and biological factors might receive a chapter of formal recognition, and the virtually obligatory formula of "the interaction of heredity and environment" usually made an appearance.

At the "higher" levels of disciplinary discourse, the period of the 1950s was dominated by debates over the structural-functional perspective which had been elaborated into a vast action systems approach by Talcott Parsons, by controversies over the question of whether "grand theory" of the Parsonian kind, or "middle range" theories of the sort advocated by Robert Merton, were more productive of useful current sociological knowledge, by the appearance of vast numbers of empirical quantitatively oriented studies in various selected and specific areas of social behavior (and the development of increasingly sophisticated techniques of quantitative measurement and inference with which to conduct such studies), and, particularly towards the end of the decade, the challenge of "conflict school" theorists who charged structural-functionalism, with its emphasis on shared collective values, consensus, and societal equilibrium, with neglecting the importance of conflict, particularly among collectivities such as social classes, in the dynamics of human behavior, and with constituting a sociological defense of the *status quo* in societal arrangements.

None of these controversies and developments brought the subject of human nature to the fore, or essentially challenged the cultural determinism perspective. Parson's work, to be sure, which he considered to be a systematic approach to the analysis of social action, contains a not inconsiderable portion of attention to the "personality system," which functions in interaction with the "social system" and the "cultural system." But in the vast Parsonian constructed edifice of categories and possibilities, biological propensities of the individual are given short shrift, and "needs" very quickly become "need-dispositions," which are now already oriented towards the social and cultural world. Parsonian personality theory, then, turns out to be a systematic analysis of the socialization process in rather standard sociological fashion,

25

coupled with certain developmental aspects of Freudian theory.[25] It does posit overall gratification tendencies in the individual, but tendencies which, again, very quickly become contained and defined by social interaction and cultural values. There are some shrewd insights into the socialization process and an important recognition of the fact that the actor chooses among and integrates both cognitive and object-related emotional inputs (Parsons calls this process "evaluation") before any given action. All in all, it is a theory of personality which in no significant way challenged the dominant current view of man as essentially plastic and overwhelmingly shaped by social and cultural forces.

In a curious fashion, neither did "conflict school" theory precipitate such a challenge. In order to explain why, we must make a conceptual distinction here between two types of theoretical approaches to the place of conflict in human societies. Type A, which I shall call "scientific conflict theory," springs out of the common sense observation that both conflict and cooperation exist in human affairs, and that the task of the sociological observer is to classify types of conflict, record their frequency relative to cooperative and equilibrium-oriented behavior, study the causes of conflict and the effects, including functions, observe how conflicts may or may not be resolved, and attempt to come to some conclusions about the institutional conditions which measurably either extend or reduce the amount of conflict in society. Answers to all these implied questions are thus left open to empirical inquiry. Type B, which may be called "eschatological conflict theory," has no such open quality about it. It springs from revolutionary ardor, or some closely allied programmatic scheme for societal change, and looks in

---

[25]See, particularly, Talcott Parsons and Edward A. Shils, eds., *Toward a General Theory of Action* (New York, Harper, 1962, original publication by Harvard University Press, 1951) and Talcott Persons and Robert F. Bales (in collaboration with James Olds, Morris Zelditch, Jr., and Philip E. Slater), *Family, Socialization and Interaction Process* (Glencoe, Ill., Free Press, 1955).

two directions, backwards and forwards. Prior to the eschatological change or upheaval, conflict abounds and is the dominant social process. After the decisive instituional change, the explicit or implicit assumption is that conflict disappears virtually to the zero point. Marxist conflict theory is clearly of the eschatological variety, a variety which lays the entire Marxist theoretical system open to the charge of utopianism, a charge which the empirical developments in Marxist societies have done nothing to dispel. Ralf Dahrendorf, a leading and, on the whole, judicious exponent of conflict theory, recognized this problem in his elegantly phrased and constructed attack on structural-functionalism in an article published in 1958. The following passage is highly relevant: "The case of Marx is even more pertinent. It is well known how much time and energy Lenin spent in trying to link the realistically possible event of the proletarian revolution with the image of a Communist society in which there are no classes, no conflicts, no state, and, indeed, no division of labor. Lenin, as we know, failed, in theory as in practice, to get beyond the 'dictatorship of the proletariat,' and somehow we are not surprised at that."[26] Indeed, we are not surprised, if the distinction between scientific and eschatological types of conflict theory is kept in mind. And, yet, Dahrendorf goes on in the same article to make the general claim that "Quite apart from its merits as a tool of scientific analysis, the conflict model is essentially non-utopian: it is the model of an open society."[27]

Another example is pertinent here. C. Wright Mills, in his celebrated attack on "grand theory" and what he pejoratively labeled "abstracted empiricism," and his plea for a socially relevant sociology, similarly faults structural-functionalism for its lack of emphasis on conflict phenomena. His own

[26]Ralf Dahrendorf, "Out of Utopia: Toward a Reorientation of Sociological Analysis," *American Journal of Sociology*, Vol. 64, No. 2 (September 1958), p. 116. See also, his *Class and Class Conflict in Industrial Society* (Stanford, Ca., Stanford University Press, 1959).
[27]"Out of Utopia: Toward a Reorientation of Sociological Analysis," p. 127.

views on the sources of conflict are clearly inferrable from the following passage from *The Sociological Imagination:* "But it is *not* true [Mills' emphasis], as Ernest Jones asserted, that 'man's chief enemy and danger is his own unruly nature and the dark forces pent up within him.' On the contrary: 'Man's chief danger' today lies in the unruly forces of contemporary society itself, with its alienating methods of production, its enveloping techniques of political domination, its international anarchy—in a word, its pervasive transformation of the very 'nature' of man and the conditions and aims of his life.'"[28] In other words, it is not human nature which creates conflict but societal institutions. In a curious symmetry, eschatological conflict theory and structural-functionalism appear to share approximately the same assumptions about the nature of man. He is basically plastic and can be overwhelmingly shaped by social and cultural influences.

Of theories of the "middle range" which occupied the attention of sociologists during the period under review, perhaps the most important, in terms of implications for a theory of human nature, was that complex of motivational analysis containing the concepts of "relative deprivation" and "reference group" behavior. The relative deprivation idea was formulated by Samuel Stouffer and associates in their analysis of data gathered on attitudes of American soldiers in World War II by the Research Branch, Information and Education Division of the United States Army.[29] Reference group theory stems from the work of several social psychologists, notably Herbert Hyman (who coined the term "reference group"), Muzafer Sherif, and Theodore M. New-

---

[28]C. Wright Mills, *The Sociological Imagination* (New York, Oxford University Press, 1959), p. 13.
[29]See Samuel A. Stouffer, Edward A. Suchman, Leland C. DeVinney, Shirley A. Star, and Robin M. Williams, Jr., *The American Soldier: Adjustment During Army Life* (Princeton, N.J., Princeton University Press, 1949); and Samuel A. Stouffer, Arthur A. Lumsdaine, Marion Harper Lumsdaine, and Leonard S. Cottrell, Jr., *The American Soldier: Combat and Its Aftermath* (Princeton, N.J., Princeton University Press, 1949).

comb, which had been carried out in this period. These related concepts were codified and elaborated on by Robert
Merton.[30] Basically, they lend themselves to the inference
that the human being is an inveterate "comparer" of his own
situation with those of others, and that his sense of satisfaction or dissatisfaction with his own condition depends heavily on such comparisons rather than exclusively on his position on some absolute scale of need deprivation-satiation.

The first effective systems-oriented breaks in the icejam
of cultural-deterministic theories which had landlocked
sociology for a generation began to appear in the late 1950s
and early 1960s. In 1958, George Homans published a paper
in the *American Journal of Sociology* called "Social Behavior
as Exchange." In the paper, Homans declared himself to be
"an ultimate psychological reductionist," thus challenging
the dominant Durkheimian view that social facts were of a
different order from psychological factors and processes, and
offering the viewpoint that the explanation of "elementary
social behavior" could probably be derived, eventually, from
the propositions of behavioral psychology. This introductory
statement was followed by the presentation of a conceptual
framework that saw human interaction as "an exchange of
goods, material and non-material," based on calculations of
profit derived from cost-reward considerations for each of the
interacting members.[31] This article was followed in 1961 by
Homans' book, *Social Behavior: Its Elementary Forms*, which
elaborated on this theoretical perspective and applied it, for
the most part, to the results of published studies of small
group behavior, the previous focus of much of Homans'
work.[32] (A revised edition of *Social Behavior* appeared in
1974.) In 1964, Peter Blau published the volume, *Exchange*

[30]See Robert K. Merton, *Social Theory and Social Structure* (Glencoe, Ill.,
Free Press, 1957). chap. 8 and 9. Chap. 8 was written in collaboration with
Alice S. Rossi.
[31]George C. Homans, "Social Behavior as Exchange," *American Journal of
Sociology*, Vol. 63, No. 6 (May 1958), pp. 597–606.
[32]George C. Homans, *Social Behavior: Its Elementary Forms* (New York,
Harcourt Brace, 1961).

and Power in Social Life, in which he acknowledged his debt
to Homans' work, and although rejecting psychological reductionism, analyzed human exchange processes and related
them to larger structural issues.[33] Although Blau's conception of "exchange" is a somewhat more restricted one than
Homans' (Blau excludes physically coercive behavior and
behavior produced entirely by internalized norms from exchange analysis), neither Homans' nor Blau's version constitutes a complete theory of human behavior involving a close
examination of indigenous psychic forces in man. In effect,
"exchange theory" assumes that, given certain "values," or
desired rewards, however derived, man will strive in his
interaction with others to achieve those values through exchange transactions which involve a calculation of the degree
of value and the amount of cost involved in attempting to
achieve the goal explicit in the value. Altruistic, as well as
hedonistic, values are included in the frame of reference. The
significance of "exchange theory" for our present analysis is
that in Homans' acceptance of psychological reductionism
and in the general theory's focus on individual motivation, at
least at an intermediate stage of its development, we can
perceive the return of the individual human actor to the
sociological stage in a programmatic way.

It is precisely the metaphor of the stage as the setting for
social interaction that has been so effectively used by Erving
Goffman in his "dramaturgical approach," which was set
forth in a series of books beginning with *The Presentation of
Self in Everyday Life,* which received its first American publication in 1959.[34] Essentially, Goffman views human interaction as a dramatic encounter wherein each actor presents his
own favorable image of himself to others, attempting through
various devices ("defensive practices") an "impression man-

[33]Peter M. Blau, *Exchange and Power in Social Life* (New York, Wiley, 1964).
[34]Erving Goffman, *The Presentation of Self in Everyday Life* (Garden City,
N.Y., Doubleday Anchor Books, 1959). See also *Encounters* (Indianapolis,
Bobbs-Merrill, 1961); *Behavior in Public Places* (New York, Free Press,
1963); *Stigma* (Englewood Cliffs, N.J., Prentice-Hall, 1963); *Interaction
Ritual* (Chicago, Aldine, 1967); and *Relations in Public* (New York, Basic
Books, 1971, also Harper Colophon paperback, 1972), among others.

agement" of the other's or others' conception of the actor. "I have suggested [he declares] that a performer tends to conceal or underplay those activities, facts, and motives which are incompatible with an idealized version of himself and his products."[35] Conflict in the interactive situation is characteristically avoided by the other's *temporary* (i.e., for the duration of the specific interaction) acceptance of the actor's claims without explicit challenge. Goffman states: "While we may be ready to see that no fostered impression would survive if defensive practices were not employed, we are less ready perhaps to see that few impressions could survive if those who received the impression did not exert tact in their reception of it."[36] While Goffman's principal concern in his series of monographs is with the permutations and combinations of devices designed to maintain some kind of equilibrium in these social interactions in various settings (although disruptions of the equilibrium also receive some attention), and while he offers no systematic analysis of human nature, the dominant impression emerges of the human actor as a person constantly engaged in the process of ego-defense. It is a conception which we shall find highly useful in subsequent analysis.

Two important papers published early in the period of sociological reassessment now under review deserve special mention here. One by Alex Inkeles, appearing in 1959, and formulating problematic issues in the area of personality and social structure, vigorously calls for a reintroduction of both a general theory of personality and attention to particular personality variables, in the study of social structural issues. While rejecting psychological reductionism, Inkeles states the need for incorporating both personality variables and social-structural variables in sociological explanations in order to reduce the amount of unexplained variance in sociological outcomes. Personality variables, including "the human personality system," are seen basically as intervening variables which mediate the impact of one structural situa-

[35]*The Presentation of Self in Everyday Life*, p. 48.
[36]*The Presentation of Self in Everyday Life*, p. 14.

tion upon another. "The central thesis of this paper," Inkeles asserts, "is that adequate sociological analysis of many problems is either impossible or severely limited unless we make explicit use of psychological theory and data in conjunction with sociological theory and data. Indeed, I would assert that very little sociological analysis is ever done without using at least an implicit psychological theory. It seems evident that in making this theory explicit and bringing psychological data to bear systematically on sociological problems we cannot fail but improve the scope and adequacy of sociological analysis."[37]

The second paper, by Dennis Wrong, incorporates its principal argument in its title, "The Oversocialized Conception of Man in Modern Sociology." The paper, which appeared in 1961, has been widely anthologized in the succeeding years and must be considered a seminal influence in the newly developing trend to challenge the dominant assumptions about man and society of the previous generation of sociological work. In this paper, Wrong declares that the tendency in contemporary sociological theory to conceive of the internalization of norms as a rather thoroughly successful process and to posit man as a creature who is motivated overwhelmingly by the desire for approval from his fellows, thus further insuring conformity to shared norms and expectations, masks, slides over, and ignores what is basically a dialectic of tension between man's biological needs and material and power motives on the one hand, and the social and cultural order on the other. "The view that man is invariably pushed by internalized norms or pulled by the lure of self-validation by others," Wrong declares, "ignores—to speak archaically for a moment—both the highest and the lowest, both beast and angel, in his nature."[38] Several other brief salient quotations from the article will allow the reader

[37]Alex Inkeles, "Personality and Social Structure," *Sociology Today: Problems and Prospects,* ed, Robert K. Merton, Leonard Broom, and Leonard S. Cottrell, Jr. (New York, Basic Books, 1959), p. 250.

[38]Dennis H. Wrong, "The Oversocialized Conception of Man in Modern Sociology," *American Sociological Review,* Vol. 26, No. 2 (April 1961), p. 191.

32

to savor the flavor of his argument: "I think we must start with the recognition that *in the beginning there is the body.* [Wrong's emphasis];" "The degree to which conformity is frequently the result of coercion rather than conviction is minimized [i.e., by current sociological theory];" "I do not see how, at the level of theory, sociologists can fail to make assumptions about human nature."[39] Wrong concedes that man's biological drives are shaped and molded by social factors, but the predominant emphasis in his attack on "the oversocialized conception of man" is on the tension created by the interplay of man's biological nature and the social and cultural forces which impinge upon it. In such a conception of man and society, stability, integration, and equilibrium become problematical, rather than taken for granted.

So far as I am aware, the first sociologist in the modern period to address the concept of human nature in a serious way and subsequently apply his formulation in highly relevant fashion to a particular substantive area of sociology is Gerhard Lenski, who, in his book *Power and Privilege,* published in 1966, developed a general theory of stratification which attempted to answer the two basic questions of why stratification exists in society and how various degrees or profiles of stratification in differing societies are related to particular causative variables.[40] Lenski begins his theoretical construction by offering several postulates concerning man and society. Three of them are of particular relevance here. They are 1) that man is essentially a selfish creature who generally acts out of self-enhancing motives where his own or his group's (usually primary groups) interests are importantly concerned. Observable altruistic human action is either reduced to unspoken selfish motivations or primary group defense, or relegated to areas of behavior in which little is at stake; 2) that most of the things that man wants are in short supply—that is, the demand exceeds the amount available—since man's desires for goods and services are insatiable

[39]These remarks will be found on pages 191, 188, and 192, respectively, of "The Oversocialized Conception of Man in Modern Sociology."
[40]Gerhard E. Lenski, *Power and Privilege: A Theory of Social Stratification,* (New York, McGraw-Hill, 1966).

primarily as a result of the status value attached to them; and 3) that men are by nature, or biologically, unequal, as individuals, in the possession of various attributes necessary for success in the struggle over scarce goods and services.

These postulates, or "constants," are then combined in a causative framework with a number of variables to predict stratification outcomes. The most important of these variables is the level of technology in the society which, in turn, largely determines the amount of economic surplus available for distribution. The combination of man's intrinsic selfishness and struggle for scare goods and services, together with inequality in individual endowments, ensures that whenever an economic surplus exists, some men will by force and power appropriate the greater part of it, then bend all efforts to legitimize their appropriation, and stratification will ensue. Other factors also play a role and, eventually, particularly in complex industrial societies, variables such as the development of constitutional government and ideologies of equality combine to produce countervailing force and power which reduce the amount of stratification, but never abolish it entirely. The workings out of this theory of stratification are tested, developed, and generally supported by reference to a broad framework of macrosocietal data taken from both historical and anthropological studies. While Lenski claims in this theory (here stated, of course, in minimal fashion which omits some of the postulates and variables and does not do justice to its full outlines) to synthesize functional and conflict theories of stratification, which he equates, roughly, with conservative and radical traditions, respectively, it would appear to me that he has, in reality, advanced a more or less distinct third theoretical perspective[41]—namely, that stratification results from human nature, since man's alleged innate selfishness, his insatiable wants, and his individual biological variability constitute the motor which sets the stratifica-

[41]In his final chapter, on page 443, Lenski seems to recognize this point in his statement: "In summary, it [his "synthesis"] is *an extremely complex mixture of elements from these two older traditions, yet at the same time unique and different.*" (Lenski's italics.).

tion machine in motion—never, incidentally, to stop, since, while substantial modifications of the stratification profile are deemed possible, and, in fact, are shown to have occurred, there is no eschatology in Lenski's theory—no golden time finally to be achieved where the struggle for power, goods, services, and prestige will cease. Lenski's theory of human nature is not a complete one (a number of dimensions are not dealt with), and it is not a proven one, but *Power and Privilege* does represent a pioneering study that lays out on the table the author's views about the nature of man and connects these views in dynamic fashion with sociological and other variables to produce a plausible general theory in an important substantive area of the sociological discipline.

Another sociologist who, in the recent period, has shown keen sensitivity to human nature considerations is Curt Tausky who, in his book *Work Organizations*, which appeared in 1970, *inter alia*, examines the assumptions about the nature of man implicit in several competing theories of how and why men are motivated to perform in the carrying out of their tasks in industrial organizations.[42] The classical or scientific management theory of Frederick Taylor, which emphasized egoistic, or selfish, motivation highly responsive to reward and punishment sanctions, is contrasted with the currently influential "human relations perspective," which sees the worker as a person who responds most effectively to considerations of job satisfaction, self-actualization, and affective relationships, all of which can orient him successfully to organizational goals. A third theory, "structuralism," is presented which constitutes a somewhat intermediate approach basing preferred motivational complexes on an analysis of the variable situational demands of particular kinds of work operations. Tausky favors the "structuralism" approach which, he notes, is closer in its assumptions about the nature of human motivations to the scientific management than the human relations frame of reference, and de-

---

[42]Curt Tausky, *Work Organizations: Major Theoretical Perspectives* (Itasca, Ill., Peacock, 1970).

clares his skepticism about the human relations perspective since he does not "share the optimism about human nature embedded in human relations writings." In a later publication, Tausky and an associate analyze several cases of job-enrichment programs which had improved production quantity or quality, cited by advocates of the self-actualization motivational model as supportive of their theory, and find incorporated into these programs factors of greater accountability or "tight reward-punishment linkages" which could have easily played a large role in producing the reported improvements.[43] These features, the authors declare, must be incorporated in order to make job-enrichment strategies successful.

An important statement calling for the application of appropriate psychoanalytic concepts to the analysis of social change and collective behavior phenomena, historically and generally, was made in the early 1970s in a collaborative and interdisciplinary effort by Gerald Platt and Fred Weinstein, the latter a historian.[44] Their position specifically rejects psychological reductionism and in fact supports, on a theoretical level, "the priority of cultural and social systems." Psychoanalytically conceived personality dynamics appear to be viewed, basically, as intervening variables explaining the impact of new developments in structure and culture upon subsequent collective outcomes. In the field of psychohistorical analysis, the work of Erik Erikson is singled out for special commendation but judged not to have gone far enough in that it concentrates on the psychological dynamics of individual historical leaders without successfully explaining why the leaders were successful in enlisting the support

[43]E. Lauck Parke and Curt Tausky, "The Mythology of Job Enrichment: Self-Actualization Revisited," Personnel, Vol. 52, No. 5 (September–October 1975), pp. 12–21.
[44]Fred Weinstein and Gerald M. Platt, Psychoanalytic Sociology: An Essay on the Interpretation of Historical Data and the Phenomena of Collective Behavior (Baltimore, Johns Hopkins University Press, 1973). See also, their earlier work, The Wish to Be Free (Berkeley and Los Angeles, University of California Press, 1969).

of mass constituencies, a goal which their own (i.e., Weinstein and Platt's) analytical scheme is designed to facilitate. The authors also, following the lead of Erikson and others, conceive of personal identity formation as a process which is not completed in the first few years of life, but as one which continues through the life-cycle and is affected by institutional complexes extending beyond the family: "Identity is comprised of internalized features," they declare, "but identity must also be re-established and can be redefined throughout life. Ego and superego processes which are established in childhood are not static; they expand and contract. The capacity for reality testing, which increases with age, and the need to examine and re-examine ideals and values in late adolescence, to cite an example we have already introduced, is indicative of this. . . . In a broader sense, *social-structural changes which affect the implementation of values and norms in a society can affect any and all age levels, systematically engendering redefinition of self and others.*"[45] (Weinstein and Platt's emphasis.)

In the field of racial and ethnic studies, I presented, in an article published in 1975, a conception of human nature dealing with several crucial dimensions as part of an attempt to construct a general theory of racial and ethnic group relations. Since that article is reprinted in this collection, and since I will enlarge and continue to develop that conception of the nature of man later on in this paper, I shall have nothing more to say about it at this point.

"What we do not like will not go away by our pretending that it is not there. We should strive for a realistic conception of human nature, realistic, in the sense that it is consistent with actual observable behavior, not with what we hope our behavior might be. We must, in short, develop an ability to take an unflinching look at what we do not like, however painful or distasteful that might be. Seeing, for example, murder, violence, snobbery, deceit, treachery, and the egotistic pursuit of self-interest occur with unflagging regularity

[45]*Psychoanalytic Sociology,* pp. 71–72.

throughout human history, we should stop considering these traits as pathological aberrations, and start entertaining the hypothesis that we are dealing with eminently normal human behavior." Can this be a sociologist speaking? Yes, it is Pierre van den Berghe who, in an article published late in 1974 entitled, provocatively, "Bringing Beasts Back In: Toward a Biosocial Theory of Aggression," and a book offered as an introductory text and published in 1975 called *Man in Society: A Biosocial View*, mounted a scathing attack on contemporary sociology, accusing it of ignoring species-wide biological factors, failing to make necessary cross-species comparisons, slighting truly cross-cultural materials from both history and anthropology, and in general presenting an optimistic view of the nature of man which is not supported either by historical or current events, or by the more recent findings of ethology, primatology, zoology, and anthropology.[46]

Van den Berghe insists that his viewpoint is not that of biological determinism but that such a phenomenon as human nature does exist, determined by "biological predispositions" common to all mankind, and that these biological predispositions are modifiable, though not eradicable, by socio-cultural learning and experiential factors and thus set limits to what human behavior can be. The overall viewpoint on this matter is not fundamentally different from that indicated by the work of Wrong, Lenski, and Tausky, reviewed earlier, or by my paper on a general theory of racial and ethnic relations mentioned above.

In terms of specifics, van den Berghe asserts the reality of biological predispositions in man toward aggression, hierarchy (based on dominance behavior), and territoriality (the defense of appropriated spatial areas). Aggression is elicited,

---

[46]Pierre L. van den Berghe, "Bringing Beasts Back In: Toward a Biosocial Theory of Aggression," *American Sociological Review*, Vol. 39, No. 6 (December 1974), pp. 777–88; and *Man in Society: A Biosocial View* (New York, Elsevier, 1975). The quotation which begins this paragraph is from *Man in Society*, pp. 18–19.

particularly, by competition for scarce resources, both material and social-psychological (man's desire for resources is regarded as insatiable). Hierarchy and territoriality function dialectically in that, once established, they reduce the amount of aggression since they establish temporary stability. Since subordinates and outsiders, however, have the capacity for resenting their inferior or excluded position, they eventually rebel against the existing state of affairs and further aggression results, presumably until a new agreed upon definition results, again, in turn, eventually to be challenged. And so the cycle continues. Population pressure exacerbates the competition for resources and thus increases the amount of aggression expressed. Additional biological predispositions of gregariousness, mother-child bonding, nuclear family incest taboo, sexual pair bonding (the development of time-extended sexual relations between one man and one woman), and play behavior are also predicated. Religious behavior is explained as arising out of man's need to answer difficult and important questions otherwise unanswerable and by his desire for immortality. The growth and development of various social institutions as they embody and are shaped by these alleged fundamental tendencies in man are described by van den Berghe in *Man in Society*.

The peremptory and salient character of van den Berghe's challenge to conventional sociology, although, as we have pointed out, work in the same direction had been making its appearance for about fifteen years, has already stirred considerable comment in professional sociological circles. The article, "Bringing Beasts Back In," became the occasion for a series of critical letters to the *American Sociological Review*, where the article had appeared, and these letters, together with a reply by van den Berghe, were published in a later issue.[47] *Man in Society* was made the

----

[47]See Claude S. Fisher, Dennis J. Moberg, and Allan Mazur, "Comments on van den Berghe" and Pierre L. van den Berghe, "Reply to Fisher, Moberg, and Mazur," *American Sociological Review*, Vol. 40, No. 5 (October 1975), pp. 674–82.

subject of a "review symposium" in the American Sociological Association's official reviewing journal and was subjected to two reviews, the first generally unfavorable in tone, the second generally favorable.[48] The controversy will undoubtedly continue in various and enlarged arenas since it is apparent that over the past decade-and-a-half serious challenges have been mounted in opposition to the dominant trends of the preceding generation of sociological work which emphasized cultural determinism, value-consensus, structural-functional explanations of social institutions, relative neglect of psychological variables, and the essential "goodness," or alternatively, plasticity of man. Some of these challenges have been motivated by a search for those universal biological factors which, we are continually told in ritualistic fashion, interact with the social and cultural environment to produce human behavior. In short, a number of sociologists are engaged in a search for a valid conception of human nature which realistically combines the biological and the social-cultural elements which interact to form the human being, and propose to use such a conception (or are already using it) to develop what they regard as a more accurate understanding of social structure and social change. It is to that task—the development of a theory of human nature for sociological use—which, in my own way and in inevitably brief compass in this paper, I now turn.

A THEORY OF HUMAN NATURE

Some Preliminary Considerations

I shall start by laying my metascientific assumptions out on the table. I am a scientific positivist in that I believe in the complete pervasiveness of causality throughout the universe (I am not concerned here, obviously, with evaluating theolog-

[48]See Roger R. Larsen and Saul Feinman, reviewers, "Review Symposium," on "Man in Society" *Contemporary Sociology: A Journal of Reviews*, Vol. 5, No. 1 (January 1976), pp. 5–9.

ical or philosophical positions concerning "first cause" or "realms beyond causality;" these are matters that are outside my province as a scientist). I believe that "pervasive causality" extends to the social world created and inhabited by human beings as well as the natural world of inanimate objects. Thus there is no room in my schema for "voluntarism," or the notion that certain spheres of human activity are determined by "free will" rather than by a complex of causational variables. Those behavioral scientists who take the voluntaristic position have quite a job on their hands, as it seems to me, in trying to separate out those areas of human behavior that are caused and those that are not. I happily leave them to their task. It is not mine.

Thus, in a strict scientific sense, I do not believe in "free will." On the other hand, I believe that as individual human begins engaged in making decisions at virtually every moment of the waking day, we *must* and *do* act as though we had free will. Any other course is, in a practical sense, impossible, even unimaginable. In other words, free will is an operationally necessary illusion. But I believe that, with regard to any human action once it has transpired, if we "knew all the variables" and their interrelationships we could give a causal explanation of the action. This is a conceptual position and in no way indicates that I am persuaded that we know enough about "all the variables" at this time, or perhaps will ever know enough, to explain all of human behavior. But this is the logical goal of social science.

It should be readily apparent to anyone who has read this far that my conception of scientific positivism is not of the variety that excludes subjective states of the actor and attempts to study man only by observing overt behavior. Quite the contrary. Subjective states and objective behavior, and the intricate and often very unobvious ways in which they relate to one another, consitute, as I see it, the irreducible subject matter of the science of man.

I believe that the science of human behavior is, in a fundamental sense, one science. Both the causes and the effects of human behavior are seamless. They do not break up by sovereign inevitability into sociology, psychology, anthropology, political science, and history. These are simply historically developed partial, and to some degree logically justifiable, separate perspectives for viewing or touching the elephant, to use the analogy of the well-known fable. But the elephant stands there in one piece and all of a piece. Since I believe that, in one sense, it is the actions of individual men and women which form the building blocks of human behavior, this would appear to push me in the direction of being a "psychological reductionist." I can accept this label with equanimity, provied that it be understood that I also believe in the reality of sociological constructs as *phenomena existing prior to the entrance on the scene of any given individual or cohort of individuals.* In this sense, I accept the position of "emergence," to use the appropriate technical term for affirming the unique reality of organized complexes at their own level of organization. Actually, my position is that sociological entities such as institutions, classes, cultural patterns, and the like, are ultimately traceable to the actions and interactions of individuals *in the past,* but since we do not normally have the time or the knowledge to trace these sociological constructs back into the myriads of individual actions and interaction from which they are eventually derivable, it makes sense to deal with them as emergent realities constituting effective variables to be used along with the psychological variables of the present to put together causal explanations of human behavior. Thus I believe it would be accurate to classify myself as a "theoretical reductionist" but a heurisitic or practical "emergentist." I reject the Durkheimian position, however, that sociology must confine itself to the study of sociological variables both as causes and effects because, theoretically, I find no justification for this position, and practically, it has led to a situation where strictly sociological explanations of human behavior have been so incomplete that only a certain portion of that behavior has been thus explained. In other words, our correlations with only sociological variables in them are too low; there is too much unexplained variance in the dependent variables, or outcomes thus explained. Thus I believe that we must combine sociological with psychological variables to raise the explanatory power of our generalizations. In fact, in principle, we should take our variables wherever we find them, in the sense that they might have explanatory value. The sociologist, in this conception of the discipline, becomes someone who is simply particularly sensitive to the existence of sociological variables, and is knowledgeable about them, and can provide necessary correctives to practitioners of the other behavioral science disciplines who may not be sensitive to, or trained in, their usability and relevance. These practitioners of the other disciplines can, in return, serve the same purpose for us as sociologists, in our endeavors.

With regard to the use of psychological variables in sociological work, even for those who concede or assert their relevance, it is clear from our just completed review of the literature, that there are still two alternative viewpoints: 1) that psychological variables should be used only as intervening variables to help explain social change, the independent and dependent variables being strictly sociological; 2) that no *a priori* assumptions should be made about the role of psychological variables, and that their possible use extends beyond (but includes) the "intervening" function and may, in many types of generalizations about human behavior, have co-equal status with sociological factors as independent variables. This model obviously envisages constant feedback effects between sociological and psychological phenomena and is open enough to entertain the possibility that certain universally found social structures or institutions have basically psychic origins in something called "human nature." This is my own position. Such universal institutional structures can certainly be modified by social-cultural and other environmental influences. All societies are not alike. Some do a better job, others a worse job of providing for the welfare of their members, and it is easy cynicism and it is wrong to refuse to make distinctions among them on the basis of valid criteria of decency, freedom, reasonable want satisfaction, and general quality of life within them. To stand a famous

43

remark from the work of George Orwell on its head by changing the focus: all societies are imperfect, but some societies
are more imperfect than others. Nevertheless, if such a thing
as human nature exists, then there are biological parameters
to cultural forms.

In the search for "human nature," the question must now
be asked: Where do we go for evidence of what its general
outlines might be? Let me say at the outset that I do not believe
that we are yet at the point where definitive evidence on this
question has been systematically gathered and is readily
available for confident use. Thus, my own theory of human
nature, which I shall present shortly, must be regarded in a
scientific sense, simply as a set of hypotheses subject, of
course, to empirical verification or non-verification. In some
ways it is similar to some theories that have been offered in
the past; in other ways it has, I believe, some distinctive
qualities, or at least some distinctive emphases. At any rate,
by discussing the possible sources of evidence, I can at least
give some clues as to where and how I derived my own views
about the nature of man, and indicate where I believe further
evidence must be sought and systematically evaluated.

First of all, I should like to make it clear that I do not share
the enthusiastic view of some social scientists, induced by the
coming into public salience in the past ten years or so of
ethological and primatological studies, written by prominent
practitioners in these disciplines such as Konrad Lorenz or by
skilled popular writers such as Robert Ardrey, that careful
observation of other animal species, particularly those closest
to man in evolutionary development, can be particularly
helpful in understanding human behavior and constructing
an accurate theory of human nature. My reason for this feeling
of dubiousness about the relevance of ethological data for the
study of man is that, as ethologists themselves concede, behavior tendencies are species-specific; that is, each species
has its own repertory of genetically programmed instincts or
predispositions for behavior. From a strictly logical scientific
point of view, there is no way to determine the nature of the
behavior of members of a particular species other than by

observing those members in action. Extrapolations from one species to another on the basis of observable evidence may help in tracing lines of evolutionary development, but such a comparative and evolutionary approach is not a substitute for observation of the particular species under study. In the case of *homo sapiens*, the development of his large and heavily convoluted brain capable of complex conceptual thought, places the members of this species light-years away in behavioral capacities and tendencies from his nearest relatives in the evolutionary scheme. This last statement should in no way be taken to mean that I am oblivious to man's evolutionary ancestry, or that I am merely repeating the familiar refrain of traditional social scientists that the behavior of the "lower animals" is determined by instincts, wheras man is entirely plastic and malleable. It should be obvious to the reader by now that I do not believe in any such sharp division in behavioral origins. Man is, obviously, much less governed by a repertory of specific instincts than other animal species and much more subject to learning and environmental influences. This does not mean, however, that he does not have his own set of biological needs, drives, predispositions, and tendencies. What is at stake, here, is the careful observation of the way in which man's specific biological inheritance interacts with his magnificent (there is no other word that will do—and the adjective is not used here simply in its laudatory implications) brain to produce characteristic human behavior. No other animal species is similarly constituted and therefore I find the results of the ethologists' studies interesting in themselves but of little value in trying to understand the behavior of the human species. Alexander Pope was more right than he knew when he advised that "The proper study of mankind is Man." It is not the study of chimpanzees, macaques, or baboons.

If not to the ethologists, then, where can we turn? To the data of psychologists is a logical answer. And it is clear that the studies of psychologists are highly relevant. Yet there are numerous problems here, and my sampling of the appropriate psychological literature persuades me that there is no generally accepted and validated theory of human nature emanating as yet from psychology. There are many *different* theories of human nature and human personality ranging from the instinct based theories of Freud and classical psychoanalysis to the environmentally oriented, stimulus-response approach of "radical behaviorism," with ego-psychology, actualization theories such as those of Carl Rogers and Abraham Maslow, and other variations in between.[49] Turning to a topical approach, a perusal of an authoritative, lengthy, and analytically sophisticated recent "review of the literature" article on "Aggression," makes it apparent that psychologists do not agree on whether aggression in man is based on instinct or drive, is a response to frustration, is acquired by reinforcement mechanisms after random occurrence, or is a function of modeling or imitative behavior.[50] There is much to be learned from the numerous reports of experimental psychologists on selected issues, the generalizations of clinical psychologists and practicing psychoanalysts, and the theoretical formulations of "personality" psychologists; but it is clear that consensus on human nature is yet to be achieved, and the range of opinion on the relevant issues is virtually as wide as that which exists among those who are not professional psychologists. Psychology, of course, is a field with many sub-specialties, and there are "cognitive" specialists who rarely or never become involved with questions of emotional motivation, or physiological psychologists whose research is concerned, for example, solely with the physiology of vision. In spite of the logic of this kind of fragmentation, which is in no way substantially different from the situation in other behavioral science disciplines, I find it somewhat strange that the development of a theory of human nature does not occupy more of the center of psychological concern than it does, or

[49]See Salvatore R. Maddi, *Personality Theories: A Comparative Analysis,* rev. ed. (Homewood, Ill., Dorsey Press, 1972).
[50]See Seymour Feshbach, "Aggression," *Carmichael's Manual of Child Psychology,* 3rd ed., Vol II, ed. Paul H. Mussen (New York, Wiley, 1970), pp. 159–259.

that so little consensus has yet been achieved in the field of psychology on what human nature actually is.

While I have benefitted from the work of psychologists and those sociologists who have begun to deal with the question of human nature, and while I have certainly developed an appropriate vocabulary and a logic and methodology of scientific inference from my professional training and experience, insofar as I can accurately introspect and trace the development of my own views on human nature, it seems to me that they have arisen largely out of day-to-day observation of successive current events over a fairly long time period, similar observations of the behavior of others (and myself) in situations where I was actually present, and the reading of history. In other words, I am suggesting that the data for a theory of human nature lie all around us in our own personal worlds, in the affairs of state, in the reports of happenings in the daily newspapers, in the visual images of the television news report, and in the easily available accounts of the trials, tribulations, and triumphs of men and women in all times and in all places in serious history, biography, and cross-cultural anthropology study. It is true that it is difficult to arrange all this data into the form of the controlled experiment, although the *ex post facto* controlled experiment model somewhat facilitates such a process. However, when one sees uniformities in behavior under particular conditions occur and reoccur with uncanny regularity, then certain insights develop. And, as I have written in some other place, an insight is simply a statistical operation performed silently in the mind. I suggest, then, that the data for a theory of human nature lie all around us. That is why, I would surmise, that the works of great literary artists such as a Shakespeare, a Melville, or a Dostoevsky, are informed with a bottom-line view of the nature of man. Nor is this process confined to writers. There is a view of man or of life, I would argue, implicit in Beethoven's *Eroica* symphony which is quite different from the one derivable from his last five string quartets. At any rate, man observing and explaining the world around him over time has the data which he needs in order to formulate a theory of human nature. With regard to the fundamental source of my own views on human nature, as the young people of today in their evocatively appropriate vernacular might put it: "That's where I'm coming from."

The Theory

Human nature is acquired developmentally. This statement is not a contradiction in terms because the capacities of the newly born child need time for maturation. During this process, the child interacts with other human beings: mother, father, siblings, substitute caretakers, and peers, so that the influences of the environment are everpresent from birth onward. Nevertheless, it is possible to conceptually distinguish the hereditary equipment from the social influences even while noting their immediate and constant interaction. The neonate cannot survive without caretaking functions from others, and thus some minimal amount of social interaction must be assumed in the maturation of the genetic capacities of all human beings.

I need four categories to describe the basic genetic equipment of the developing child relevant to human nature analysis. These are 1) physiological needs; 2) capacities for emotional or affective expression; 3) cognitive capacities; and 4) overarching drive motivations. I need three stages to demonstrate the appearance and functioning of the overarching drive motivations, and I need one category which I shall call "derived behavioral patterns" to refer to the behavioral tendencies which result from the operation of this genetically developing behavioral motor in interaction with the social environment. I shall consider these categories and stages serially, although interactive processes occurring among them will require some discussion even in this serial description.

The irreducible core of physiological needs are hunger, thirst, and sexual desire. One can add oxygen need, eliminatory need, and temperature control to this list, but since these latter needs are rather universally fulfilled without occasioning much in the way of behavior dynamics, not being in short supply or subject to value elaboration, they need not further concern us. I remain unpersuaded by much of Freudian psychology, so that, while concurring with Freud's basic view concerning the inevitable tension between human desires and societal requirements, and finding some of his conceptualizations and vocabulary useful, I do not attach as much significance to infantile sexuality as he did and frankly confess that I find the idea of a universal or even society-wide "Oedipus complex" untenable. I defer to no one in my estimation of the importance of the sexual drive and the crucial role of its degree of fulfillment in human happiness, but I believe that its dynamic importance emerges largely only at puberty, then to continue unabated for a lifetime.

Emotional or affective expression capacities can probably be conceptualized and specified in several alternative ways, none of which differ greatly from each other in essential meaning, but I suggest that the following classification is reasonably accurate and sufficiently comprehensive. The human infant is capable of feeling anger, fear, anxiety, attachment, and dependency. In the developmental process, after socialization has effectively begun, the crystallization of the sense of self and the experience of being evaluated by significant others leads to the emergence of capacities for feeling shame and pride. Fear and anxiety are closely related emotions but theoretically somewhat separable by the specificity of the stimulus in fear and the diffusion of the stimulus in anxiety.[51] Attachment and dependency feelings share the common attribute of favorable feeling toward the relevant human target, but differ in the amount of ego sufficiency involved in the respective feelings. Pride and shame await the development of the sense of self and the appearance of the super-ego, or conscience, as the child internalizes values imposed by powerful and valued others—in the first

---

[51]See on this point Paul Henry Mussen, John Janeway Conger, and Jerome Kagan, *Child Development and Personality*, 4th ed. (New York, Harper, 1974), p. 387.

instance, of course, the parents, but expanding to a larger and larger group of effective judges, including peers, and finally the society itself as expressed through its dominant norms. It should be added, however, that, particularly in large and complex societies containing many subgroups with varying values, the pool of significant others may shrink as the individual comes to realize that options for collective support exist, and he may do some picking and choosing based on his particular needs and values of the moment.

The cognitive capacities of the developing child and, to a lesser degree, the mature adult, have received considerable attention from psychologists. Much of the results of this attention, however valuable in itself, is too detailed and of insufficient relevance for my purposes here. Also, there is one cognitive function, of crucial value for personality development and social interaction, which appears to have been substantially neglected. I shall explicate this point shortly. At any rate, I would classify cognitive capacities into five categories: 1) conceptualization; 2) means-ends apprehension; 3) self-conception; 4) evaluation; and 5) rationalization. The first two require little comment. They are obviously at the core of cognition and involve the ability to organize sensory stimuli into appropriate categories formulated by noting relevant similarities and dissimilarities, to thus carry on symbolic communication by means of language, and finally to discover plausible or probable cause and effect sequences. With this basic portion of the cognitive apparatus, man has cumulatively achieved wonders in the material and technical realm culminating in our time in the delivery of men to the moon equipped with an honored, safe-return ticket. That this same brilliant success of cognitive functions in the technical area also has equipped major nation-states with weapons capable of producing virtually complete mutual destruction should alert us to the possibility that there are other cognitive functions and interrelationships of cognitive functions with other aspects of human personality that need further attention—that, in other words, man's cognitive operations in the social world of interpersonal and intergroup relations have been conspicuously less successful than in the technical world. Let us proceed.

The third category of cognitive functioning which I have listed is "self-conception." This category refers to the development of a sense of self in the child. The infant at birth and for a time thereafter is a rather inchoate constellation of bodily and feeling states which demand gratification. Child psychologists are pretty much agreed that at this stage the neonate does not differentiate himself from the surrounding environment of human beings and objects which serve to succor, nourish, clean, and restrain him. Somewhere between one year and one year-and-a-half, the infant cognitively, and presumably gradually, develops a conception of himself as separate from his environment, an entity in himself distinct from the other entities, human and material, which surround him. In other words, he becomes able to see and contemplate himself as an object existing in a field of other objects. In the description of the child's cognitive development provided by psychology's most famous student of the subject, Jean Piaget, and his associate, the process is described as follows: "The child's initial universe is entirely centered on his own body and action in an egocentrism as total as it is unconscious (for lack of consciousness of the self). In the course of the first eighteen months, however, there occurs a kind of Copernican revolution, or, more simply, a kind of general decentering process whereby the child eventually comes to regard himself as an object among others in a universe that is made up of permanent objects (that is, structured in a spatio-temporal manner) and in which there is at work a causality that is both localized in space and objectified in things."[52]

The development of the sense of selfhood, the realization that one is a separate creature with executive function pos-

---

[52]Jean Piaget and Bärbel Inhelder, *The Psychology of the Child* (New York, Basic Books, Harper Torchbooks, 1969), p. 13. See also, Arthur T. Jersild, *Child Psychology*, 6th ed. (Englewood Cliffs, N.J., Prentice-Hall, 1968), pp. 165–70; and Elizabeth B. Hurlock, *Child Development*, 4th ed. (New York, McGraw-Hill, 1964), pp. 525–26.

sibilities and with emotional feelings that emanate from one-self is, of course, the first step in the process of mastering skills which prepare the child for adult life and which can eventuate, in the case of extremely gifted individuals, in the noblest creations of science, the arts, and human leadership in matters of societal welfare. However, in all individuals the development of the self concept brings into being an entirely new dimension in the area of interpersonal relationships. No longer is the infant simply a conglomeration of specific needs which demand fulfillment. Now there is a self which interacts with other selves—at first, of course, the parents—which are consciously perceived as making demands and providing approval, disapproval, and punishment for compliance or lack of it. Now there are siblings who emerge as entities in themselves which compete for parental attention. In short, *now there is a self to be defended,* against competitors, against power-holders, against authority figures, and, most of all against those who have the audacity to value us less highly than we value ourselves.

This last statement should prepare the way for the fourth category of cognitive capacities and functions which I wish to distinguish. So far as I am able to discover, it has not been adequately conceptualized and emphasized, or placed in a systematic framework, in the social science literature, and yet it is one of the most important mainsprings in human behavior. I call it simply "evaluation." Man's cognitive capacities allow and impel him to make the finest of distinctions in virtually every area of human life. Some people offer us pleasure, others pain. Some people are taller, others short-er. Some individuals charm us by their personalities, others repel us. Some members of the opposite sex are more attrac-tive physically, others less attractive, still others are not at-tractive to us at all. Some persons are highly intelligent, others are average, or below average in intellectual abilities. Some people impress us with their leadership and executive qualities, others do not. This listing of traits could obviously be extended indefinitely. The various positions on each of these implicit scales are evaluated by Ego so that they become informed with relative degrees of positive or negative affect. To be sure, social and cultural factors play some role in shaping the criteria used in these evaluations, but a) no cultural system can eliminate the human propensity to make the evaluations; and b) I have a strong hunch that appropriate study of the cultural variations would show that these variations deal with rather superficial aspects of human qualities and that the evaluative scales of people all over the world and throughout history have been remarkably similar. If my general hypothesis here is valid, then every individual is at one and the same time an evaluator and an object of evaluation— that is, an evaluatee. Every human interaction, then, contains a process of mutual evaluation. This process is most salient, of course, when strangers meet, and interaction among familiars is characterized by a relatively stabilized, or temporarily stabilized, set of mutual evaluations, but this does not gainsay the continuous and omnipresent nature of the process nor guarantee in any way that the "stabilized" mutual evaluations are optimally satisfactory to the interactive participants. This constant process of mutual evaluation, I would suggest, constitutes the theoretical background for the dramaturgical "presentation of self" in most favorable terms that informs Goffman's analysis of human interaction, and is also the more general process out of which emanate the subprocesses of "reference group" and "relative deprivation" behavior. I should add, with particular reference to the last point that the individual not only evaluates other individuals but also evaluates himself, whether such self-evaluation is accurate or not. Or, to use a conceptualization offered by the psychologist, Seymour Epstein, he has a "self-theory," a theory about himself.[53] I shall leave this point now, temporarily, in order to complete my enumeration of cognitive traits, but it should already be apparent that since no individual is likely to rate unusually high on all dimensions of possible evaluation, and

[53]Seymour Epstein, "The Self-Concept Revisited: Or a Theory of a Theory," *American Psychologist*, Vol. 28, No. 5 (May 1973), pp. 404–16.

since, according to my hypothesis, the process of mutual evaluation is pervasive, continuous, and ineradicable by any cultural system, the potentiality for anger, hostility, and conflict arising out of disparate mutual evaluations is very great.

My fifth and last category among the cognitive capacities is "rationalization," a term which I use in its generally understood psychological meaning of providing a socially approved reason or explanation for a given action when the real reason or explanation for the action is negatively evaluated by the criteria provided by societal or group norms. Let us consider. Man's "magnificent" brain is *at the service of* his needs, emotions, and his "overarching drives" (which I have yet to come to). Why should we ever have assumed that anything else was the case? Man's powerful cognitive abilities can be used instrumentally to strive for satisfaction of his needs, emotions, and drives, and is so used, but in the process, his wishes, more often than not, come in conflict with those of others and with society's normative structure for regulating this conflict or otherwise restricting his elemental or derived wants (as in the case, for instance, of "victimless crimes"). What is more natural than for man, so beset, to use his intricate mental capacity which can split hairs, twist meanings, self-delude, and consciously or unconsciously dissemble motives till the cows come home, to present a "sanitized" version of his reasons and behavior which will avoid the censure or punishment of his fellows. "Use every man after his desert, and who shall 'scape whipping?" notes Hamlet with dolorous mockery in converse with Polonius. And who wants a whipping! And Hamlet's reply to Rosencrantz who has just announced that the world had grown honest is the ironic "Then is doomsday near." Some such conception of man's rationalizing propensities also seems to inform Dennis Wrong's concluding sentence in his well known essay, dealt with earlier, when he refers to "man, that *plausible* creature whose wagging tongue so often hides the despair and darkness in his heart [my emphasis]." Finally, it is precisely this tendency of man to use his cognitive abilities to justify himself, to avoid censure, and to deflect negative evaluations, which supplies a crucial missing link in Pareto's analysis of man and society. Pareto's *magnum opus*, as we have already indicated, is virtually a great set of variations on the theme of man's attempt to "logicalize," to present in logical or pseudo-logical terms his behavior, which is really motivated by the "residues," or instinctive instigators. But when he deals with the question of why this constant attempt takes place, his answer is simply, and unpersuasively, that the tendency is part of the instinctive framework itself. The tendency to "logicalize" is one of the residues. Not so. It is part of the protective mechanism which goes into operation when man's cognitive apparatus sets up defenses to enable him to forestall adverse judgments and societal censure.

I come now to the category of "overarching drive motivations." These differ from the specific needs, emotions, and cognitive capacities in that they represent the implacable tendencies of the *total* organism and are not traceable to any specific neurological mechanisms or sources but are presumably products of evolutionary development which, in the lower animals manifest themselves in self-preservative tendencies but which in man must be conceptualized and described in much more complex terms. To a certain extent, they have appeared by implication in our previous discussion, but they must be explicated now in precise formulation and in developmental fashion since they appear in stages. These stages are not to be thought of as supplanting each other, but as cumulative, highly related, and interactive, as will shortly become apparent.

Stage 1 is simple hedonism, or the seeking of pleasure-avoidance of pain principle, which impels the human organism to seek gratification of his specific physiological needs and to respond in similar fashion to his emotional states by appropriate avoidance, physically manipulative, or attachment behavior. This is the overarching drive motivation in the infant prior to the development of the sense of self. Stage 2 appears after the self-concept has developed, somewhere within the first eighteen months of life, and devolves exactly on defending the self as a total entity against adverse

55

psychological judgments by significant others in the form of disapproval and denigration. This stage, as we have already noted, brings with it not only a sense of self, but increasingly as the child gradually expands his apprehension of the various criteria on which he is being evaluated, a conception of the worth of his own self qualities, each one of which is theoretically and empirically subject to favorable or unfavorable evaluation. This stage brings into play the mechanism of ego-defense, the defense of the self, which Gregory Rochlin, the psychoanalyst, regards as the dominant motive in human behavior and the sovereign source of aggression.[54] While I concur with Rochlin in many of his formulations, I shall deal with aggression in a somewhat more expansive framework, to be discussed below. At any rate, consideration of ego-defense has necessarily already entered our discussion in previous pages. I have no doubts about its salient and pervasive presence in human life.

Stage 3 makes its appearance as soon as the child becomes aware of his mortality. It is the desire for eternal self-preservation—the desire for immortality. Man, so far as we know, is the only creature who is aware of the fact that death is inexorably his ultimate fate. He does not face this state of affairs with equanimity nor with stoic resignation, but turns to theological or philosophical ideologies which promise him eternal life, salvation, resurrection, or reincarnation, and assure him that his apparent cessation from life's activities is not an abrupt ending but a passage to a greater glory. This confrontation of man with his own mortality is a phenomenon which has occupied the attention of all great artists who have probed the depths of human consciousness, as well as of behavioral scientists. The time of its incipient awareness as well as the dynamic operation of its effects undoubtedly vary with different individuals, but Rochlin, on the basis of his clinical experience asserts that its cognitive presence appears quite early in the life of the child. "My own studies," he

---

[54]Gregory Rochlin, *Man's Aggression: The Defense of the Self* (Boston, Gambit, 1973).

declares, "have shown that the knowledge of death, including the possibility of one's own death, is acquired at a very early age, and far sooner than is generally supposed. By the age of three years the fear of one's own death is communicable in unequivocal terms. How much earlier than three years of age this information is acquired is a matter of tenuous speculation. Communication with a younger child on the subject is unlikely. It also would be much too fragmentary. What is more important is that in a child three years old death as a fear, as a possibility, has already begun to produce significant effects."[55] Ernest Becker, the anthropologist, has explored this theme with remarkable virtuosity in two recent books, his Pulitizer Prize-winning *The Denial of Death* and *Escape from Evil*.[56] "The idea of death," Becker asserts, "the fear of it, haunts the human animal like nothing else; it is a mainspring of human activity—activity designed largely to avoid the fatality of death, to overcome it by denying in some way that it is the final destiny for man."[57]

The attachment to immortality granting belief systems probably merges imperceptibly, as a scientific phenomenon, with immersion in social and political ideologies which at least guarantee the survival of the chosen or favored group or system of ideas. The latter is a kind of "immortality once removed," and if one must die, how much better it is to "die for a cause." Political and social ideologies, however, I believe are not entirely explained by immortality seeking, but also contain strong elements of cumulative anger and rage based on a sense of violation of justice norms. How much of this outrage derives from objective conditions, how much from internal personality dynamics in reality unrelated to the social conditions, and how much from immortality striving is difficult to say. Undoubtedly all of these factors are at work in

[55]Gregory Rochlin, *Griefs and Discontents* (Boston, Little Brown, 1965), p. 67.
[56]Ernest Becker, *The Denial of Death* (New York, Free Press, 1973); and *Escape from Evil* (New York, Free Press, 1975).
[57]*The Denial of Death*, p. ix.

varying combinations of causal relevance in particular cases. It is difficult not to be impressed, however, with the way in which each person's projected utopia (I include my own) turns out to be a place where its creator, with his particular virtues and defects, would do well. If one is a philosopher, the ideal state is to be ruled by a philosopher-king.

All three of the stages of overarching drive motivations can, of course, be subsumed under the heading of the effectuation and the preservation of ego-welfare. To separate them, conceptually, however, is to pay appropriate attention to their developmental aspects and to the somewhat different dynamics and contents which their analytical distinctiveness implies.

I now come to my final category of "derived behavioral patterns." They are derived in that they are not contained, as entities, in man's original biological equipment of needs, emotional capacities, cognitive capacities and overarching drive motivations, but are produced by the interaction of some part or parts of this equipment with the social and cultural environment. This does not mean in any way that they are unimportant or even that they are not pervasive. Quite the contrary. What it does mean is that they are elicited from the biological organism by socio-cultural forces acting upon it. The two most important derived behavioral patterns are aggression and cooperation.

Aggression, which is behavior, must be distinguished from aggressive feelings, which are attitudes. Motivated behavior of any degree of complexity at all requires, as we shall see, an intricately formed and functioning decisional process which produces varying outcomes in situations involving similar stimuli, depending upon a whole host of additional variables such as, for instance, fear of punishment. Furthermore, aggressive behavior can arise from many different motivations and capacities. Aggression, in other words, is preceded by varying causal sequences which in some cases are little related to each other. This fact becomes quite apparent if we distinguish among at least four different types of aggression—that is, aggressive behavior, I shall call them 1) anger-induced aggression; 2) instrumental aggression; 3) authority-induced aggression; and 4) force-induced aggression. Let us consider them serially.

Anger-induced aggression is the type most commonly thought of and involves the transformation of anger into hostility—that is, anger directed at a particular person or group—usually, but not always, the source which has produced the anger-hostility syndrome in the first place. This source may have blocked physiological need satisfaction, it may have interfered with the successful completion of attachment or dependency behavior, it may have devalued Ego's self conception, or it may have threatened or appeared to threaten by verbal attack or by behavior, Ego's constructed immortality-granting system. This type of blockage calls into play the well-known, frustration-aggression mechanism, which had been noted in the early work of Freud, described in somewhat different terms by McDougall, and conceptualized and developed in systematic fashion in the modern period in the work of John Dollard and associates.[58] This is, of course, a very common type of aggression, but it should be noted that the instigated anger and hostility can be directed as aggressive behavior at various targets: a) the source of the frustration, b) a scapegoat, or c) the self, depending upon a calculation of the reality power forces operative in the situation, and upon internal personality dynamics. It is also possible, I believe, for the hostility to be kept dormant and not be expressed at all as aggressive behavior if the power forces arrayed against it are perceived as overwhelming in all directions. There is a lot of aggressive behavior in the world, but the amount of hostility lying broodingly in the actor but unexpressed in behavior exceeds the latter by far.

Instrumental aggression is aggressive behavior carried out in the pursuit of scarce and evaluated goods and services

[58]See John Dollard, Neal E. Miller, Leonard W. Doob, O. H. Mowrer, and Robert R. Sears, in collaboration with Clellan S. Ford, Carl Iver Hovland, and Richard T. Sollenberger, *Frustration and Aggression* (New Haven, Yale University Press, 1939).

which gratify physiological needs and which become elaborated by status attributes into self-enhancing valued objects as well. Warfare between small groups of hunters and gatherers in man's early history may have approximated this type of aggression. On an individual level, this type of aggression is commonplace among children but becomes more restricted as adult mechanisms for maintaining law and order come into play in a society. However, it is obviously not eliminated entirely. Common assault and robbery on the streets of our modern metropolises is probably not usually committed with great emotional aggressive affect. The main motive of the perpetrator is simply to get the wallet, and particularly the cash within it. Of course, the possibility for instrumental aggression to turn into the anger-induced type is always present, if effective resistance on the part of the target or victim ensues.

Authority-induced aggression is aggressive behavior ordered by an authoritative source and carried out as a result of obedience to the authority. It has been demonstrated experimentally by the psychologist, Stanley Milgram, in his series of simulated situations where an inordinately high percentage of his subjects were induced to administer what they thought were pain-producing electric shocks to a confederate of the experimenter acting as an innocent co-subject in an alleged "learning experiment."[59] The experiment was designed, of course, to shed some light on the psychological aspects of the bureaucratic mechanisms and manifestations which were a necessary part of the Holocaust, the Nazi murder of six million Jews—the most evil manifestation of aggression of our time or, as yet, any other time. While Milgram's experimental situation did not, of course, call for the infliction of severe injury or death, and there were other important differences between life in Nazi Germany and his experimental laboratory, this research has implications for the question of the extent to which individuals may be induced to commit acts which they theoretically and affectively

[59]See Stanley Milgram, *Obedience to Authority* (New York, Harper, 1974).

regard as immoral but which the show of authority and the situational pressures may bring to fruition. On the basis of twentieth century history and Milgram's ingenious experiments, we may confidently assert that while all people are not uniformly subject to it, authority-induced aggression is a formidable phenomenon to be reckoned with.

If authority can induce men to commit aggressive acts, consider how much more potent force or the threat of force is likely to be in eliciting such behavior. William Goode has recently written persuasively on the importance of force and force-threat as a form of social control, and the tendency among modern sociologists to ignore or de-emphasize this powerful but frequently obscured or disguised source of human action.[60] It is clear, then, that we may speak of force-induced aggression, my fourth category. The appearance as an institutional form of the conscript army within the last two centuries of Western history illustrates clearly that modern warfare is fought by millions of men who are influenced to "join up" not simply through authority (though this factor probably plays some role), but because, at the bottom line, if they refuse to enlist, they face the wrath of the state in the form of imprisonment (unless, in democratic societies, they can convince local draft boards that they are legitimate conscientious objectors), or, doubtless, in some nations, death. While emotions of potential shame at disobeying moral norms of "fighting for one's country," and fears of disapprobation from one's family, neighborhood, and other primary group sources also play a role, along with authority, the success of the modern conscript army in filling its ranks rests, in the last analysis, on force threat. This is particularly true, of course, when the moral issues at stake in the contemplated or ongoing war are ambiguous or have distinctly negative connotations, as they did for many American young people in the recent war in Vietnam. Highly intense civil wars in small nations, such as the one which recently raged in Lebanon,

---

[60]William J. Goode, "The Place of Force in Human Society," *American Sociological Review*, Vol. 37, No. 5 (October 1972), pp. 507–19.

where such emotional issues as ethnic identity and ethnic power are salient, undoubtedly spring from, and bring into play, aggression emanating from anger and hostility. But large-scale modern military conflict need not count heavily on emotion-induced aggression from the rank and file. The power of the state is sufficient for the purpose. In totalitarian societies the enormous concentration of the means of enforced social control, including both weapons and information, and the lack of any political mechanism for instituting countervailing power, provide its rulers with the means of enforcing effective group aggression against any conceivable outsider nation, or any subgroup or individual within its population which it singles out for punishment or destruction. Force-induced aggression is not a figment of the analyst's imagination. It is a grim reality of the modern world.

We come, finally, to our second major "derived behavioral pattern," namely cooperation. By cooperation, I mean simply any form of behavior which allows human beings to interact without aggression or the threat of aggression. In a sense, it is a residual category, but none the less important for that. In fact, it is, of course, absolutely necessary for human survival. It allows us to play established roles in a predictable manner; it permits us to mingle on the street as passers-by without fear of attack; it is both a prerequisite and a consequence of the division of labor that allows some of us to function as teachers and writers, while others ply their trades as carpenters, plumbers, salesmen, and politicians. It ranges as far on one side, as behavior arising out of familial or conjugal love and, on the other, as the sullen and unhappy compliance of a child ordered by his mother to be "nice to the doctor" who is plunging a needle into his arm for the purpose of vaccinating him against a deadly disease.

Like aggression, cooperation is behavior. Like aggression, it may be produced by different motivations. In fact, like aggression, cooperation may be divided into four types defined by the particular motivational and cognitive forces which bring it into being, supplemented by one additional and important type induced by the internalization of norms.

The first four categories are the same, with the exception that one of the motivational forces is replaced by two others. We may then, "*in totum*, speak of 1) attachment and/or dependency-induced cooperation; 2) instrumental cooperation; 3) authority-induced cooperation; 4) force-induced cooperation; and 5) normative, or super-ego-induced cooperation. These meanings, particularly after my discussion of types of aggression and the previous paragraph delineating the range of types of cooperative behavior, are sufficiently obvious so that I need not belabor the reader with a serial exposition of each type. Before concluding this paper I would like, however, to emphasize three points. First, instrumental cooperation plays a very large role in human affairs. We are smart enough, we members of *homo sapiens*, to know that we need each other in a wide variety of endeavors necessary to our own welfare. We act accordingly a great part of the time. Secondly, we are taught from childhood to eschew aggression and enjoined to "act nice" to other people in ordinary situations. To a considerable extent we do internalize these norms and function as instructed. Thirdly, society has enacted a network of controls in the form of law and custom which induce us to act cooperatively in a great many situations whether we like it or not. Thus, cooperative behavior makes up a large part of the daily activities of most people. On the other hand, as I have previously pointed out with some emphasis, the forces making for aggression and hostile feelings and thus laying the groundwork for aggressive behavior lie pervasively in the human environment and in ourselves. Thus we are faced with that complex mixture of cooperation and aggressive feeling and behavior which makes up the tension-laden human scene. It is this tension, provided by the interaction of every man's "human nature" with every other man's "human nature" that constitutes the most telling aspect of society and social institutions. Unless we comprehend it, our sociological analyses will be incomplete and our proffered sociological solutions to pressing human problems will fail. Only by understanding human nature and its role in sociological processes can we make lasting progress in societal welfare—progress which will not be undone or twisted into retrogression or transmuted into deleterious unanticipated consequences because we ignored, were unable to discern, or were unwilling to face the true complexity of the nature of man.

2
Toward a General Theory of Racial & Ethnic Group Relations

In *Assimilation in American Life,* published in 1964[1] I presented a multidimensional model of the assimilation process and applied it to the American scene historically and contemporaneously. This model distinguished seven assimilation dimensions or variables: cultural, structural, marital, identificational, attitude receptional (absence of prejudice), behavior receptional (absence of discrimination), and civic (absence of value and power conflict). Certain hypotheses about the relationship of these variables were advanced; these were (1) that in majority—minority group contact cultural assimilation or acculturation would occur first; (2) that acculturation may take place even when none of the other types of assimilation has occurred; and this situation of "acculturation only" may continue indefinitely; and (3) that if structural assimilation occurs along with or subsequent to acculturation, all the other types of assimilation will inevitably follow. This theoretical model of variables and propositions was used to analyze the meaning of the traditional American ideologies

Note: I wish to thank W. Clark Roof for a careful reading of an earlier draft of this paper and for some useful suggestions.

[1]Milton M. Gordon, *Assimilation in American Life* (New York, Oxford University Press, 1964). In two earlier publications, one going back to 1954, I had made the distinction between cultural and structural assimilation which is basic to the model. See my "Social Structure and Goals in Group Relations," *Freedom and Control in Modern Society,* ed. Morroe Berger, Theodore Abel, and Charles H. Page, (New York, Van Nostrand, 1954), pp. 141–57; and "Assimilation in America: Theory and Reality," *Daedalus* (Spring 1961), 263–85.

of "Anglo-conformity," the "melting pot," and "cultural pluralism," and the historical and current realities of American racial and ethnic group life. It was concluded that massive (although not complete nor uniform) acculturation to Anglo-Saxon norms and patterns had in fact taken place historically, while structural separation of racial and religious groups, and to some degree national origins groups, still remained. One important exception to this generalization were intellectuals and artists among whom a new subsociety appeared to be forming which largely ignored ethnic considerations in the formation of primary group relationships and organizational membership. To this overall picture of American racial and ethnic relations in the early 1960s, which it seemed to me would continue indefinitely, I applied the term "structural pluralism." This analysis contributed to the unfolding realization among students of race and ethnicity that the optimism of an earlier generation of sociologists concerning the inevitable assimilation or "melting" of American minority groups into some common framework which would effect their disappearance was distinctly unwarranted and that, in the words of Glazer and Moynihan, "the persisting facts of ethnicity demand attention, understanding, and accommodation."[2]

Subsequent events in American intergroup relations during the latter half of the 1960s and into the 1970s, the deepening of racial and ethnic conflicts throughout the world during this period, and my concurrence in the cogency of the call to both comparative research and the formulation of more general theories of intergroup relations by such writers as van den Berghe, Blalock, and Schermerhorn have led me to reexamine the assimilation process in a context somewhat more expanded than that of my previous formulation.[3] The

[2]Nathan Glazer and Daniel Patrick Moynihan, *Beyond the Melting Pot* (Cambridge, Harvard University Press and MIT Press, 1963), p. v.
[3]Pierre L. van den Berghe, *Race and Racism: A Comparative Perspective* (New York, Wiley, 1967); H. M. Blalock, Jr., *Toward a Theory of Minority-Group Relations* (New York, Wiley, 1967); R. A. Schermerhorn, *Comparative Ethnic Relations* (New York, Random House, 1970).

domestic events referred to above center particularly on the rise of the "black power" movement, Afro-American cultural nationalism, rioting by blacks in major American cities, efforts to institute community control over public institutions in black neighborhoods, and the presumed effects of these developments on the heightening of group consciousness and collective action among Mexican-Americans and Puerto Ricans, and possibly "white ethnic" groups as well.

The balance of this paper will first consider the relationship of assimilation analysis to the concepts of power and conflict which were relatively ignored (or, more accurately, perhaps, taken for granted) in my previous study, and second, will attempt to place considerations of assimilation, pluralism, power, and the like, into the more general framework of a multi-causal model for the prediction of particular outcomes in majority-minority group relations. The assimilation paradigm itself and its application to the American historical experience up until the early 1960s I find no reason to materially alter.

Blalock has made a useful distinction between competitive resources and pressure resources and, drawing upon social psychological theory, has conceptualized power as a product of resources and the mobilization of those resources.[4] We may, then, speak of competitive power—the ability to compete as individuals in the rewards system of the society—and pressure power—the power to effect change in the society in a collective fashion. I find it additionally useful to subdivide pressure power into two subtypes: (1) political pressure, narrowly defined, in the form of action by means of voting and litigation to induce favorable action on the part of the legislature, the courts, and the executive branches of government, and (2) disruptive pressure, consisting of acts which disrupt normal and expected routines of social intercourse; these could range from peaceful nonviolent demonstrations at one end of the spectrum through angry and

[4]*Toward a Theory of Minority-Group Relations,* chap. 4.

violence-threatening confrontations, up to sporadic rioting, and finally to the ultimate extreme of violent revolution.

With these distinctions in mind, I turn now to a reconstruction of the expectancies about the manner of social change in the area of racial and ethnic relations in the United States which prevailed in this country around the middle of the twentieth century among the liberal leadership of the movement for racial equality, both Negro and white, and among men of good will generally. These expectations were approximately as follows: that because of what appeared to be overwhelming white dominance, demographically, economically, and politically, the attempt to improve the lot of racial and ethnic minorities would have to be made by a massive effort to activate the consciences of white Americans to implement the American creed of democracy and equalitarianism, to eliminate Jim Crow laws in the South through litigation at the Supreme Court level, to fight for legislation in the North (and nationally) to legally bar discrimination in employment and housing, to break down the extra-legal barriers to voting by Negroes in the South and to encourage the use of the ballot by minority group members generally for the achievement of equal rights, and finally to work for federal and other governmental efforts to deal effectively with poverty and urban blight in a manner which would benefit all the poor in the population impartially, but which would, clearly, have particular impact, because of generations of past discrimination, on submerged racial groups.

Even the peaceful demonstrations of civil disobedience which became a part of the civil rights movement in the early sixties did not, on the whole, challenge these expectancies. The demonstrations, while often drawing violent reactions from hostile whites, were, at least so far as the demonstrators were concerned, generally nonviolent and were aimed at obtaining rights for Negroes which had already been granted by law in the wake of the Supreme Court decision against segregated public education in 1954, or were otherwise well within the boundary of practices sanctioned by American democratic values.

In summary, the proclaimed goal of both blacks and white liberals was equal treatment by the law, integration, the raising of the competitive resources of blacks by the corrective means of governmental aid programs and the opening up of white institutions to all, regardless of race, who could now or later qualify by meeting universalistic standards—in short, the use of competitive resources plus political resources, with nonviolent demonstrations viewed not so much in terms of disruption as a call to the conscience of America, and with the pace of progress seen as inevitably determined by the overwhelmingly greater power of the white majority. Within this context, the prediction of indefinitely continuing structural separation, or structural pluralism, was seen as a concession to the realities of both existing (though hopefully lessening) attitudes of prejudice and avoidance, and the factual presence of an already built-up institutional structure within the communities of racial minorities.

What actually happened, of course, in the subsequent period was not only an intensification of structural separatism, but, along with *some* of the developments mentioned above in what might be called "the liberal expectancy," the generally unanticipated emergence of the black power movement, black cultural nationalism, sporadic rioting in the black ghettoes, and the gradual supplanting (though not completely) of old-style liberal black leadership by a more militant type advocating and using disruptive pressure resources. Thus, there has developed, in a pluralist context, something close to a real power struggle with both potential and actual outbreaks of conflict signifying the uneasy race relations climate of the current American scene and which could conceivably, although not inevitably, reach the stage of what Lewis Killian has called "the impossible revolution."[5] At the same time, some of the processes encompassed in the "liberal expectancy" also continue to operate so that the picture is a mixed one. For an analysis of this complex

[5]Lewis M. Killian, *The Impossible Revolution?* (New York, Random House, 1968).

situation the variables of power and conflict must be attached or built into assimilation theory. This, however, is only another way of saying that *assimilation theory must, for purposes of achieving greater explanatory power, be placed in the framework of a larger theoretical context which helps explain the general processes of racial and ethnic group relations.* [6] What is required, then, is a more general theory of intergroup or racial and ethnic group relations, one which includes not only sociological but also psychological variables, a consideration of power relationships, and an examination of relevant basic social-psychological processes of human interaction. In the next portion of this chapter, I shall attempt to suggest the outlines of what, as it seems to me, such a theory should contain.

The first task in constructing a causal theory is to designate the effect, or dependent variable. While this attempt to extract such a temporarily static phenomenon from the ceaseless ebb and flow of human interaction is bound to be less than perfectly successful because of both "chain" and "feedback" effects, such an attempt must, clearly, be made if any theory at all is to be developed. The problem is also made more difficult by the fact that often the effect we are interested in is not a single or unfactorable variable but a complex of variables, whose total variation is a function of varying com-

---

[6]It should go without saying that assimilation theory, as presented in my earlier model, was never meant to advance the thesis that complete assimilation inevitably occurred in contact between ethnically diverse population groups—quite the contrary: the multidimensional approach to assimilation provided by my model allowed the various subtypes of assimilation to be conceptually distinguished from each other, advanced hypotheses about the interrelationships of these subtypes, allowed for the possibility of varying rates of progress toward assimilation among the various dimensions, or on some dimensions virtually no progress at all, and, in fact, predicted the indefinite continuance of structurally separate ethnic groups on the American scene. Nor did my discussion of assimilation assign absolute positive valuation to either the assimilationist or pluralist ends of the continuum. It did, however, present the hypothesis that there were boundaries to the process of separation of ethnic groups within the same society beyond which disfunctional effects were likely to occur.

binations of positions of its components. In such a situation, it is entirely possible that no overall quantitative measure of position on a unidimensional scale is possible at all, and the varying possible outcomes must be designated as a qualitative typology in which the subtypes of effects are separated not by quantitative units but by differences in kind. Such must certainly be the case in a first approximation of the designation of the dependent variable in a theory of intergroup relations.[7]

My thesis, then, is that the most useful dependent variable or attribute in a theory of racial and ethnic intergroup relations is a construct which consists of four subvariables. These are: (1) *Type of assimilation*, with the major distinction being that between cultural and structural assimilation. Each type can, in theory, of course, be thought of as quantifiable along a single scale or dimension ranging from complete assimilation on one end of the scale to complete pluralism on the other. (2) *Degree of total assimilation*. This variable would consist of an index combining scores for each subtype of assimilation. Theoretically, such scores could be assigned for each of the seven assimilation subtypes in my original assimilation model. For purposes of research economy, cultural and structural subtypes alone might be used, or more desirably, four subtypes: cultural, structural, marital, and identificational. There might be good theoretical reasons for assigning variable weights to scores on the different types, although this is not an issue that need concern us here. (3) *Degree of conflict* existing in the society between the minority group or groups in the society and the majority group and among each other. (4) *Degree of access to societal rewards*—economic, political, institutional, and so on—for the minority group or groups in comparison with the majority group. This is an equality dimension.

For purposes of expository economy, we may arbitrarily trichotomize each of the continuous variables in this complex

[7]See, for instance, the typology developed by Schermerhorn in *Comparative Ethnic Relations*.

into high, moderate, and low to illustrate some possible outcomes. One outcome for minority group *A* might be high cultural assimilation, low structural assimilation, moderate degree of total assimilation, high degree of conflict, and low degree of access to societal rewards. Another outcome for minority group *B* might be high cultural assimilation, moderate structural assimilation, moderate total assimilation, low degree of conflict, and high degree of access to societal rewards. This type of constellation or profile, in my opinion, identifies the essential features of the minority group's position in the society at a given time. The research strategies for obtaining the requisite measures, while posing difficulties, offer no insuperable theoretical obstacles. Their discussion, however, is not within the scope of this chapter. It will be noted that this scheme, while it incorporates the variable of conflict in the dependent variable complex, by implication places power on the independent variable side of the casual equation.

Let us turn now to a consideration of the more important independent variables relevant for a general theory of racial and ethnic group relations. In fact, what I shall attempt to do is to make a classification of the types of appropriate variables, list some that belong in each type, and discuss one or two from each list that seem to deserve particular attention. Finally, on the basis of the foregoing, I shall attempt to illustrate the possible nature of such a general theory by suggesting several hypotheses and questions which would properly derive from it.

I would classify the relevant independent variables under three rubrics: *bio-social development variables, interaction process variables*, and *societal variables*. Bio-social development variables refer to those relating to the biological organism which is man, and the shaping of that biological organism, within conceivable limits, by the social environment in the process of attaining adulthood. Interaction process variables refer to social psychological processes of interaction among adults, and societal variables refer to collective structures and phenomena pertaining to the demographic, ecological, institutional, valuational, cultural, and stratificational features of a society which are the sociologists' stock in trade and need no further definition here.[8]

Bio-social Development Variables. The biological organism of man contains capacities, indeed imperatives, for acting on three levels: the satisfaction of physiological desires, cognition, and emotional or affective response. This bundle of imperatives is acted upon by the social environment in the attempt to effect a socialization which will allow the developed person to function within the bounds of societal and subsocietal demands. This process, I believe, is rarely completely successful and the resulting tensions and dynamics both make and record the relation of man to his social milieu. In this ongoing process the human organism develops a sense of self. Since society is constantly and, in my opinion, inevitably evaluative and value-giving, the protection of the self, not only in the physical and physiological sense, but at least as importantly, in the social-psychological sense, becomes the dominating theme of personality development and human interaction. The capacities to be both cooperative and aggressive, altruistic and selfish, are all contained within this framework. This significance of this viewpoint for intergroup relations is that the sense of ethnicity (in the larger definition of racial, religious, or national origins identification), because it cannot be shed by social mobility, as for instance social class background can, since society insists on its inalienable ascription from cradle to grave, *becomes incorporated into the self.* This process would appear to account for the widespread, perhaps ubiquitous presence of ethnocentrism, and perhaps even more crucially means that injury to the ethnic group is seen as injury to the self, and the intensity of the passions engendered by ethnic conflict becomes of a magnitude comparable to those engendered by threats to the individual.[9] In other words, man defending the

---

[8]Obviously, interaction processes take place among children and adolescents, as well. The distinction made here is for the purpose of separating out the developmental stage from a later stage.

[9]See the role of ethnocentrism in Donald L. Noel's paper, "A Theory of the Origin of Ethnic Stratification," *Social Problems,* Vol. 16 (Fall 1968), 157-72.

honor or welfare of his ethnic group is man defending himself.

A consideration of the role of self in the process of biosocial development inevitably raises questions about the concept of "human nature" and its potential connection to a theory of racial and ethnic intergroup relations. Virtually since its inception, the discipline of sociology, attempting to carve out a distinct field of inquiry for itself, reacting against a naive biological determinism that had traditionally dominated man's thinking about human behavior, and, later, rejecting the proliferating "instinct" theories of some early psychologists, has with few exceptions resolutely turned its back on the question of human nature, assuming implicitly or explicitly either that man was infinitely plastic and malleable, and thus basically formed for better or worse by the particular social and cultural environment in which he was socialized, or alternately, that the question was not relevant.[10]

It has become more and more apparent, however, that the question of human nature is relevant—that it must be faced—since any theory of social action must inevitably deal with the nature of the social actor, however formed; and some observers, including myself, have become increasingly struck by the persistent similarities in human behavior across cultural lines and historical epochs and have begun to wonder whether there are not biological constants or propensities in human behavior which fall short of the "instinct" category but which predispose the actor to certain kinds of behavior in a more forceful fashion than the tenets of conventional cultural determinism would allow. Thus a pair of contemporary anthropologists speak of a biologically programmed "behavioral infrastructure of human societies," and point out that "This view of human behavior . . . makes the organism an active, searching, and stubborn participant in the learning process, rather than just a receiver; it suggests that the teacher

[10]An early critic of alleged overemphasis on cultural conditioning in the sociological discipline was A. H. Hobbs, *The Claims of Sociology* (Harrisburg, Pa., Stackpole, 1951). See particularly his chapter 3 on "Personality."

is as moved to teach in a certain way as the pupil is to learn. The slate [the familiar *tabula rasa*] here is not blank at all; it is doing a lot of its own writing."[11]

At least two important sociological works of the past few years, in which the authors dealt with standard theoretical issues in sociology, have recognized the necessary link between the problems they were respectively dealing with and the question of human nature. Gerhard Lenski in *Power and Privilege: A Theory of Social Stratification* integrates in his theory of why social stratification exists and at what magnitude it exists under varying conditions a variety of cultural, social, and environmental variables with certain postulates or "constants" concerning man and society.[12] One of these postulates is that man is predominantly selfish or self-seeking when it comes to areas of choice of large importance to himself or his group.[13] This postulate plays a decisive part in Lenski's theory, since he conceives of it as the major motivational force in the differential appropriation of economic surplus which produces social stratification.

Similarly, Tausky, in his analysis of major theoretical perspectives about the behavior of men in work organizations,[14] compares the classical or scientific management theory of Frederic Taylor, based on a conception of man as motivated by self-interest, with the "human relations perspective" which focuses the worker's motivation by means of affective relationships and "self-actualizing" on organizational goals, and himself opts for the "structuralism perspective," a somewhat intermediate view which, he notes, is "closer to that of scientific management than to human

[11]Lionel Tiger and Robin Fox, *The Imperial Animal* (New York, Holt, 1971), pp. 13, 15.
[12]New York, McGraw-Hill, 1966.
[13]Lenski's exact statement reads as follows: "Thus, when one surveys the human scene, one is forced to conclude that when men are confronted with important decisions where they are obliged to choose between their own, or their group's, interests and the interests of others, they nearly always choose the former—though often seeking to hide this fact from themselves and others." *Power and Privilege*, p. 30. (Partly italicized in original.)
[14]Curt Tausky, *Work Organizations* (Itasca, Ill., Peacock, 1970).

relations." Which view one takes, Tausky points out, is predicated to a considerable extent upon one's conception of human nature as either based primarily on self-interest and thus essentially indifferent to organizational needs, or the contrary. "Try as I might," Tausky states, "I remain skeptical about human relations. Research which attempts to validate the human relations perspective has not, in my judgment, successfully done so. Let me state baldly the basis for my skepticism. It is simply that I do not share the optimism about human nature embedded in human relations writings."[15]

Any attempt to formulate a conception of human nature which can be used as a primary building block in a theory of social action must deal not only with a selfish-altruistic dimension but also with the crucial and ubiquitous phenomenon of human aggression. Psychoanalysts, psychiatrists, psychologists, and sociologists have struggled with this issue for several generations with indecisive results. Some see man as basically non-aggressive but seduced into aggressive behavior by corrupt institutions and defective socialization. Others, following Freud, find aggression to be deeply embedded in the early development of the psyche as a result of incoporation into a "death wish" or through a relationship with sexuality. Some ethologists posit a specific instinct for aggression as a function of man's close evolutionary relationship to other animal species (this assumes, of course, the presence of an instinct for aggression in these other species). Still others, in a thematic development which goes back to the work, a generation ago, of John Dollard, and also has roots in Freudian psychology, consider aggression among human beings to be a likely response to situations of frustration. The theory of the origins of aggression in man, however, which I find most persuasive and congruent with my own observations has recently been brilliantly stated in a new book by the psychiatrist Gregory Rochlin.[16] In a sense, Rochlin's formulation appears to be closely related to the frustration-aggression

[15]*Work Organizations*, p. viii.
[16]*Man's Aggression: The Defense of the Self* (Boston, Gambit, 1973).

theory mentioned above; however in Rochlin's hand the frustration-aggression mechanism is put into a larger framework with an organizing principle of its own.

Briefly stated, Rochlin's thesis is that aggressive behavior among human beings is not instinctive, but rather derives from the fact that man, unlike other animal species, has a distinct psychological concept of self; that love of the self, or narcissism, is the most basic human feeling; and that injuries or threats to the self, which are omnipresent in human life, evoke aggressive responses. In short, aggression is the inexorable response to continually embattled narcissism. "Neither metaphor nor a mere label," writes Rochlin, "narcissism, this love of self, is the human psychological process through which preserving the self is assured. In infancy, childhood, maturity and old age, the necessity of protecting the self may require all our capabilities. And, when narcissism is threatened, we are humiliated, *our self-esteem is injured, and aggression appears.*"[17] And in a more rhetorical vein he declares:

> The compelling imperative for self-preservation is self-love. It expresses itself in an endless lust for a rewarding image of oneself, whether that image is seen in a glass or in another's eye. The further passion for praise, honor and glory makes for an endless marathon. We enter it remarkably early in our existence and leave it only when we expire. Self-love . . . is a governing tyrannical principle of human experience, to which aggression responds as a bonded servant.[18]

Another area of human functioning, as we have mentioned before, is the cognitive one. While emotional tendencies and predispositions may well be of greater importance in the formation of racial and ethnic prejudice, still it would appear that the ability to avoid stereotyping by noting distinc-

---

[17]*Man's Aggression*, p. 1. (Italics as in original.)

[18]*Man's Aggression*, p. 1. Rochlin, like most social scientists, acknowledges that human aggression is not always destructive—that, in fact, it can play a creative role in societal affairs. Nevertheless, it is the destructive aspects of aggression which occupy most of his attention.

tions among people in an outgroup, to discern connections between historico-cultural experience and group behavior, to think of groups in terms of the distribution of individuals along the normal or bell-shaped curve, to imagine the functional value of cultural diversity, to foresee the disfunctional consequences of unchecked and exacerbated conflict—are all characteristics related in some measure to level of intellectual functioning. We should all like to believe that the general or average level of human intellectual capacity is quite sufficient to encompass all these tasks; but the dominant role of racism and intergroup conflict in the Western world in the several centuries ushered in by the Enlightenment should give us at least some pause before making this assumption with extreme confidence.

To hypothesize or to assert as postulates that man is basically selfish, narcissistic and perpetually poised on the edge of aggression, and intellectually somewhat wanting, is not, of course, to prove these conceptions of the human condition. Numerous illustrative examples in life, literature, and history can be quickly adduced, but so can some examples on the other side. We are clearly dealing here with matters of statistical frequency, central tendency, more or less, mostly or partly, differences of degree, and so on. Moreover, as I have mentioned before, there are socializing forces and institutions in society which begin the process of controlling, taming, and shaping man from the day of his birth onward designed to predispose him to display cooperation, altruism, and socially beneficial behavior toward his fellow human beings and to develop attitudes of sympathy, concern, and responsibility which would make such behavior a function of internal attitudes as well as external sanctions. Even here, however, one must reckon with certain capacities of the individual, classically identified in the psychological literature, for (among others) rationalization, self delusion, selective perception, and hysterical repression, which allow, in Freudian terms, the id to outwit the superego while ostensibly accepting the socially certified comfort of the latter's hegemony.

In any event, the process is a dialectic one. Where to categorize the presumed statistical result determines one's judgment about the character of the individual actor whose multiple interactions make up the social process. Unfounded optimism in this matter will do no service for the cause of improved intergroup relations and will inhibit the scientific understanding on which true and lasting progress must be based. Total pessimism would foreclose all actions designed to alleviate racial and ethnic tensions, and seems to me also unjustified as a scientific judgment. It is my view, however, that the conception of man as basically motivated by self-interest, irresistibly narcissistic and protective of the self, ready to defend the self by aggressive behavior (however defined and however circumscribed), and possessed of not unlimited intellectual capacity, is a more plausible portrait of the human being than any others which have as yet been advanced. When we add to this conception of the resolute defender of the self and the vigilant watcher over its well-being the hypothesis which I stated earlier—namely, that the sense of ethnicity, by virtue of its totally ascriptive nature, becomes incorporated into the self—we are then ready to insert into a theory of racial and ethnic contact the actor who, with his fellow actors, is at one time part of the cause and at another time, or perhaps simultaneously, part of the effect in the ever recurrent drama of intergroup relations.

Interaction Process Variables

Those that seem particularly important with regard to intergroup relations would include stereotyping, which stems from what would appear to be rather widespread cognitive inadequacies reinforced by affective tendencies and lack of equal-status primary group contact between groups; frustration-aggression mechanisms in which aggression is easily produced by frustration and directed, depending upon accessibility, either toward the perceived source or toward scapegoats; felt dissatisfaction phenomena based on the mechanisms of relative deprivation, rising expectations, status inconsistency, and cognitive dissonance (it is this cluster which has been most successfully adduced to date to explain the rise of the Negro Protest and Black Power movement in the late 1960s);[19] calculation of success chances in goal-attainment based on conflict—an intellectual or cognitive phenomenon which is not unaffected by emotional considerations but which also operates in the context of estimation of the amount and kind of restraint or punitive forces which are likely to be brought to bear; and, finally, a process which appears to me to be well-nigh universal in human interaction, namely, that of conflict escalation—the tendency for parties in conflict to react to each other's threats and reprisals by escalating the level of aggression, punishment, and revenge unless checked by either overwhelming power, exhaustion, or conflict-reducing mechanisms which we at present know too little about.[20]

Stereotyping and the frustration-aggression dynamic have received considerable attention in the sociological and psychological literature on intergroup relations.[21] It is the last

[19]See the excellent and groundbreaking discussion of these phenomena in James A. Geschwender, "Explorations in the Theory of Social Movements and Revolutions," Social Forces, Vol. 47 (December 1968), 127–35.

[20]See Lewis Coser's comment that "In the state of nature, to use Hobbesian terminology, conflict, whether it be waged for gain, for safety, or for glory, 'ceaseth only in death.' Hobbes' philosophical vision can be translated into modern sociological terminology when we note that social conflicts tend to continue or to escalate, and to end with the total destruction of at least one of the antagonists, when unchecked by societal regulation and by deliberate actions of the contenders. Social structures always contain or create mechanisms that help control and channel conflicts through normative regulation. Yet the degree to which conflicts are so regulated varies considerably." Continuities in the Study of Social Conflict (New York, Free Press, 1967), p. 37.

There is a growing and interesting literature that embraces conflict escalation from the point of view of game theory and/or the analysis of war and international relations. See, for example, Herman Kahn, On Escalation (New York, Praeger, 1965); Thomas C. Schelling, The Strategy of Conflict (Cambridge, Harvard University Press, 1960); and Amitai Etzioni, The Hard Way to Peace (New York, Collier Books, 1962).

[21]For a classic statement, see Gordon W. Allport, The Nature of Prejudice (Cambridge, Addison-Wesley, 1954).

three processes: felt dissatisfaction phenomena, calculation of success chances, and conflict escalation—and particularly their interrelationships—which I should like to explore in greater detail in this chapter.

Man is apparently and irretrievably a comparer.[22] That is, he makes judgments about his own needs and their satisfaction not only on the basis of absolute criteria—I am hungry; I am fed and thus satisfied—but on the basis of comparisons with others—he is better fed than I; or I am better fed than he. This mechanism applies, of course, not only to material satisfactions, but also to status issues where the range of possible positions is virtually limitless. The points of reference in this endless process may be not only the individual and other individuals, but his group or groups and other groups. Empirically, the individual and group referents are likely to become inextricably intertwined. Thus the individual is potentially in the situation of comparing the material or status position of himself and his ethnic group with the material and status achievements of members of other ethnic groups and of the other ethnic groups as entities.

With the issue posed in this way, the question we need to ask is why such endless invidious comparisons and their implicit strivings do not produce a level of conflict among individuals and groups which bursts the bonds of societies asunder. The answer, it seems to me, is that the transmuting of felt dissatisfaction into conflict depends on three other factors, two of which play a strong role in determining the level of felt dissatisfaction itself, and the third of which powerfully determines whether felt dissatisfaction will actually turn into overt conflict. Let us examine these stages in the process serially.

The two factors which produce the level of felt dissatisfaction itself are the value system, and the attendant ideologies, of the respective comparing individuals or groups and the actual nature or profile of the reward system. Even

[22]See Robert K. Merton, *Social Theory and Social Structure* (Glencoe, Ill. Free Press, 1957), chap. 8 and 9. Chap. 8 was written in collaboration with Alice S. Rossi.

these two factors interact with each other in myriad ways, since the values and ideologies concerning the just distribution of rewards will influence feelings about the reward system, whatever it may be. An individual in a low economic and status position in a caste or estate form of society may accept his position with equanimity as foreordained by the gods or the divinity. Or one in an open class society may believe that he has a sturdy chance for upward mobility if he is industrious and thrifty or acquires the requisite educational skills. In these two instances felt dissatisfaction is kept at a low level by acceptance of the prevailing ideology by all parties. And in the latter case where the reward system actually provides perceived cases of upward mobility, this perception adds to the forces which minimize felt dissatisfaction. Translated into group terms, a suppressed ethnic group in a racist society which accepted the usually prevalent ideology in such a society which stigmatized it as inferior would conceivably have a low degree of dissatisfaction (scholars are coming to question the actual substantive existence of such acceptance historically, but here we are for the moment concerned with theoretical possibilities in a model), or a suppressed ethnic group in a somewhat open society with substantial upward mobility opportunities which in practice were continually being exercised by members of all groups would presumably also have relatively low rates of dissatisfaction.

If the value systems of the respective individuals and groups do not simultaneously legitimate the given rewards system, however, or if the rewards system is so extreme in its manifestations of inequality that any value consensus would be continually thwarted by the sheer pressure of lack of satisfaction of human needs at a bearable level, then the third factor, if present in the situation, will come into play to reduce over conflict; that factor is the system of perceived sanctions based on force or power aimed at suppressing revolt, threatening physical attacks on the system, disruptive demonstrations, and so on. In other words, there is, to use my previously suggested phrase, a "calculation of success chances" prior to the projected action which will play a powerful role in determining whether the action will, in fact, be undertaken. The entire process of combining value impetus with a judgment of the probability of carrying out the action without incurring prohibitive punishment is somewhat similar to the concept of the "dynamic assessment" immediately prior to the initiation of action which was advanced by MacIver a generation ago in his analysis of action and causality.[23]

There is a pronounced tendency in recent sociological writings to minimize the role of perceived sanctions in human action and to conceive of the human actor as responding largely to valuations, ideology, and emotional forces in actualizing behavior. While these forces clearly do make up a significant portion of the field of stimuli which propel behavioral responses, given the perpetual tension between human desires and societal restraints, it seems illusory to me to ignore the important role which perceived power sanctions play in governing the passions of men.[24] This formula applies, I believe, both at the micro level of individual action and the macro level of group action. It is certainly true that both individuals and groups may at times under situations of extreme stress act violently or disruptively to relieve their anger or frustrations, or their sense of being unfairly treated, regardless of perceived probable consequences. But our hypothesis is that, statistically speaking, perceived power sanctions substantially reduce the level of overt violent conflict between competing or potentially conflicting individuals and groups. It should go without saying that this is a sociological statement, not a value judgment bearing on the question of the desirability or undesirability of using violence or disruption to redress grievances under particular circumstances. The attempt here is to suggest a processual model of

[23]R. M. MacIver, *Social Causation* (Boston, Ginn, 1942). See particularly chap. 11 and 12.

[24]These sanctions may, of course, be either legal or illegal. For an important recent and more extensive statement of a similar viewpoint, see William J. Goode, "The Place of Force in Human Society," *American Sociological Review*, Vol. 37 (October 1972) 507–19.

human behavior which actually has application to both micro and macro situations of human contact and to many fields besides that of racial and ethnic relations.

If conflict does erupt between contending individuals or groups, it has a distinct tendency to escalate, all other things being equal. This proposition follows from our discussion of the overriding nature of the propensity to defend the self—and the ethnic group which becomes incorporated into the self. Conflict, virtually by definition, is viewed, usually quite correctly, by each of the contending parties as either a physical attack on the self, a threat of physical attack on the self, or a psychological attack on the self. The emotional anger engendered by this attack syndrome dictates a counterattack of some kind, which is then viewed by the other of the contending parties as an attack on *his* sense of selfhood. This first party will then reattack with even greater vehemence. And so the escalation of conflict proceeds. If escalating conflict is not to reach the point of annihilation of one or both of the contending parties, some conflict-reducing mechanism or mechanisms must be brought into play. Such mechanisms consist of institutional arrangements supported by societal power for the resolution of certain kinds of conflict—for instance, legal adjudication, arbitration, decision by the rules, so to speak (but the rules supported by authority, or legal power), internal controls in the personality implanted by the socialization process, or by the signalized retreat or submission, however temporary, of one of the contesting parties in the face of power "calculated" to be for the time being insurmountable and even more threatening to the self, physically or psychologically, than continuance of the conflict.

In the case of disadvantaged ethnic groups in a given society, understandably dissatisfied with their disadvantaged position, if they can count on a favorable ideological climate and operate through legitimated parliamentary channels to press their claims for an end to discrimination and prejudice and for special programs of aid to effect their normal distribution into the economic and political institutions of the society, the eruption of overt power conflict with its escalating tendencies can probably be avoided. If the dominant tendency in ethnic relations becomes an overt power struggle, however, the escalating tendencies in such a struggle project a precarious future—one in which the costs are unknown and the benefits uncertain.

Societal Variables

These variables include a cluster of demographic phenomena such as absolute size of the majority and minority groups, their relative size, and their comparative rates of natural increase. Included in this group are also territorial dispersion and concentration of minority groups by region, rural-urban residence, and section of city.[25] Another cluster of societal variables consists of value consensus or dissensus between the majority and minority groups and specifies the particular areas where such consensus or dissensus exists. This cluster has already been examined in connection with its role in felt dissatisfaction phenomena. Still a third group of variables is made up of cultural differences between the majority and minority groups existing at the time of initial contact. For instance, differences in language or religion which existed at the time of first meeting presumably would have a cumulative influence on the extent of cultural assimilation conceptualized as a dependent variable at the time of study. A fourth variable is the nature of ideologies about racial, religious, and ethnic groups present in the general population and concerns the degree of equalitarianism and humanitarianism present in these ideological systems and also the degree and type of assimilation or pluralism desired. A fifth major group of variables devolves around the distribution of power between majority and minority groups. The distribution of

[25]See, for instance, Karl E. Taeuber and Alma F. Taeuber, *Negroes in Cities* (Chicago, Aldine, 1965); Stanley Lieberson, "The Impact of Residential Segregation on Ethnic Assimilation," *Social Forces,* Vol. 40 (October 1961), 52–57; and W. Clark Roof, "Residential Segregation of Blacks and Racial Inequality in Southern Cities: Toward a Causal Model,"*Social Problems,* Vol. 19 (Winter 1972), 393–407.

competitive power, political power, and disruptive power quite clearly affects the outcome of our designated dependent variable profile. Here, however, the analysis becomes even more complex, since the mobilization of power resources does not operate in a structural vacuum but depends on the perception of threatened restraints, punishment, and application of countervailing power which help to make up what might be called "the field of power vectors." Frustration and perceived need provide the motive power for action toward desired goals, but such action, as I have pointed out, also has a cognitive component of estimation of the probable degree of negative sanctions.

Sixth, the degree of access to societal rewards (the equality-inequality dimension) available to the minority ethnic group affects the degree of felt dissatisfaction of the group and thus affects the dynamics of social change which determine the outcome at any given time. That this variable thus appears on both the dependent and independent variable sides of the causal chain should produce no great methodological disquietude, since this simply attests to the constant feedback and interaction effects of factors in societal processes.

Seventh, the political nature of the society with regard to the democratic-totalitarian scale or dimension should be recognized as an important variable for outcomes in intergroup relations.[26] This variable interacts with the power variable, since its position determines whether ideological and value positions and their behavioral implications for ethnic group relations can be fought out in the legislative and public opinion arenas by concerned citizens' groups, or whether such decisions are made by a small group of rulers at the top and handed down and enforced by the concentrated power of governmental control in the hands of the totalitarian state.

I have already discussed the "distribution of power" variable at several points and noted its useful categorization into competitive, political, and disruptive subtypes. Another

[26]See *Comparative Ethnic Relations*, chap. 5, and particularly pp. 186–87.

dimension of power which it is necessary to isolate and sub-classify, with regard to the ethnic group context, is whether the power of the group, whatever its degree, comes exclusively from inside the society in which it is located (either from its own power base or with internal allies), or whether its power is augmented by allies from outside the sovereign host society. Many or most ethnic groups within a given society or state have ancestral ties of language, religion, race, or national origins with some other sovereign state. If the ancestral sovereign state is militarily powerful, or has strategic interests or ideology in common with the host sovereign society, the latter may be constrained to attentuate or eliminate discriminatory measures against the minority ethnic group within its borders. In other words, ethnic group relations in the modern interconnected world operate within an international as well as an internal context (under conditions of actual international conflict—that is, war—this fact can operate, of course, to hinder as well as help a given minority—in this case one which is ancestrally derived from the now defined "enemy"). We may thus distinguish between "inside power" derived from the minority's own power position plus that of internal allies, if any, and "outside power"—that augmentation of power stemming from the friendly interest in the minority's welfare of another sovereign state, or, conceivably, an international body (for example, the United Nations), the degree of such augmentation being a function of the actual power such a state or body has and is willing to use in order to influence relevant events in the host society.

The final point which I should like to raise and discuss briefly in this consideration of social variables takes us back to the issue of ideologies about racial and ethnic group relations present in the society and held respectively by the majority and the minority groups. As I have indicated, these can be categorized along an equality-inequality dimension. In this sense, we can distinguish very roughly between ideologies which are essentially inequalitarian or racist and those which are essentially equalitarian and non-racist. Within the latter group, however, three subtypes seem to have particular relevance in the contemporary world. One is an assimilationist structure in which the presumed logical goal would be eventual complete assimilation along the various dimensions previously distinguished in the assimilation process. The two others are essentially pluralist structures which need to be carefully distinguished from each other, since their differences constitute crucial points of current controversy in many pluralistic settings over the world, and their actual respective implementations could well have differential consequences for outcomes in intergroup relations.[27]

The first type I would call "liberal pluralism." It is characterized by the absence, even prohibition, of any legal or governmental recognition of racial, religious, language, or national origins groups as corporate entities with a standing in the legal or governmental process, and a prohibition of the use of ethnic criteria of any type for discriminatory purposes, or conversely for special or favored treatment. Many members of such groups would, of course, receive benefits provided by legislation aimed at the general population in connection with problems produced by lack of effective economic participation in the society: for example, anti-poverty measures, housing, education and welfare measures, and so on. Members of disadvantaged ethnic groups would thus benefit as individuals under social programs in relation to their individual eligibility, but not in a corporate sense as a function of their ethnic background. Structural pluralism under these circumstances would exist voluntarily, as an unofficial societal reality in communal life, as would also some measure of cultural pluralism, at the will of the ethnic group members, and subject to the pressures toward conformity to general societal norms implicit in whatever degree of industrialization and urbanization was present in the society. Equalitarian norms in such a society would emphasize equality of opportunity and the evaluation of individuals on the basis of universalistic standards of performance. Such a model of society

---

[27]Some of the distinctions noted below are insightfully discussed by Daniel Bell in his essay "On Meritocracy and Equality," *The Public Interest*, No. 29 (Fall 1972), 29–68.

is very close, it will be recognized, to that implicitly envisaged by the "liberal expectancy" mentioned earlier in this chapter.

The contrasting pluralistic structure may be called "corporate pluralism." Under corporate pluralism racial and ethnic groups are formally recognized as legally constituted entities with official standing in the society. Economic and political rewards, whether in the public or private sector, are allocated on the basis of numerical quotas which in turn rest on relative numerical strength in the population or on some other formula emanating from the political process. Equalitarian emphasis is on equality of condition rather than equality of opportunity, and universalistic criteria of reward operate only in restricted spheres themselves determined in a more particularistic manner. Structural pluralism is officially encouraged, and indeed becomes the necessary setting for individual action, and cultural pluralism tends to be reinforced even in urban and in industrial settings.

Putting together the equality dimension with the structural dimension, we may thus distinguish four types of societies with regard to ethnic orientation: (1) racist, (2) assimilationist, (3) liberal pluralist, and (4) corporate pluralist. In practice, of course, elements of several types may exist at any given time in combination. Nevertheless, in a theoretical sense, these four types need to be distinguished from each other. Both as ideological goals of either minority or majority, and as actual conditions of given societies in a particular period, they may influence the outcome of racial and ethnic group relations in the next stage of the society's existence.

APPLICATIONS:
SOME THEORETICAL PROPOSITIONS

Within the appropriate limits of this chapter, I shall be able to select only a few major variables which seem to me most salient and construct some plausible causal chains. As an initial strategy, I shall consider some actual historical situations of intergroup relations and apply the variables previously adumbrated. Most observers would agree that the two most devastating and horrendous examples of intergroup relations in the past four hundred years were the enslavement of four million Negroes of African descent in the American colonies and American state prior to the Civil War and the murder of six million Jews by the Nazis in the twentieth century. We begin with the bio-social development variables (or relative constants, if one prefers) of the human being conceived as essentially a narcissistic defender of the self, aggressively ready to defend the self, incorporating the sense of ethnicity into the self and displaying the usual ethnocentrism. In the interaction process we focus on the tendency to compare the self invidiously with others, the tendency to conflict escalation, and the potential tempering of this process by the field of power vectors which produces a calculation of success chances prior to the initiation of a given contemplated action. These relative "givens" may be thought of as present in all the causal chains I shall adduce below, although for purposes of conserving space I shall not necessarily refer to them again in the formal propositions.

Within the American colonies, from an ideological point of view, although democratic and relatively equalitarian values applied to whites, they distinctly were not considered relevant to blacks. The overwhelmingly prevalent view of whites toward blacks was racist. With regard to power, the blacks had virtually none. Internally, they were fragmented, socially and culturally, carefully kept uneducated, and unable to acquire by virture of their bondage the military technology which would have enabled them to revolt with any possibility of success against their masters. Externally, the societies in Africa from which they had been seized had neither the organizational unity nor the military technology with which to even attempt the mounting of a power threat against the technologically advanced white civilization. The use of black slave labor in the South was economically advantageous. Thus we might say in summation: American colonial whites, infused with a racist ideology (equalitarian and democratic values applying to whites only), finding it

economically advantageous and thus self-enhancing to en-
slave blacks, unopposed by countervailing power on this
issue from the outside world, moved inexorably into the enslavement of the black population. In propositional terms,
this historical example suggests the following:

> Racist ideology pervading the majority group plus low degree
> of "inside" minority ethnic power, plus low degree of "out-
> side" minority ethnic power plus felt opportunity to enhance
> the self through economic means by massive discrimination
> *leads to* low degree of access to societal rewards by the minority
> ethnic group ranging from second class citizenship to slavery
> plus minimal conflict (at least, in the short run).

In the case of the Jews in Nazi Germany, we note the
presence of an endemic racism (anti-Semitism), again a
minority relatively powerless internally in either a numerical
or potentially military sense, a quickly emerging totalitarian
state, and no threat of effective countervailing military sanctions from the outside (World War II did not begin until
Germany invaded Poland). In this situation, a genocidal
ideology was promulgated by totalitarian rulers who made
use of both endemic anti-Semitism and the overwhelmingly
effective social control mechanisms and institutions of the
modern industrialized totalitarian state to engender support
and terrorize any potential opposition to their policy of extermination of the Jews. In propositional terms, we emerge
with the following:

> Intermediate degree of racist ideology permeating the majority
> group plus low degree of "inside" minority ethnic group power
> plus low degree of "outside" minority ethnic group power plus
> totalitarian government *leads to* low degree of access to societal
> rewards by the minority ethnic group, quick and intense
> mobilization of hatred toward the minority group at gov-
> ernmental will, plus massive and quickly terminated conflict
> ranging in outcome to the point of expulsion or extermination.

It will be noticed that for the purpose of brief exposition
here I have chosen to focus, among the dependent variables,
on access to societal rewards and degree of conflict, and

among the independent variables on ideology, power (both "inside" and "outside"), and the political nature of the society on the democratic-totalitarian scale. I should like to add a further comment on the individual and simultaneous effects of ideology and power on particular outcomes in intergroup relations. In both examples I have used to suggest theoretical propositions, the minority had low "inside" power. In the face of a distinctly racist ideology converted into action on the part of a highly discriminatory majority, an ethnic minority clearly needs augmented power in order to redress the balance and secure its rightful opportunity for an equitable distribution of rewards and respect. It might be inferred from this that I am suggesting that an optimal situation in all pluralistic societies is an equal distribution of power among all groups, majority and minority. I do not, in fact, advance this hypothesis for the following reason, or complex of reasons. In a pluralistic society which operates in a democratic ethos and with equalitarian ideals, albeit with ever present modest degrees of ethnocentrism, a situation of equal power for all groups in the society, given the volatile and escalating nature of ethnic passions will probably be inherently unstable and conflict producing. The optimal situation in a democratic-egalitarian pluralistic society, I would hypothesize, is one in which the minority group has an *intermediate degree of power*—less than that of the majority, so that it cannot disrupt the society completely, but enough so that it can levy strategic influence to protect its rights—"cause trouble," so to speak, in areas of discriminatory treatment, and in which it is supported by "outside" power in the face of a violent threat of attack by the majority on its existence and legitimate aspirations. "Outside" power—that is, power wielded by another sovereign entity—cannot, in the very nature of things, be wielded often or indiscriminately, or on every or even most day-to-day issues of political conflict inevitably arising in a pluralistic society. It can serve, however, as a "backup" threat in the face of extraordinary danger to the minority, and, perhaps more usually, in the form of special diplomatic negotiations relating to specific issues of unusually grave concern. A latter recent case in point would be the presumptive influence of American détente and trade relations with the Soviet Union on that country's relaxation of emigration restrictions on its Jewish population.

One final point. I have deliberately refrained from inserting into any causal hypothesis which I have hitherto advanced the influence of the type of pluralism ideologically supported by either majority or minority group, or experienced by the society to date. These two types, in the equalitarian setting, are the liberal type and the corporate type. Most nations in the world either are now or are becoming pluralistic in nature. Even if the battle against outright and overt racism can be won, a conflict between policy choices tending toward either liberal pluralism or corporate pluralism will constitute a significant portion of the dynamics of racial and ethnic group relations in the decades ahead. Which type produces better outcomes in terms of the general welfare—the welfare of all—we do not as yet know. Not enough of the data has yet transpired, much less been studied. My own guess— and it is only a guess—is that, for reasons I do not have space to elucidate here, the liberal variety promises better results. But I may be wrong. History will write its answer. Sociologists will read it, one hopes, correctly. Or, as is said, time will tell.

part II
Subsocieties, Subcultures, & Ethnicity

The Concept of the Sub-Culture & its Application

3

One of the functions of any science, "natural" or "social," is admittedly to discover and isolate increasingly smaller units of its subject matter. This process leads to more extensive control of variables in experiment and analysis. There are times, however, when the scientist must put some of these blocks back together again in an integrated pattern. This is especially true where the patterning reveals itself as a logical necessity, with intrinsic connections which create something more, so to speak, than the mere sum of the parts. Specifically, in the social sciences, this patterning is necessary where the impact of the nexus on the human being is that of a unit, and not a series of disconnected social situations. This paper represents an attempt to delineate such a nexus by a logical extension of the concept of culture.

American sociologists, on the whole, have seemed reluctant to extend the concept of culture beyond the point where it has already been developed and more or less handed to us by the anthropologists. We hear an occasional reference to "urban culture," or "rural culture," or "the culture of the middle class," but these references have seemed to represent sporadic resting-places of semantic convenience rather than any systematic application of the term to well-defined social situations. Broadly speaking, we have been content to stop the concept of culture at national boundaries, and engage in our intra-national analyses in terms of the discrete units of ethnic background, social class, regional residence, religious affiliation, and so on. It is the thesis of this paper that a great deal could be gained by a more extensive use of the concept of the *sub-culture*—a concept used here to refer to a sub-division of a national culture, composed of a combination of factorable social situations such as class status, ethnic background, regional and rural or urban residence, and religious affiliation, but *forming in their combination a functioning unity which has an integrated impact on the participating individual*. No claim is made here for origination of the term. Although its use has apparently not been extensive enough to merit it a place in the *Dictionary of Sociology*, edited by Fairchild,[1] a recent and perceptive use of the term has been made in a paper by Green, where he speaks incidentally of "highly organized subcultures," and, in connection with the question of neuroses, phrases a query in the following manner: "Since in modern society no individual participates in the total cultural complex totally but primarily in a series of population segments grouped according to sex, age, class, occupation, region, religion, and ethnic group—all with somewhat differing norms and expectations of conduct—how do these combine in different ways to form varying backgrounds for individual etiologies of neurotic trends?"[2]

Green, by implication, uses the terms "subculture" and "population segment" interchangeably. Nomenclature is relatively unimportant so long as it is consistent, but we prefer

[1]*Dictionary of Sociology*, Henry Pratt Fairchild, ed. (New York, Philosophical Library, 1944); the nearest concept in the *Dictionary* is that of the "culture-sub-area," which is defined as "a sub-division of a larger culture area, distinguished by the comparative completeness of the development of a particular culture trait, or the comparative readiness with which such a trait will be diffused" (p. 83). The emphasis here is obviously on *area*—physical contiguity, which factor may, or may not, or may only partially be present in the *sub-culture*. Thus groups of lower-class white Protestants may live in different sections of the same city. Or middle-class Jews may be scattered over a medium-sized city and still form a social entity (see, for instance, W. Lloyd Warner and Leo Srole, *The Social Systems of American Ethnic Groups*, Yankee City Series, Vol. 3, New Haven, Yale University Press, 1945, p. 51).
[2]Arnold W. Green, "Sociological Analysis of Horney and Fromm," *The American Journal of Sociology*, Vol. LI (May 1946), p. 534.

the former term since it seems to emphasize more directly the dynamic character of the framework within which the child is socialized. It is a world within a world, so to speak, but it *is* a world. The emphasis on this paper, then, is simply on the unifying and transmuting implications of the term "sub-culture" for such combinations of factors as ethnic group, social class, region, occupation, religion, and urban or rural residence, and on the need for its wider application.

A primary and major implication of this position is that the child growing up in a particular sub-culture feels its impact as a unit. For instance, the son of lower-class Italian immigrants, growing up in New York's upper East Side, is not a person who is simultaneously affected by separable items consisting of ethnic background, low-economic status, and a highly urbanized residential situation. He is a person whose environmental background is an interwoven and variegated combination of all these factors. Each of the elements has been somewhat transformed by virture of its combination with the others. This fact must be taken into consideration in research procedures dealing with environmental backgrounds and their effects. A corollary of this position is that identically named factors in different sub-cultures are not interchangeable. Thus being a middle-class Jew is not the same thing as being a middle-class Gentile except for the additional factor of being Jewish.

A wider use of the concept of the *sub-culture* would, in the opinion of this writer, give us a keen and incisive tool which would, on the one hand, prevent us from making too broad groupings where such inclusiveness is not warranted (we would, for instance, refer not so much to "the Negro," as to "Southern, rural lower-class Negroes," or "Northern, urban, middle-class Negroes," etc.[3]), and on the other hand, enable us to discern relatively closed and cohesive systems of

[3]The writer is aware of the increasing attention which is being given, especially to class-differentiation in the Negro group. Progress in this direction with other ethnic groups, such as, for instance, the Jews, has not been so marked.

social organization which currently we tend to analyze separately with our more conventional tools of "class" and "ethnic group." The writer, for instance, has been interested to observe in the city of Philadelphia a not entirely cohesive, but unmistakably present, sub-culture composed of members of the Society of Friends (Quakers), and ranging in class position from upper-middle to upper-upper. More conventional objects of sociological attention, second and third generation Jews, would seem, for the most part, to be neither "marginal men" in the Park and Stonequist phrase, nor competitors in the social class system with white Gentiles, but rather members of highly integrated "marginal sub-cultures" (called marginal here because, like the "marginal man," these sub-cultures composed of the descendants of immigrant Jews lie somewhere between the immigrant culture and the native Gentile culture and contain cultural contributions from both) whose variable elements are size of community of residence and social class.

A distinction must, of course, be made between separate sub-cultures and separate units of the same sub-culture. Thus lower-class white Protestants in one medium-sized New England city would presumably belong to the same sub-culture as lower-class white Protestants in another medium-sized New England community hundreds of miles away, though each group would constitute a separate unit. Whether lower-class white Protestants in a medium-sized community in the Middle-West would form a different sub-culture is a more difficult point. The question of whether variation of one factor is sufficient to set up a separate sub-culture would have to be answered empirically by a field study of the community situations in question.

A comprehensive application of the sub-cultural concept to the American scene would, in time, lead to the delineation of a fairly large number of sub-cultures of varying degrees of cohesiveness and with varying patterns of interaction with each other. Among the many further research problems which such an analysis would pose, six of particular interest to the writer are mentioned here:

1. How do the various sub-cultures rank on a scale of differential access to the rewards of the broader American culture, including both material rewards and status?

2. How is the experience of growing up in a particular sub-culture reflected in the personality structure of the individual? Is there a portion of the personality which is roughly equivalent to a similar portion of the personality of every other individual who has matured in the same sub-culture, and which might, then, be referred to as the "sub-cultural personality"? If Kardiner's hypothesis of a common "basic personality structure" for all participants in the same national culture[4] is valid, it would seem equally likely that a second tier of the personality, so to speak, would consist of the "sub-cultural personality structure."[5]

3. In what way are identical elements of the national culture refracted differentially in the sub-culture? We have been prone, perhaps, to assume uniformities which do not entirely exist. Football, to male adolescents of one sub-culture may mean the chance to hawk programs and peanuts and make some money, to those of another, enthusiastic attendance at the High School game on Saturday afternoon, and to those of still a third, inviting girls up to the campus for a houseparty week-end.

4. What are the most indicative indices of participation in a particular sub-culture? If any one had to be singled out,

[4]Abram Kardiner, *The Individual and His Society* (New York, Columbia University Press, 1939). See particularly p. vi, and p. 12.

[5]The Warner and Lunt concept of the "social personality," which this writer would like to have seen more fully developed than it was in the Yankee City Series, seems to fluctuate between the idea of the sub-cultural personality offered here, and something different. For instance, in one paragraph they state, "Because a given individual occupies a particular place in the social space of a given society, out of the multitude of places it would be possible for him to be in, and participates in this one place, he has a social personality *different from that of anyone else.*" (Italics my own.) On the other hand, in another passage they speak of "Individuals with similar social personalities." W. Lloyd Warner and Paul S. Lunt, *The Social Life of a Modern Community,* Yankee City Series, Vol. 1. (New Haven, Yale University Press, 1941), pp. 26–27. Again the writer would reiterate that he has no emotional stake in any specific nomenclature.

the writer would offer speech patterns (particularly pronunciation and inflection) as at once the easiest to "observe" and the most revealing. Clothes would probably rank next in indicativeness and ease of discernability—contrary to casual opinion, for men as well as women.

5. What explains the "deviant," that is, the person who does not develop the sub-cultural or social personality characteristic of the particular sub-culture in which he was born and nurtured? An interesting question here is whether there are particular combinations of biological characteristics which would adjust more or less easily to the sub-cultural personalities specifically demanded. What about the above-average in intelligence and sensitive boy, for instance, born into a sub-culture of low-status and rather rough behavior patterns? or, conversely, the son of professional parents who cannot make the grade at college but would much rather be out tinkering with the motor of his automobile?

6. In upward social mobility, does a change of "sub-cultural personality" invariably accompany acquisition of some of the more objective indices of higher status, such as wealth or more highly valued occupation? If not, what stresses and strains result? This last question, in the writer's opinion, is a most interesting one, and in the growing literature on social mobility, to his knowledge, has barely been touched.

4

The Subsociety & The Subculture

What does a man answer when he is asked, or asks himself, a question as old as the time when some Pleistocene hunter, strayed far from his reassuring campfire and making his way fearfully through the dark tree-dense forest, came upon a stricken man, bested by his quarry, and realized that he had never seen him before—the first stranger? That question is "Who are you?"

If the stranger is a member of an Old, or more assuredly New, Stone Age band he will reply I am a Zuni, or an Arapesh, or a Kariera—these are my people—*the* people—so-and-so is my mother and thus-and-so is my mother's brother and this is our land, which is the world. In other words, he places himself in a group which is a political unit, which is culturally uniform, and which occupies a definite geographical place (at the center of the universe), and within this group he occupies more specific relationships of kinship.

The subsequent history of mankind, apart from those isolated pockets of pre-literate society, steadily and irretrievably dwindling in number, which have been by-passed by what we immodestly choose to call civilization, is from one point of view a record of a series of events which have challenged with ever-increasing force and complexity this simple model of self-identification.

The coming of settled agriculture and animal domestication brought with it the possibility of accumulating food surpluses, which, in turn, allowed some members of the society to withdraw from the previously society-wide demand of hunting and gathering or fishing for the daily supply of edibles, and to devote themselves to the specialized pursuits which a better-fed and growing population required: the ex-traction and smelting of ore to create more efficient metal tools, the propitiation and cultivation of the gods, the govern-ing of the larger and more complex community. These occu-pations tended to become differentially evaluated and re-warded and to create various life-styles, and the occupational specialization might be passed down to the sons and the sons of sons, and thus social class divisions arose. Ultimately these agricultural surpluses made it possible for some men to live apart from the agricultural community itself, to reside to-gether in walled towns and cities where busy markets al-lowed them to trade their services and handmade goods for the agricultural staples brought in by farmers from the outly-ing area, driving their donkeys and camels along with a stick and muttering suspiciously of the flesh-pots and wicked dis-tractions to be found in this community of men who did not labor and sweat in the sun to grow their daily food—who did not "work." As the farmers entered the city, they would see the Ruler's soldiers, haughty in their special garb, with swords clanking at their sides.

And from inside the palace there came occasionally in the clear night to these peasants, sleeping fitfully on beds of straw in the ill-smelling stable beside their beasts of burden and the wheat as yet unsold, the sound of the voices of the courtiers, high-spirited but thick with wine, and the tantaliz-ing musical laughter of beautiful women—women dressed in fine linen and rubbed with fragrant ointments—women such as they knew they would never see in their own village and by their own hearthsides.

Now what was a man to answer when asked who he was? I am an Assyrian, yes, but I am also a scribe in the palace and sit at the right hand of the King. My companions at table are priests and nobles and my daughter shall marry one of their sons. I live in the city and know nothing of the way in which barley is sown and reaped. Those who labor in the fields or clean out my stable are of my people, and yet we are not the same, and it is good that each of us knows his special place, for is this not the way it was decreed by the great god Ashur? And so he identifies himself as a member of a people, but also of a particular social class within that group and in a particular ecological segment of the society—that is, the urban segment.

As if this were not complex enough, simultaneously came the wars and conquests and migrations, and here is now a *people* subjugated by another *people* and transferred to the conquerors' land space, some as slaves, some not. I am a Jew but I dwell in Babylon. God speed the day of my return to the land of my fathers. Or the conquerors come and establish their rule in the land. I am a Hellene but the governor of my city and the collector of my taxes are Romans. And complexity compounded! Whereas in the days of my ancestors all of us worshipped the gods of Olympus, now there are some of us who have transferred their allegiance to the Roman gods, others who adhere to the commands of Mithras, and I have heard tell of a new cult in our city which follows the teachings of one Jesus of Nazareth, a Jew who was crucified during the reign of Tiberius and whose disciples call themselves Christians.

In distant India, under Hinduism, a religion which had developed, scholars speculate, out of the civilization of invaders from the northwest, there was taking form a rigidly hierarchical and hereditary system of castes and subcastes which carefully marked out a person's status, his life-space, his occupation, and his sense of identity. I am a Brahman, a keeper and interpreter of the sacred lore. All who are not Brahmans are my inferiors and must defer to me.

The winning of Europe by Christianity after the fall of Rome eventually imposed a substantial measure of religious uniformity over the peoples of Western Europe. Eastern Europe went its own way under the banner of Byzantium and Eastern Orthodoxy. The political units, however, such as the Holy Roman Empire and the Frankish Kingdom, were loosely organized, vast sprawling affairs which, of necessity, allowed considerable cultural autonomy to their heterogeneous array of ethnic societies, each, for the most part, occupying its own land base.[1] The feudal order, with its system of "estates" in

---

[1]There are exceptions to this last point, to be sure. Spain, with its mixture of Christians, Moors, and Jews, is a conspicuous example. The Jews, of course, constituted small enclaves throughout Europe at this time.

which nobles and clergy dominated the vast peasant mass, emphasized identity with the semi-heritary social class to which a man belonged, over and against the cross-cutting loyalties of ethnic background and budding nationhood. "Oh! you are an Englishman, are you?" Shaw has his nobleman twit the Chaplain in *Saint Joan*. "Certainly not, my lord: I am a gentleman," the cleric hastens to reply.

The momentous schism which we call the Protestant Reformation, and the rise of the nation-state, usher us into the modern era where national boundaries and concepts of statehood began to enclose groups of widely different ancestral heritages and variant and, initially, sharply conflicting, religious affiliations. The discovery and conquest of the Western hemisphere by the white-skinned Europeans brought them into contact with a new racial group, the Indian aborigines, and created the demand for cheap and heavy labor which caused the slave trade with Africa to flourish and resulted in the forced transportation to the New World of thousands of black men. The final developments of the modern era—the industrial revolution, which made both possible and necessary large-scale voluntary migration of peoples from Europe (and to a smaller extent Asia) to the Americas, the rapid growth of cities to the point where Western life is predominantly and increasingly urban life, and the substantial widening of the channels for social mobility under free private enterprise capitalism so that a man could well change his social class position during his own lifetime—provide the setting for our contemporary inquiry. What now was a man to say when asked, Who are you?

THE ETHNIC GROUP

Before we endeavor to wrestle decisvely with this question, let us look back at the brief historical survey with which we have opened this discussion and extract its relevant conceptual points. First and foremost, we note that early man identified himself as a member of a group, his "people," and that this "peoplehood" was, roughly, coterminous with a given rural land space, political government, no matter how rudimentary, a common culture in which a principal element was a set of religious beliefs and values shared more or less uniformly by all members of the group, and a common racial background ensuring an absence of wide differences in physical type. These are elements of the classic model of the "folk society," to use Robert Redfield's term,[2] a type of society which produces the characterological configuration described by David Riesman as fitting the "tradition-directed" person.[3] For my somewhat different purposes here, I wish to focus attention on the sense of "peoplehood" which, under the circumstances described, is unitary and uncomplicated. A convenient term for this sense of peoplehood is "ethnicity" (from the Greek word "ethnos," meaning "people" or "nation"), and we shall refer to a group with a shared feeling of peoplehood as an "ethnic group."[4]

The subsequent march of civilization, with its population increases, stimulation to social class formation, wars, migrations, creation of cities, proliferation of religious variation, and grouping in progressively larger political units has, in accelerating tempo, shattered and fragmented this sense of peoplehood—this ethnicity—detaching one by one each of the elements which composed the once unified whole, and isolating each element from the other. Accompanying these changes there have grown up ideologies which correspond to them. In the modern industrialized urban state, such an

[2]Robert Redfield, "The Folk Society," *American Journal of Sociology*, Vol. 52, No. 4 (January 1947), 293–308; *Tepoztlan, A Mexican Village* (Chicago, University of Chicago Press, 1930); and *The Primitive World and Its Transformations* (Ithaca, N.Y., Cornell University Press, 1953). Of course, there are other elements contained in the "folk society" model as discussed by Redfield and others; important among them are the absence of literacy and relative isolation from other groups.

[3]David Riesman, with the collaboration of Nathan Glazer and Reuel Denney, *The Lonely Crowd: A Study of the Changing American Character* (New Haven, Yale University Press, 1950).

[4]Cf. E. K. Francis, "The Nature of The Ethnic Group," *American Journal of Sociology*, Vol. 52, No. 5 (March 1947), 393–400.

ideological model, stemming from classic eighteenth and nineteenth century liberalism blended with nationalism, views the huge nation as "the people"; the remnants of former types of ethnicity are then regarded as inconvenient vestiges—to be tolerated, if the state is democratic—but not to be encouraged. In the more extreme rationalist-liberal "one-world" or "federation of nations," "world government" ideological system, the ultimate point is reached: even nations are regarded as outmoded socio-political entities and the projected ideal sense of peoplehood is one which embraces the entire population of the world—the "brotherhood of man" knowing no boundaries, national or otherwise. Ethnicity, as representing a sense of special ancestral identification with some *portion* of mankind has, in this conception, disappeared entirely.

It is not my purpose at this point in the discussion to pass judgment on the desirability or undesirability of ethnicity or to evaluate its various forms, but rather to attempt to ascertain the realities as they exist. My essential thesis here is that the sense of ethnicity has proved to be hardy. As though with a wily cunning of its own, as though there were some essential element in man's nature that demanded it—something that compelled him to merge his lonely individual identity in some ancestral group of fellows smaller by far than the whole human race, smaller often than the nation—the sense of ethnic belonging has survived. It has survived in various forms and with various names, but it has not perished, and twentieth-century urban man is closer to his stone-age ancestors than he knows.

Here we must digress for a moment to point out that the fragmentation of ethnicity left competing models of the sense of peoplehood, so that men were forced either to choose among them or to integrate them in some fashion—to arrange them, perhaps, in a series of concentric circles each a step farther removed from the core of personality and self-identification. Our knowledge of the social psychology of historical populations is not extensive, but we may speculate that the feudal peasant of the later Middle Ages, for instance,

108

thought of himself as a member of Christendom, and that within this outer layer of group self-identification there were slight—probably very slight—overtones of identification as a Burgundian or a Sussexman, perhaps even as a Frenchman or an Englishman, but that closer to the core of his personality was his self-identification as a serf or a villein who lived in this particular village or as a part of the peasant group who served this particular lord of the manor. Peasant life in all ages is notoriously isolated and self-contained and relatively unaware of the larger world around it. The course and boundaries of empire, state, and nation might swirl and change above him, but what was this to the humble tiller of the soil? Life went on much as it did before—the oxen must be harnessed to the plough at dawn and driven over to the liege lord's acres regardless of whether the Anglo-Saxon Edward or the Norman William wielded the royal scepter.

In the above example, the sense of social class identity, which I wish to keep conceptually separate from ethnic identity, bulks larger than ethnicity itself, although it is still a social class contained within the white race, within Christendom, and more immediately, fused with the local village and manorial group all of whose members spoke the same dialect.

In the twentieth-century nation-state, and particuarly in the United States, the competing models of ethnicity are the nation-state itself, race, religion, and national origin or nationality background. By the last term I mean the nation which our ancestors who first came to this country came from. The American who answers Who He Is, answers, then, from an ethnic point of view, as follows: I am an American, I am of the White or Negro or Mongoloid race, I am a Protestant, Catholic, or Jew, and I have a German, or Italian, or Irish, or English, or whatever, national background. While we can only speculate as to the order in which these layers of ethnic identity are arranged around the self, it is convenient to diagram the situation as in Figure 1.

In practice, it is probable that these discrete categories are attached to the self not separately or serially but in combination. Our conventional language of ethnic identification

109

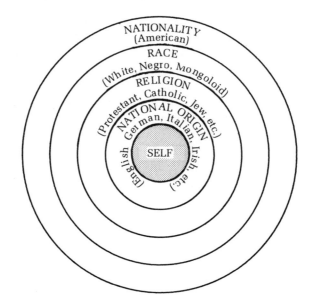

. Fig. 1   Ethnic identity of an American

within the nation suggests as much. This American is a white Protestant Anglo-Saxon; that one is an Irish Catholic (white race understood), this one is a Negro Protestant (African background understood), that one is a Russian Jew (white race understood). This is the way we identify each other and ourselves when we think, ethnically, about Who We Are within the national boundaries. These are the labels of group-hood which history made sure would eventually be attached to our psychological self as we arrived in the world within the confines of this family rather than that one. "John Doe," rhapsodizes the newspaper editorial somewhat patronizingly about the American Negro who has gained respectable fame or fortune, "is a credit to his people." What "people" does the editorialist refer to? Not, we know, to his country, but to his race.

When I use the term "ethnic group," then, to refer to a type of group contained within the national bundaries of America, I shall mean by it any group which is defined or set off by race, religion, or national origin, or some combination of these categories. I do not mean to imply that these three concepts mean the same thing. They do not. Race, technically, refers to differential concentrations of gene frequencies responsible for traits, which, so far as we know, are confined to physical manifestations such as skin color or hair form; it has no intrinsic connection with cultural patterns and institutions. Religion and national origins, while both cultural phenomena, are distinctly different institutions which do not necessarily vary concomitantly. However, all of these categories have a common social-psychological referent, in that all of them serve to create, through historical circumstances, a sense of peoplehood for groups within the United States, and this common referent of peoplehood is recognized in the American public's usage of these three terms, frequently in interchangeable fashion. Our point, then, is not that we wish to legitimize confusion by giving it a name, but that there is a common social-psychological core to the categories "race," "religion," and "national origin"—the sense of peoplehood—and the term "ethnic group" is a useful one for designation of this common element.[5]

This "sense of peoplehood" itself deserves further examination. Of what does it consist? What are its component elements? To a member of a stone-age society—the man of prehistory—such a question would have been incomprehensible since, for him, all the potential elements of peoplehood were joined together in a unitary whole. The members of the small band of which his family was a part lived together on the land, worshipped in the same manner, had roughly similar views of right and wrong, hunted, fished, or planted in the

---

[5]Some sociologists use the term "ethnic group" to refer to a national origins group—thus the Italian or Polish ethnic group. I prefer the broader use of the term because we have a specific phrase, "national origin" or "nationality background" and we need the broader term because of the common sense of peoplehood running through race, religion, or national origin—the common social-psychological referent. It is thus simply a matter of semantic convenience. My usage is in accord with that of E. K. Francis in the work cited above.

same way, looked very much alike, and governed themselves. While there were individual differences in personality type or physical prowess, or skill, these differences remained on an individual basis; they did not mark off groups beyond kinship lines. Ethnicity, then, was simply the human environment in which one breathed and functioned.

The man who has entered history, however, the man of cities, occupational specialization, war, conquest, migration, and religious variation, while clinging tenaciously to the sense of ethnicity, is literally forced to mould its nebulous shape more narrowly in accordance with the vagaries of the history of which he is a part. At one time he may feel his peoplehood on the basis of present or past national grouping, at another on the basis of common religious adherence, and at still another, on the basis of common racial identity. Common to all these objective bases, however, is the social-psychological element of a special sense of both ancestral and future-oriented identification with the group. These are the "people" of my ancestors, therefore they are my people, and they will be the people of my children and their children. With members of other groups I may share political participation, occupational relationships, common civic enterprise, perhaps even an occasional warm friendship. But in a very special way which history has decreed, I share a sense of indissoluble and intimate identity with *this group* and *not that one* within the larger society and the world.

Once these attitudes of special ethnic group identity develop, it is obvious that they reinforce each other through the system of mutual expectations that grow up. As Will Herberg has pointed out, it is *expected* in American society that we be either a Protestant, a Catholic, or Jew, whether we are formally connected with a church or synagogue or not.[6] And the "status" of being Negro or a White or a Mongoloid Oriental is not one from which one may voluntarily resign. The occasional individual who may have determined independently

---

[6]Will Herberg, *Protestant-Catholic-Jew* (New York, Doubleday, 1955), chap. 3.

that he will wear none of these labels—religious or racial—finds that the institutional structure of the society and the set of built-in social and psychological categories with which most Americans are equipped to place him—to give him a "name"—are loaded against him. Group categorization, then, has its own social momentum once it is set in motion and is by no means purely a matter of individual volitions acting in concert. Herberg put it this way: "The way in which one identifies and locates oneself ('Who, what, am I?') is closely related to how one is identified and located in the larger community ('Who, what, is he?'). Normally they reflect, sustain, and illumine each other; it is only in abnormal situations that they diverge and conflict."[7] It was the perception of this sociological fact and its implications that underlay the social psychologist Kurt Lewin's suggestion that "interdependence of fate" rather than similarity or dissimilarity in characteristics of individuals was the basic component of group constitution.[8] Considering it further, we may say that the similarities and dissimilarities of the past, which certainly played some role in group formation at any given time, both persuade and force us through the social grouping precipitations of history and the social-psychological expectations concerning group identity which these precipitations have created in the present, to take on group identifications which may or may not be congenial to our individual interests, preferences, and idiosyncrasies.

SOCIAL STRUCTURE AND CULTURE

The ethnic group, besides being based on a social-psychological sense of peoplehood stemming from history, has another major characteristic which distinguishes it from all "small groups" and from most other "large groups." This is the nature of its relationship to the various phenomena

[7]*Protestant-Catholic-Jew*, p. 25.
[8]Kurt Lewin, *Resolving Social Conflicts* (New York, Harper, 1948), pp. 163–66, 183–85.

which may be subsumed under the term "social structure." I propose now to define this term closely since its elucidation is crucial to the entire argument of the book. By the social structure of a society I mean the set of crystallized social relationships which its members have with each other which places them in groups, large or small, permanent or temporary, formally organized or unorganized, and which relates them to the major institutional activities of the society, such as economic and occupational life, religion, marriage and the family, education, government, and recreation. To study a society's social structure is to study the nature of its family groups, its age and sex distribution and the social groupings based on these categories, its social cliques, its formal and informal organizations, its divisions on the basis of race, religion, and national origin, its social classes, its urban and rural groups, and the pattern of social relationships in school and college, on the job, in the church, in voting behavior and political participation, and in leisure time activities. It is a large definition but a consistent one in that it focuses on *social relationships*, and social relationships that are *crystallized*—that is, which are not simply occasional and capricious but have a pattern of some repetition and can to some degree be predicted, and are based, at least to some extent, on a set of shared expectations.

Of the various ways of classifying the groups which represent the crystallization of social relationships there is one which is of particular interest to us here. It is based on the concept of the "primary group," suggested by the pioneer American sociologist, Charles Horton Cooley,[9] and in its extended form includes the obverse concept of the "secondary group." The primary group is a group in which contact is personal, informal, intimate, and usually face-to-face, and which involves the entire personality, not just a segmentalized part of it. The family, the child's play group, and the

[9]Charles Horton Cooley, *Social Organization* (New York, Scribner's, 1909), chap. 3. See also, Leonard Broom and Philip Selznick, *Sociology: A Text with Adapted Readings* (Evanston, Ill., Row, Peterson, 1955), Chapter 5.

social clique are all examples of a primary group. They are primary in that they are first both from the point of view of time in the "socialization" process—that is, the process by which the growing child is indoctrinated into the values of his culture—and first from the standpoint of their importance in moulding human personality.

In direct contrast, the secondary group is a group in which contacts tend to be impersonal, formal or casual, non-intimate, and segmentalized; in some cases they are face-to-face, in others not. We belong to many an "interest" organization, for instance, in American society, most of whose other members we never see, but whose annual bill for dues arrives promptly. The intimate friends we invite to our house regularly for dinner and to whose parties we are invited in return constitute a primary group. The civic committee for the preservation of the community's parks to which we belong and which meets twice a year is a secondary group. And, obviously, there will be groups which will be hard to classify but which will appear to have both primary and secondary aspects—to fall somewhere in the middle of a scale built on this dimension. To put the matter in another way, we may speak of *primary relationships* with other persons, which are personal, intimate, emotionally affective, and which bring into play the whole personality, as contrasted with *secondary relationships*, which are impersonal, formal, and segmentalized, and tend not to come very close to the core of personality.

Social structure, man's crystallized social relationships, is one side of the coin of human life, the other side of which is *culture*. Culture, as the social scientists uses the term, refers to the social heritage of man—the ways of acting and the ways of doing things which are passed down from one generation to the next, not through genetic inheritance but by formal and informal methods of teaching and demonstration. The classic definition of culture is that of the early anthropologist, E. B. Tylor, who described it as "that complex whole which includes knowledge, belief, art, morals, law, custom, and any other capabilities and habits acquired by man as a member of society."[10] Culture, in other words, is the way of life of a society, and if analyzed further is seen to consist of prescribed ways of behaving or norms of conduct, beliefs, values, and skills, along with the behavioral patterns and uniformities based on these categories—all this we call "non-material culture"—plus, in an extension of the term, the artifacts created by these skills and values, which we call "material culture."

Culture and social structure are obviously closely related and in a constant state of dynamic interaction, for it is the norms and values of the society which, for the most part, determine the nature of the social groupings and social relationships which its members will create; and, conversely, frequently it is through the action of men in social groups that cultures undergo change and modification. To illustrate the first point we need only think of the adult organizations so characteristic of American life (and which we take for granted) composed of adults of both sexes, married and unmarried, who come together because of some common interest. An example would be a municipal choral society, a poetry club, or a chapter of the American Civil Liberties Union. An organization composed in this fashion would be unthinkable in a traditional Moslem society. To illustrate the second point, we may note that it was an organization, the Bolshevik Party under Lenin, which provided the dynamic thrust that produced the vast cultural changes that consitute the enormous behavioral gap between Czarist Russia during World War I and the Soviet Union of the 1960s.

When used in the general sense, the term "culture" refers to the sum of man's social heritage existing over the world at any given time. More frequently, however, the term is used specifically to refer to the social heritage or way of life of a particular human society at a particular time. Thus one speaks of American culture in the twentieth century, as differentiated, for instance, from French culture in the

[10]E. B. Tylor, *Primitive Culture*, 3rd ed. (London, John Murray, 1891), Vol. I, p. 1. The first edition appeared in 1871.

eighteenth century, or from contemporary Chinese culture. It is obvious, then, that the term may be applied to human groupings of various dimensions, whenever these groupings involve shared behavioral norms and patterns that differ somewhat from those of other groups. Thus in one sense, America, France, and Italy are all a part of Western culture because of certain behavioral values shared by Americans, Frenchmen, and Italians as the result of their common social heritage of European life—values which they do not share with peoples of Oriental or African cultural background. By the same token, groups *within* a national society may differ somewhat in their cultural values since in a large, modern, complex, multigroup nation, cultural uniformity of the type approximated in a primitive society is impossible of attainment. Thus we may speak of the culture of a group smaller than the national society.

The Subsociety and the Subculture

With these concepts of "social structure" and "culture" in mind, we may now go on to develop the argument. The ethnic group, I have said, bears a special relationship to the social structure of a modern complex society which distinguishes it from all small groups and most other large groups. It is this: *within the ethnic group there develops a network of organizations and informal social relationships which permits and encourages the members of the ethnic group to remain within the confines of the group for all of their primary relationships and some of their secondary relationships throughout all the stages of the life-cycle.* From the cradle in the sectarian hospital to the child's play group, to the social clique in high school, the fraternity and religious center in college, the dating group within which he searches for a spouse, the marriage partner, the neighborhood of residence, the church affiliation and the church clubs, the men's and the women's social and service clubs, the adult clique of "marrieds," the vacation resort, and then as the age-cycle nears completion, the rest

117

home for the elderly and, finally, the sectarian cemetery—in all of these activities and relationships which are close to the core of personality and selfhood—the member of the ethnic group may, if he wishes, and will in fact in many cases, follow a path which never takes him across the boundaries of his ethnic subsocietal network.

In addition, some of the basic institutional activities of the larger society become either completely or in part ethnically enclosed. Family life and religion are, virtually by definition, contained within the ethnic boundaries. Education becomes ethnically enclosed to the extent that "parochial" school systems are utilized. Even within public and nonsectarian private schools and colleges, a system of social cliques and voluntary religious organizations set up for educational and social purposes may effectively separate the students from each other in all but formal classroom instruction. Economic and occupational activities, based as they are on impersonal market relationships, defy ethnic enclosure in the United States more than any institution except the political or governmental, but even here a considerable degree of ethnic enclosure is by no means a rarity. The white Christian who works for an all-white Christian business concern, or the Jew who is employed by an all-Jewish firm, labors at the points of intersection of the economic institution and ethnicity. Even in the "all-ethnic" business concern, impersonal secondary relationships across ethnic group lines may take place in wholesale purchasing or in sales. However, if the clientele of the concern is also of the same ethnic group— examples would be the kosher butcher shop or the retail store whose only merchandise is religious objects for Catholic consumption—then the isolation from inter-ethnic contacts even on the job is virtually complete.

Governmental relationships to the larger society are, by definition, non-ethnically oriented. That is, barring the exceptions noted earlier, the politico-legal system of the United States recognizes no distinctions on the basis of race, religion, or national origin, and a citizen's obligations, responsibilities, and relationships to the laws of the state are not ethnically qualified.[11] Active work in political parties, if it is above the local neighborhood level (and frequently even there), takes one across ethnic group lines. "Bloc voting" on an ethnic basis has, of course, played an important part in American political affairs, and although the day of herding masses of unknowing immigrants to the polls is past, ethnic background still influences voting preferences in substantial fashion,[12] even though it is a reasonable guess that, over the long run, time and increasing socio-economic differentiation within each ethnic group will gradually dilute the ethnic impact on politics. Military service, since the banishment of racial segregation from the armed forces, mixes people of varying ethnic backgrounds indiscriminately.

I shall return to this subject in greater detail later and discuss exceptions, individual and patterned, to the "model" of American society which I am presenting, but here my purpose is to paint the picture in broad strokes. In these terms, as far as we have gone, the American social structure may be seen, then, as a national society which contains within its political boundaries a series of *subsocieties* based on ethnic identity. The network of organizations, informal social relationships, and institutional activities which makes up the ethnic subsociety tends to pre-empt most or all primary group relationships, while secondary relationships across ethnic group lines are carried out in the "larger society," principally in the spheres of economic and occupational life, civic and political activity, public and private nonparochial education, and mass entertainment. All of these relationships, primary

[11]A further exception should be noted here: the federal government's recognition of religious belief and background as relevant in the case of the conscientious objector to war and military service. Even here, the exemption is not absolute; "alternative service" of a non-military nature is required.

[12]See Paul F. Lazarsfeld, Bernard Berelson, and Hazel Gaudet, *The People's Choice*, 2nd ed. New York, Columbia University Press, 1948); Bernard R. Berelson, Paul F. Lazarsfeld, and William N. McPhee, *Voting* (Chicago, University of Chicago Press, 1954); Angus Campbell, Gerald Gurin, and Warren E. Miller, *The Voter Decides* (Evanston, Ill., Row, Peterson, 1954); and Samuel Lubell, *The Future of American Politics* (New York, Doubleday, Second edition, Doubleday Anchor Books, 1956).

and secondary, are contained within the boundaries of common political allegiance and responsibility to the politico-legal demands and expectations of American nationality. The structure is shown in Figure 2. Table 1 presents the relation-

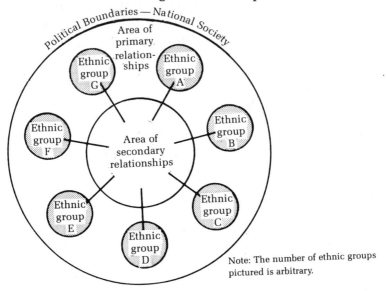

Note: The number of ethnic groups pictured is arbitrary.

Fig. 2. American society

TABLE 1. Ethnicity and Institutional Activity

INSTITUTION	ETHNICITY
Political	Mostly mixed
Economic	Mostly mixed, with significant exceptions
Education	Partly mixed—parochial schools and some segregation in social activities qualify mixing influence of formal structure of public and private non-parochial school systems
Religion	Ethnically enclosed
Family	Ethnically enclosed
Recreation	Ethnically enclosed in participation, except for impersonal relationships at mass entertainment functions

ship of ethnicity to institutional functioning in America in summary form.

Thus far we have called attention to two functional characteristics of the ethnic group or subsociety. First, it serves psychologically as a source of group self-identification—the locus of the sense of intimate peoplehood—and second, it provides a patterned network of groups and institutions which allows an individual to confine his primary group relationships to his own ethnic group throughout all the stages of the life cycle. Its third functional characteristic is that it refracts the national cultural patterns of behavior and values through the prism of its own cultural heritage. This unique subnational heritage may consist of cultural norms brought over from the country of recent emigration, it may rest on different religious values, or on the cumulative domestic experiences of enforced segregation as a group within American borders over a number of generations, or on some combination of these sources of cultural diversity. It is this phenomenon which is patently the basis for the term "cultural pluralism," used to describe the model of American society as a composite of groups which have preserved their own cultural identity.[13] The question of the actual extent of this cultural diversity in contemporary American society I wish to leave for later discussion. My purpose here is simply to point out that provision for the possibility of cultural diversity within the larger national society is the third major functional characteristic of the ethnic subsociety. In this sense, then, just as we speak of the national culture as representing the cultural way of life or cultural patterns of the national society, one may think of the ethnic subsociety as having its own cultural patterns, these patterns consisting of the national cultural patterns blended with or refracted through the particular cultural heritage of the ethnic group; this blend or amalgam we may call, in preliminary fashion, the *subculture* of the ethnic subsociety.

---

[13]The historical development of this concept will be traced elsewhere.

The term "subculture" has been used by a number of sociologists to refer to the cultural patterns of any subgroup or type of subgroup within the national society. One may speak of the subculture of a gang, a neighborhood, a factory, a hospital, etc. Albert K. Cohen's excellent study of delinquency in which he analyzes the cultural patterns of the delinquent gang is based on such a use of the term.[14] We prefer, however, to reserve the term "subculture" to stand for the cultural patterns of a subsociety which contains both sexes, all ages, and family groups, and which parallels the larger society in that it provides for a network of groups and institutions extending throughout the individual's entire life cycle. For the cultural patterns of a group more restricted in scope than an entire subsociety we suggest the term "group-culture."[15] The distinction allows us to isolate and distinguish from each other phenomena of different scope and import. It is summarized briefly in the paradigm presented in Table 2.

Thus far I have spoken of the subsociety as though it were equivalent to the ethnic group. However, if we stop to consider the functional characteristics of the subsociety—its salience as a locus of group identification, its network of groups and institutions which allow primary group relationships to be confined within its borders throughout the life cycle, and its role as a carrier of particular cultural patterns, then it becomes clear that other sociological categories, in addition to the ethnic group, demand consideration. The rise of the city

[14]Albert K. Cohen, *Delinquent Boys* (Glencoe, Ill., Free Press, 1955). See also, for such a use of the term, several papers by Alfred McClung Lee: "Levels of Culture as Levels of Social Generalization," *American Sociological Review,* Vol. 10, No. 4 (August 1945), pp. 485–95; "Social Determinants of Public Opinions," *International Journal of Opinion and Attitude Research,* Vol. 1, No. 1 (March 1947), pp. 12–29; and "A Sociological Discussion of Consistency and Inconsistency in Intergroup Relations," *Journal of Social Issues,* Vol. 5, No. 3, pp. 12–18.

[15]Compare use of this term in Alfred McClung Lee, "Attitudinal Multivalence in Relation to Culture and Personality," *American Journal of Sociology,* Vol. 60, No. 3 (November 1954) pp. 294–99. Lee uses the term to refer to the particularized culture of any group, regardless of scope.

TABLE 2. Social Units and Their Cultures

SOCIAL UNIT	CULTURAL TERM
The National Society (or The Society): (the nation with its political boundaries)	The National Culture (or The Culture)
The Subsociety (the social unit, smaller than the national society, which contains a large network of groups and institutions extending through the entire life cycle of the individual)	The Subculture
The Group (groups of segmental import; for example, the gang, the play-group, the factory, the hospital, the office)	The Groupculture

created differences between the urban dweller and the farmer which were also reflected in the areas of group identification, social relationships, and cultural behavior. The eventual creation of the large nation meant that people living in areas widely distant from one another would develop regional differences in behavior and self-identification, as well as regionally contained social systems. But most important of all in this connection was the rise of *social classes,* to which we referred in our historical summary.

Social class phenomena refer to hierarchical arrangements of persons in a society based on differences in economic power, political power, or social status.[16] (I have defined "social status" elsewhere as "a psychological system

[16]For general analyses of social class research and theory in the recent sociological literature, see Bernard Barber, *Social Stratification* (New York, Harcourt Brace 1957); Milton M. Gordon, *Social Class in American Sociology* (Durham, N.C., Duke University Press, 1958); Joseph A. Kahl, *The American Class Structure* (New York, Rinehart 1957); Leonard Reissman, *Class in American Society,* (Glencoe, Ill., Free Press, 1960); and Kurt B. Mayer, *Class and Society* (New York, Doubleday, 1955). For a popular account with emphasis on social status, see *The Status Seekers,* by Vance Packard (New York, David McKay, 1959).

of attitudes in which superiority and inferiority are reciprocally ascribed.")[17] Usually these three categories or "variables" of class hierarchy vary together to a considerable extent—that is, those who are high in economic power tend to be high in political power and in social status, and so on. Each of the variables, in other words, "converts" easily to the other, and there is a process of constant interaction in which greater economic power allows one to secure higher social status, while higher social status, in turn, makes it easier to secure additional economic power. However, the variables do not vary together perfectly and there is always some overlapping or lack of synchronization when large numbers of people are being considered. For instance, the average clergyman has higher social status than he has economic power. Consequently, it is necessary to decide which of the variables or dimensions we will demarcate in order to designate groups in American life to which we attach the term "social classes." There is some reason to believe that the social status dimension is the most closely related to the variables of sense of group identification, confinement of intimate social relationships, and particularized cultural behavior—all criteria of the subsociety. Accordingly, we will use social status as our direct basis for social class division. When we speak of social classes, then, we shall mean the hierarchy of social status groups in American society, and it will be understood that these differences in social status also imply, on the average, differences in wealth and income—i.e. economic power— and differences in political power in the community and the nation.

The precise number of hierarchical status groups on the American scene has been a matter of dispute among sociologists, and there are a few who even describe the American status system as one vast hierarchical continuum without any groupings at all but simply individual differences in position on the continuum. My own view is that the idea of broadly conceived status groups gives a better fit to the

[17]*Social Class in American Sociology,* p. 245.

124

realities of the American status system than the unbroken continuum theory.[18] These groups do not have hard and fixed boundaries but shade off imperceptibly into each other. As Vance Packard has well put it: "While there is a continuum, it is also true that people will tend to cluster so that the continuum is actually a series of bulges and contractions. The major bulges might be called the major class groupings."[19] The existence of these groups is based on the social-psychological constructs or categories in people's minds as they think about their own and other people's social status directly or obliquely, and on the social relationships and types of cultural behavior that develop in conjunction with these subjective categories. Some subgroupings of status are probably made within the major social classes so that there are internal status differentiations of lesser magnitude within each class. It is possible, provided the correct steps are taken, to move up in the class system, and this is what is referred to as upward social mobility. Downward mobility may also take place under certain circumstances.

While there will be variations depending on the type of community, the general social status structure in the United States may, in the present stage of our knowledge, most satisfactorily be described, with certain qualifications, as one made up of six classes. I follow the terminology of W. Lloyd Warner, a pioneer student of the American social status structure, and his associates in designating these classes as the upper-upper, lower-upper, upper-middle, lower-middle, upper-lower, and lower-lower.[20]

I shall discuss the American class system, and particularly its relationship to ethnicity, in more detail later; at this point it will be sufficient for our purposes to characterize

---

[18]For my reasons, see *Social Class in American Sociology*, chap. 6 and 8.
[19]*The Status Seekers*, p. 30.
[20]See W. Lloyd Warner and Paul S. Lunt, *The Social Life of a Modern Community*, Yankee City Series, Vol. 1 (New Haven, Yale University Press, 1941). For a detailed criticism and evaluation of the Warner method of studying social classes and of his findings, see *Social Class in American Sociology*, chap. 4.

these classes briefly. The upper-uppers are the "old family" aristocrats, to be found especially in the class systems of the larger cities of the eastern seaboard where long histories of settlement have made their claims to ancestral prestige possible. They are usually wealthy, but more importantly, they can point to a family tradition of wealth and leading social position in the community. This background of wealth and position transmitted over a number of generations has resulted in the development of cultural patterns of behavior in dress, clothes, and manner which mark them subtly as having been born and reared in the world of power, privilege and "good taste." The men are bankers, owners and directors of important businesses, or work in high prestige professions such as medicine, law, and architecture. The families are listed in the city's *Social Register* or its equivalent, and they have been so listed since these compilations of the names, addresses, and schools of the elite began to appear in the late nineteenth century. They are the unostentatious but firmly established leaders of the "society" world of their city.

More and more, however, the upper-uppers find themselves sharing power, privilege, and social relationships with the families who have amassed substantial wealth and power more recently. These are the "newly rich," the lower-uppers, whose fortunes date from the post-Civil War industrial expansion of America or the even more recent industrial and military developments of the twentieth century and thus have not yet received the ultimate accolade of gentility which time, in sufficient quantity, will doubtless eventually bestow. The lower-uppers, however, although coolly received at first, gradually make their way into the organizations, social cliques, and institutions of the upper-uppers, this infiltration gradually being reflected for many in *Social Register* listing. Intermarriage and the passage of time establish many of the "newer" families securely in the upper class as the still later developments of American industrial life cast up a fresh lower-upper group. Time, then, tends to blur the distinction between the upper-upper and the lower-upper groups, and many communities outside of the East, because of their foreshortened history, have never had an upper-upper class in the terms described, and can best be characterized as possessing a five-class system headed by a relatively undifferentiated and unseparated upper class.[21]

The upper-middle class in American communities may best be described as the "solid substantial citizens," who, for the most part, are comfortably well off or have reasonably adequate incomes but are not wealthy or "social." If they are below forty-five years of age, they have probably been to college. Increasingly, a college education is the passport to upper-middle class status. They are the community's business executives and professionals—owners of middle-sized business concerns, middle-level executives of the large corporations, doctors, lawyers, architects, engineers, scientists, clergymen, college professors (the last two groups being among the relatively low-paid members of the class), and executives of the various service and civic bureaucracies that are becoming more and more numerous. This is only a partial occupational listing for the good-sized corps of largely (and increasingly) college-trained men who "run things" at the middle levels of power and decision-making in American communities of various sizes and who, in the metropolitan areas, ride the commuting trains home to their nightly refuge in the Scarsdales, Montclairs, and Ardmores of the nation.

Below the upper class and the upper-middle class, which W. Lloyd Warner groups together as "the Level Above the Common Man" and Vance Packard refers to collectively as

---

[21]Thus W. Lloyd Warner and his associates and August B. Hollingshead, in separate studies of the same small midwestern community carried out in the early 1940s, each divided the community into five classes, the upper class being undifferentiated into subclasses. See W. Lloyd Warner and Associates, *Democracy in Jonesville* (New York, Harper, 1949); and August B. Hollingshead, *Elmtown's Youth* (New York, Wiley, 1949). For an excellent study of a metropolitan upper class, see E. Digby Baltzell, *Philadelphia Gentlemen* (Glencoe, Ill., Free Press, 1958). For a stimulating general discussion of the upper class in American life, with emphasis on the power rather than the status dimension, see C. Wright Mills, *The Power Elite* (New York, Oxford University Press, 1956).

"the Diploma Elite," are the lower-middle class and the two lower classes. The line between the lower-middle and the upper-lower class (these two constituting Warner's "Level of the Common Man") is becoming increasingly blurred as blue-collar workers in the huge production industries, organized into powerful labor unions, increasingly surpass lower-level white-collar workers in income and the material possessions which income can buy. Perhaps the matter can be put in this way. Historically, the lower-middle class was predominantly a class made up of white-collar people of the lower ranks—clerks, salespersons, secretaries, owners of small businesses, and the like—together with a few "aristocrats" of the blue-collar world doing highly skilled work. The upper-lower class was then solidly composed of the bulk of skilled and semi-skilled manual workers, plus those unskilled workers who maintained minimum standards in lifestyle. The income gains of the blue-collar workers under powerful post-World War II unions, at the expense of the largely unorganized white-collar workers, raise questions about the subsequent interplay of income, power, status, and style of life at these class levels—questions which are as yet largely unanswered by sociological research. The issues are doubtless still in the process of resolution. In terms of status all we can safely say is that traditionally the bulk of the blue-collar workers have been classified in the upper-lower or "working" class and that social class dynamics currently at work may modify this situation eventually for the reasons mentioned—to what degree, we can only speculate.

The lower-lower class is composed of the unskilled manual laborers and the frequently unemployed who inhabit the slums of the nation's cities, towns, and rural areas. Their living standards are low, they are looked upon with either contempt or pity by the rest of the community, and their way of life rarely breeds ambition in either themselves or their children. Family desertion by the male is common in this class, and frequently public relief is called upon to maintain the mother and her children.

Farm owners may be thought of as belonging to either the lower-middle, upper-lower, or in some cases upper-middle class, depending on the size and scope of their farm operation and the way of life they and their families engage in.

The significance of social class analysis for our argument is that social classes, though not as precisely bounded as ethnic groups, also become sources of group identification, social areas of confinement for primary group relations, and bearers of particular cultural patterns of behavior. This, in fact, from one point of view, is the most important set of findings which has emerged from the vast accumulation of research and inquiry into social class phenomena in America which social scientists, which accelerating tempo, have been carrying out during the past thirty years. The social class, in other words, while not formally delineated, tends to have its own network of characteristic organizations, institutional activities, and social cliques. These are created because people who are approximately in the same social class have similar interests and tastes, have a common educational background, and work at occupations which bring them in touch with one another in various ways and which involve common types of experience. Thus they feel "comfortable" with each other. These reasons are probably more compelling than sheer "social snobbery" or status consciousness itself in keeping people of widely separated social classes apart from each other in primary group relationships, although doubtless all these reasons interact with one another to produce social separation.

The child, then, grows up in a particular family which is part of a particular class and learns the cultural values of that class as those values are brought home to him in family training, neighborhood play groups, and class-oriented educational patterns. Men and women of the same social class will thus share certain cultural values and patterns which distinguish them from Americans of other class backgrounds. Upward social mobility, then, involves the need for learning and adopting values and behavior in accordance with the standards of the class into which the upwardly mobile person is moving.

We have now isolated four factors or social categories which play a part in creating subsocieties within the national society that is America. They are ethnic group, social class, rural or urban residence, and region of country lived in. In the original form in which I first published this theory in 1947, my essential thesis was that these four factors do not function in isolation, or serially, but *combine or intersect* to form the basic large social units which make up American society and which bear and transmit the subcultures of America.[22] While the factors are theoretically discrete, they tend to form in their combination *"a functioning unity which has an integrated impact on the participating individual."*[23] Thus a person is not simply a white Protestant. He is simultaneously a lower-middle class white Protestant living in a small town in the South, or he is an upper-middle class white Catholic living in a metropolitan area in the Northeast, or a lower-class Negro living in the rural South, and so on. To put it in another way, the stratifications based on ethnicity are intersected at right angles by the stratifications based on social class, and the social units or blocks of bounded social space created by their intersection are contained in an urban or a rural setting in a particular region of the country. The analytical scheme is summarized in Table 3.

Central to this type of analysis is, of course, the relationship of the ethnic group stratification system to the social class stratification system. In 1951 I wrote: "American society is 'criss-crossed' by two sets of stratification structures, one based on social status, economic power, and political power differences, regardless of ethnic background, the other a set of status and power relationships based precisely on division of

[22]See Milton M. Gordon, "The Concept of the Sub-Culture and Its Application," *Social Forces*, Vol. 26, No. 1 (October 1947), pp. 40–42. See also, "A System of Social Class Analysis," *Drew University Studies*, No. 2 (August 1951), pp. 15–18; *Social Class in American Sociology*, pp. 252–56; and for a fuller exposition, "Social Structure and Goals in Group Relations," *Freedom and Control in Modern Society*, ed. Morroe Berger, Theodore Abel, and Charles H. Page (New York, Van Nostrand, 1954). In these publications I used the term "subculture" to stand elliptically for both the subsociety and the subculture as defined here.

[23]"The Concept of the Sub-Culture and Its Application," p. 40 (Italics as in original).

130

TABLE 3. The Subsociety and the Subculture

Factors Combining to Form
   the Subsociety
   Ethnic Group
     race
     religion
     national origins   The Subsociety
                                  with its particular

   Social Class   Subculture

   Rural-Urban Residence

   Regional Residence

     Examples of particular subsocieties characterized by particular subcultures:

   Upper-middle class white Protestant, southern urban
   Lower-middle class white Catholic, northern urban
   Lower-lower class Negro Protestant, southern rural
   Upper-middle class Negro Protestant, northern urban
   Lower-middle class white Jewish, western urban
   Upper class white Jewish, northern urban

the population by racial, nationality background, and religious categories into 'Old Americans,' Negroes, Jews, Catholics, Japanese-Americans, Italians, French-Canadians, etc."[24] In effect, this means that each ethnic group may be thought of as being divided into subgroups on the basis of social class, and that theoretically each ethnic group might conceivably have the whole spectrum of classes within it, although in practice, some ethnic groups will be found to contain only a partial distribution of social class subgroups.

    In the meantime, sociologists August B. Hollingshead and Jerome K. Myers, at Yale University, had been studying the social structure of the city of New Haven and had come to

[24]"A System of Social Class Analysis," pp. 15–16; see also, *Social Class in American Sociology*, p. 252.

a similar conclusion about the relationship of the ethnic group and the social class systems in American communities. In 1952, in a paper reporting on this research, Hollingshead stated:

> The data indicate that the community's current social structure is differentiated *vertically* along racial, ethnic, and religious lines, and each of these vertical cleavages, in turn, is differentiated horizontally by a series of strata or classes that are encompassed within it. Around the socio-biological axis of race two social worlds have evolved—a Negro world and a white world. The white world is divided by ethnic origin and religion into Catholic, Protestant, and Jewish contingents. Within these divisions there are numerous ethnic schisms.[25]

Reviewing the evidence dealing with the nature of institutional and organizational life within some of the bounded strata created by this system, Hollingshead referred to "the development of *parallel class structures* within the limits of race, ethnic origin, and religion."[26]

The role of regional and rural-urban factors in contributing to the differential nature of the subsocieties of America is doubtless decreasing with each passing decade, yet they cannot be ruled out entirely in a discussion of this topic even today. The vast differences in the cultural system of white attitudes and behavior toward the Negro which exist between North and South constitute an effective reminder that diversities of geography, climate, and historical experience have placed their respective marks on Americans of various regional localities. At least since the days of the great historian, Frederick Jackson Turner, these diversities and their effects

[25]August B. Hollingshead, "Trends in Social Stratification: A Case Study," *American Sociological Review*, Vol. 17, No. 6 (December 1952), p. 685. (Italics as in original.) See also, August B. Hollingshead and Frederick C. Redlich, *Social Class and Mental Illness* (New York, Wiley, 1958); and Jerome K. Myers and Bertram H. Roberts, *Family and Class Dynamics in Mental Illness* (New York, Wiley 1959).

[26]"Trends in Social Stratification: A Case Study," p. 686. (Italics as in original.) The term "ethnic" is obviously used here in the narrower sense of "national origin."

have been matters of considerable concern to historians, social scientists, and literary critics.[27] As Robin Williams has put it, "Not only are there systematic regional differences in overt patterns of behavior, but there are different 'historical memories' and collectivity sentiments that persist with a strength sometimes disconcerting to makers of national policy. . . ."[28]

However, these regional differences, along with the differences in way of life between a shrinking rural America and an expanding urban America, are subject to the accelerating onslaught of rapid transportation, mass communications, and the increasing mechanization of a vast array of productive enterprises, including farming.[29] These forces continually narrow the cultural gap between farm and country or Midwest and Far West. Perhaps we can put it this way. In attempting to predict the cultural behavior patterns of any given person on the basis of the factors making up his subsocietal participation, to know his "region" and whether he is rural or urban (or his position on a scale representing the rural-urban dimension), along with his ethnic group and social class, increases the accuracy of the prediction of his subcultural behavior. However, after one has ascertained his ethnic group and social class, the increase in accuracy of prediction obtained by adding his region and his position on the rural-urban scale is probably not now great, and this increment of predictive accuracy is decreasing with the years. Thus, ethnic group and social class will become increasingly important as the principal background factors making up the subsociety with its subculture in American life.

---

[27]See Merrill Jensen, ed., *Regionalism in America* (Madison, University of Wisconsin Press, 1951); and Howard W. Odum and Harry Estill Moore, *American Regionalism* (New York, Holt, 1938).

[28]Robin M. Williams, Jr., "Unity and Diversity in Modern America," *Social Forces*, Vol. 36, No. 1 (October 1957), p. 2.

[29]For a discussion of recent changes in the rural way of life in the United States, see Charles P. Loomis and J. Allan Beegle, *Rural Sociology: The Strategy of Change* Englewood Cliffs, N.J., Prentice-Hall, 1957), especially chap. 14.

THE ETHCLASS

If the portion of social space created by the intersection of the ethnic group with the social class is fast becoming the essential form of the subsociety in America, then we need a name for convenient reference to this subsocietal type. I have no great affection for neologisms and am pleased to do without them whenever possible; moreover, the one I am about to suggest has a quality about it which faintly calls to mind the Newspeak of Orwell's society of 1984. Nevertheless, I have thus tried to disarm my potential critics in advance because the need for some term of reference is great and because the term I am proposing has, at least, the virtues of simplicity and clarity of origin. I propose, then, that we refer to the subsociety created by the intersection of the vertical stratifications of ethnicity with the horizontal stratifications of social class as the *ethclass*. Thus a person's *ethclass* might be upper-middle class white Protestant, or lower-middle class white Irish Catholic, or upper-lower class Negro Protestant, and so on.

We must now inquire into what happens to the three crucial variables of group identity, social participation, and cultural behavior as they pertain to the subsociety of the ethclass, and thus discern how the ethclass functions differentially from the ethnic group itself. I shall offer the following remarks as a set of hypotheses which will be considered elsewhere in relation to such empirical evidence as is available. These hypotheses apply to American society at mid-century.

1) With regard to cultural behavior, differences of social class are more important and decisive than differences of ethnic group. This means that people of the same social class tend to act alike and to have the same values even if they have different ethnic backgrounds. People of different social classes tend to act differently and have different values even if they have the same ethnic background.

2) With regard to social participation in primary groups and primary relationships, people tend to confine these to their own social class segment within their own ethnic group—that is, to the ethclass.

3) The question of group identification must be dealt with by distinguishing two types of such identification from one another—one the sense of peoplehood to which we referred earlier, the other a sense of being truly congenial with only a social class segment of that "people." I can best articulate the distinction by quoting in full from one of my previous writings: "The matter of psychological orientations, that is, group identification and patterns of 'in-grouping' and 'out-grouping,' is complicated by the fact that we are dealing here with more than one dimension. Although a person may participate largely in a social field circumscribed by both ethnic group and social class borders, the attribution of ethnic group membership *by itself* is a powerful pattern in our culture—a pattern generated both by pressure from within the ethnic group and from without. Rare is the Negro, or the Jew, for instance, who can fail to respond affectively to events or to evaluative allegations which concern, respectively, Negroes or Jews as a group. Nevertheless, the participation field and the field of close behavioral similarities are likely to be class-confined, as well as ethnic-confined. Thus we may distinguish two types of psychological constellations corresponding to these respective experience patterns. 'I am ultimately bound up with the fate of these people' is the type of constellation attached to the ethnic group as a whole [See Kurt Lewin's concept of "interdependence of fate," referred to above]. We may call this *historical identification* since it is a function of the unfolding of past and current historic events. On the other hand, 'These are the people I feel at home with and can relax with' is the type of constellation attached to those persons with whom one participates frequently and shares close behavioral similarities. According to the subcultural hypothesis, these persons are likely to be of the same ethnic group *and* social class (and regional and rural-urban categories). This constellation we may call *participational identification*. To sum up: in terms of psychological orientations, the ethnic group is likely to be the group of historical identification, whereas the subculture [read "ethclass"] will be, in the majority of cases, the group of participational identification. It should be pointed out that identification with larger units—that is,

American society as a whole, 'Western society,' 'all humanity,' are likely to be present at different levels of structuring."[30]

Succinctly, then, one may say that the ethnic group is the locus of a sense of *historical identification*, while the ethclass is the locus of a sense of *participational identification*. With a person of the same social class but of a different ethnic group, one shares behavioral similarities but not a sense of peoplehood. With those of the same ethnic group but of a different social class, one shares the sense of peoplehood but not behavioral similarities. The only group which meets both of these criteria are people of the same ethnic group *and* same social class. With these "birds of our feather" we truly share a sense of what the early sociologist, Franklin Giddings, called "consciousness of kind"—with these particular members of the human race and no others we can really relax and participate with ease and without strain.[31]

DEVIANCE AND MARGINALITY

I have stated this last hypothesis in unqualified fashion only for the sake of conceptual clarity. At most, it is true, of course, only in degree—something which may be said for all the hypotheses (depending on the method of statement) which constitute the theory of subsocietal and subcultural life in America. Any theory of this kind must include categories and concepts which allow for the inevitable exceptions to the main pattern. Such exceptions to the pattern of primary group relationships postulated by the theory of American sub-

---

[30]"Social Structure and Goals in Group Relations," pp. 146–47. (Italics as in original.)

[31]E. K. Francis describes the ethnic group as a "secondary community" to which, by a process of abstraction and transposition, the qualities of primary group relationships have been attached. (See "The Nature of the Ethnic Group," p. 399). This puts the matter rather well except that we would add two qualifications: 1) it is the ethclass rather than the ethnic group itself to which primary group qualities are transposed; and 2) in the strict sense the ethclass does not have primary group qualities itself—it is too large for that. Rather it becomes the psychologically recognized *potential source*, or population pool, for whatever primary groups and primary group relationships are to be formed.

societies and subcultures may be rather simply cross classified under two dimensions; their degree of frequency and whether they involve participation in primary relationships across class lines or across ethnicity lines. On the frequency dimension, such primary group contacts across subsocietal lines may be conveniently divided into two categories: exceptional and systematic. The resulting typology of exceptions, then, gives us four dimensions: 1) Exceptional—across class lines; 2) Exceptional—across ethnic lines; 3) Systematic—across class lines; and 4) Systematic—across ethnic lines.

Let us look at these types separately. "Exceptional" or occasional primary group contacts across either social class or ethnic group lines occur in American life because of its multiplicity of opportunities for initial secondary contacts on the job, in the school, in the civic organization, and so on, and because of factors of individual congeniality and attraction which may come to the fore on such occasions. Thus we have the white Protestant who has one close Jewish friend, or one close Negro friend—or the small-town lawyer who plays poker once a month with a group of cronies which include a factory worker who had gone to high school with him. Such occasional forays across the lines which divide primary group life in America are only exceptions to the general pattern—for the person participating in them they do not involve breaking ties with his ethnic group or his social class or threaten his general immersion in the subsocietal life of either his ethnic group or his social class. Resting comfortably and securely in the subsocietal network of groups and institutions of his ethclass, as it were, this person simply ventures across group lines as an interesting and perhaps flavorful exception to the usual pattern of his social movement. His exceptions are those that "prove the rule."

By "systematic" contacts across social class and ethnic group lines in primary relationships, I mean those that are frequent and persistent and that make up a significant portion of the person's total primary group contacts. The two subtypes here demand individual and separate discussion.

Systematic primary group contacts across social class lines usually are an indication of vertical social mobility. That is, the person whose contacts are largely, or in a major way, with persons of the adjoining class above him in the hierarchy of social classes is probably engaged in the process of consolidating his position in the class of higher rank. This is a routine step in social mobility as educational, occupational, and economic changes are reflected in changes in interests, tastes, and values, and eventually the formation of relationships with those who occupy the superior and more powerful positions in the class structure and display the newly favored cultural patterns. Downward vertical mobility similarly involves changes in primary group relationships. Since upward mobility in social class position is a well-recognized and generally approved phenomenon as a result of the American value system's emphasis on "bettering oneself," the "rags to riches" theme, the triumph of "individual merit," and so on, it is probable that problems of changing social relationships in upward social class mobility, while they are not entirely absent by any means, are not of the same magnitude as the problems involved in frequent inter-ethnic primary group relationships. The more formidable problems of "marginality" (we shall discuss this term below) are found in substantial primary relationships across ethnic group lines.

The individual who engages in frequent and sustained primary contacts across ethnic group lines, particularly racial and religious, runs the risk of becoming what, in standard sociological parlance, has been called "the marginal man."[32] The marginal man is the person who stands on the borders or

[32]The concept was first presented by Robert E. Park in "Human Migration and the Marginal Man," *American Journal of Sociology*, Vol 33, No. 6 (May 1928), pp. 881–93. It was developed and elaborated by Everett V. Stonequist in "The Problem of the Marginal Man," *American Journal of Sociology*, Vol. 41, No. 1 (July 1935), pp. 1–12; and The *Marginal Man* (New York, Scribner's 1937). Some later discussions are Arnold W. Green, "A Re-examination of the Marginal Man Concept," *Social Forces*, Vol. 26, No. 2 (December 1947), pp. 167–71; Everett C. Hughes, "Social Change and Status Protest: An Essay on the Marginal Man," *Phylon*, Vol. 10, No. 1 (First Quarter 1949). pp. 58–65; David Reisman, *Individualism Reconsidered (Glencoe, Ill., The Free Press*, 1954), pp. 153–78; David I. Golovensky. "The Marginal Man Concept; an Analysis and Critique," *Social Forces*, Vol. 30, No. 3 (March 1952), pp. 333–

margins of two cultural worlds but is fully a member of neither. He may be the offspring of a racially mixed or interfaith marriage, or he may have ventured away from the security of the cultural group of his ancestors because of individual personality and experience factors which predisposed him to seek wider contacts and entry into social worlds which appeared more alluring. In the latter case, most frequently he is a member of a minority group attracted by the subsociety and subculture of the dominant or majority group in the national society of which he is a part. Frustrated and not fully accepted by the broader social world he wishes to enter, ambivalent in his attitude toward the more restricted social world to which he has ancestral rights, and beset by conflicting cultural standards, he develops, according to the classic conception, personality traits of insecurity, moodiness, hypersensitivity, excessive self-consciousness, and nervous strain. While the personality consequences of marginality have never been decisively proven, and while at least one acute observer of the contemporary American scene has pointed to the possible desirable personality results of marginality, such as greater insight, self-understanding, and creativity,[33] the sociological *position* of marginality may certainly be discerned. In the type most pertinent for our discussion, it is the position occupied by the social deviant from standard ethnic behavior—the person who ventures across the subsocietal lines of ethnicity in substantial fashion to seek the friendships, social cliques, and organizational affiliations that make up the world of his primary group relationships.

In some cases the marginal man may remain in his marginal position for an indefinite period; in others, he may eventually retreat to the comfort and familiarity of the ethnic group from which he originally ventured with high hopes. We must not overlook still a third possibility, however, and that is the gradual formation of a subsociety composed pre-

39; and Aaron Antonovsky, "Toward a Refinement of the 'Marginal Man' Concept," *Social Forces*, Vol. 35, No. 1 (October 1956), pp. 57–62.
[33]See *Individualism Reconsidered*, pp. 153–78.

cisely of marginal men as here defined.[34] It is my contention that, to some degree, this eventuality is taking place in American society today, in one area particularly—the social world or worlds of "the intellectual" and the creative and performing artist, whether literary, musical, theatrical, or visual. In the situation of men and women coming together because of an overriding common interest in ideas, the creative arts, and mutual professional concerns, we find the classic sociological enemy of ethnic parochialism. The forces interested in maintaining ethnic communality recognize the danger and attempt to counter it by providing for the satisfaction of intellectual, artistic, and professional concerns within the boundaries of the ethnic group. This counterattack is only partially successful, however, since the main currents of intellectual and artistic activity flow unconcernedly on in the broader world beyond ethnicity. The marginality thus created and the kind of social world generated by the interaction of marginal intellectuals constitute topics of considerable interest.

With this discussion of marginality we conclude the presentation of the theory of the subsociety and the subculture. We began with the sense of peoplehood, simple, unitary, and unfragmented in the life of stone-age man. We saw how the development of cities, occupational specialization, social classes, conquest, migration, industrialization, and the huge nation-state transformed the sense of peoplehood but did not destroy it, and we speculated on its survival in the racial, religious, and national background collectivities which compose the larger American society. We observed the outlines of a powerful system of horizontal stratification—the social class system—which transects the ethnic groups, and, now that rural-urban and regional differences are becoming increasingly minimized, leaves the social unit which we have called the "ethclass" as the effective model of the subsociety

[34]See "Social Change and Status Protest: An Essay on the Marginal Man" "Social Structure and Goals in Group Relations"; and Milton M. Gordon, "Social Class and American Intellectuals," *American Assocation of University Professors Bulletin*, Vol. 40, No. 4 (Winter 1954–55), pp. 517–28.

with its characteristic subculture in America—the social unit which allows for the maintenance of primary group relationships through the life cycle within its network of social organizations, cliques, and institutions, and which carries its characteristic system of cultural behavior. We discussed the differences between the ethnic group and the ethclass in the several dimensions of identification, social participation, and cultural behavior. And, finally, we took into consideration the deviant, or marginal man, who defies or ignores the conventional boundaries and behavior of subsocietal life. The theory has been painted in broad strokes as a set of hypotheses concerning the nature of American social life. Hopefully, the foregoing exposition has brought us, if not to the answer, at least farther along the road of appreciation of the necessary complexity of the answer to the question of social identity which opened our inquiry, this complexity itself constituting a significant measure of the vast distances of social history which stand betweeen our Pleistocene hunter and the man of the modern world.

part III
Assimilation & Pluralism

Social Structure & Goals in Group Relations

In the voluminous literature on racial and cultural group relations in American life, two basic related considerations appear to have received a minimum of attention, both in terms of theory and research. These considerations, in brief, are (1) the outlines of American social structure within which attitudinal and behavioral relationships between persons of varied ethnic backgrounds occur,[1] and (2) the various possible goals in the area of reduction of group tensions articulated with reference to the kind of social structure they respectively imply.

The minimal attention given to these topics, both demanding close attention to social structure, can hardly be justified on theoretical grounds, since relevant description and causational theory alike logically demand their articulation. An intermediate explanation, which itself merits further investigation, is that societal analysis in the science of sociology has long been institution-centered, with secondary focus on social processes, and (apart from the elementary age and sex categories) tertiary and residual attention relegated to social structure. Interestingly enough, the beginnings of a change in this emphasis emerge not from ethnic group analysis, from which they might be expected, but from the community studies in social stratification. The yet prevailing dominance of the institutional approach, however, may be quickly ascertained from an examination of current textbooks

[1] E. Franklin Frazier, in his Presidential Address before the American Sociological Society in December, 1948, called attention to this fundamental omission. See "Race Contacts and The Social Structure," *American Sociological Review*, Vol. 14 (February 1949), pp 1–11.

in the various fields of sociology and is strikingly confirmed in the contents of a recent volume designed as an overall survey of American society by one of the most careful and nonidiosyncratic of American sociologists.[2] This dominance is regrettable, since social structure is the basic framework within which institutions function and social processes take place; it is not merely a casual addendum to them.

An adequate theory of social structure for modern complex societies must go far beyond age and sex categories to ascertain the broad social units within the national culture, each of which may allow for the unfolding of the life-cycle within its invisible but operationally functioning borders. Such analysis must carefully investigate clique and associational memberships, ecological concentration, occupational relationshps, courtship and marriage practices, and psychological orientations with respect to the degree of their delimitation within broad social categories. Such investigation, moreover, cannot afford to rest with one-category analysis. It is not enough to know, for instance, that X per cent of marriages in American Town is ethnically endogamous and Y per cent is endogamous with respect to social class. An equally important question for the student of social structure is the distribution of endogamous marriages within each "social box" set up by combining the ethnic and class categories.[3] If other social factors prove relevant, their addition to the correlational structure is indicated. Such analysis extended along the entire gamut of institutional and associational life would eventually provide a relatively precise outline of American social structure, the varied effectiveness of its dividing lines, and finally a sociological setting for the analysis of the problems of persons who are marginal or mobile with regard to the various internal structures.

As a name for these internal structures, made up of a combination of social categories and usually providing for

[2]Robin M. Williams, Jr., *American Society, A Sociological Interpretation* (New York, Knopf, 1951).

[3]For an empirical study which shows awareness of the need for such analysis, see August B. Hollingshead, "Cultural Factors in the Selection of Marriage Mates," *American Sociological Review,* Vol. 15 (October 1950), pp. 619–27.

the unfolding of the life-cycle, the term *subculture* is approp-riate. Although this term has found casual and not infrequent usage heretofore, it appears to have stood, usually, for dis-crete units (that is, ethnic group alone, social class alone, etc.), occasionally for temporary groupings touching only one phase of the life-cycle, such as play groups and gangs, and sometimes for area-localized groups.[4] The present writer of-fered in a paper several years ago a systematic presentation of a theory of subcultural structure which has specific articula-tion and delineation.[5] The paradigm presented there, with minor modification, is as follows: a subculture is a social division of a national culture made up by a combination of ethnic group (used here as a generic term covering race, religion, or national origin[6]), social class, region (North-East,

---

[4]An early use of the term is that of Ralph Linton in *The Study of Man* (New York, Appleton-Century, 1936), pp. 275ff. Linton's analysis is focused largely on area-localized groups within a tribal culture. Alfred McClung Lee, in several papers, has used the term to refer to subgroups within a national culture and has related the analysis to norms and behavior patterns. See his "Levels of Culture as Levels of Social Generalization," *American Sociologi-cal Review*, Vol. 10 (August 1945), pp. 485–95; "Social Determinants of Public Opinions," *International Journal of Opinion and Attitude Research*, Vol. 1 (March 1947), pp. 12–29; and "A Sociological Discussion of Consis-tency and Inconsistency in Intergroup Relations," *Journal of Social Issues*, Vol. V, No. 3, pp. 12–18. A completely different meaning of the term "subcul-tural" is Joseph K. Folsom's. Folsom uses it to refer to behavior patterns which are below the level of cultural choice and are the inevitable products of human bodily structure and a given environment. See his *The Family* (New York, Wiley, 1934), pp. 46ff.

This list is by no means exhaustive.

[5]Milton M. Gordon, "The Concept of The Sub-Culture and Its Application," *Social Forces*, Vol. 26 (October 1947), pp. 40–42.

[6]Some writers use "ethnic group" to refer specifically to a national origin group. However, there is a need for a generic term to embody the common grouping principle involved in race, religion, and national origin divisions. Since "national origin," while a bit cumbersome, is already available for its specific, a "neutral" term such as "ethnic group" seems appropriate for generic usage. This usage is in accord with that of E. K. Francis in "The Nature of The Ethnic Group," *American Journal of Sociology*, Vol. LII (March 1947), pp. 393–400. (This article is particularly noteworthy for its cogent theoretical analysis of structural and psychological aspects of the "ethnic group.")

Mid-West, South-East, etc.), and rural or urban residence. Examples of a specific subculture would be the following: Negro, upper-class, North-East, urban; white Protestant, lower-class, South-East, rural; Jewish, upper-middle class, Mid-West, urban; and so on.

The theory of subcultural structure posits that, in "ideal type" terms, the four major factors listed above form in their combination a functioning unity which has an integrated impact on the participating individuals, in relation to both social structure and psychological orientation. With respect to social structure, they constitute the social setting within which the socialization process and the majority of later primary contacts take place. Psychologically, they provide the "social field" with which subnational identification and "consciousness of kind" constellations are joined.

The evidence which lends support to the subcultural theory varies widely in the preciseness of its focus in subcultural terms but is impressive in its cumulation when examined with this focus. It consists in large part of the monographs detailing community studies in social stratification and or ethnic group life.[7] On the whole, the most cogent

[7]Some examples are: W. Lloyd Warner and Leo Srole, *The Social Systems of American Ethnic Groups* (New Haven, Yale University Press, 1945); Allison Davis, Burleigh B. Gardner, and Mary R. Gardner, *Deep South* (Chicago, University of Chicago Press, 1941); St. Clair Drake and Horace R. Cayton, *Black Metropolis* (New York, Harcourt Brace, 1945); Elin L. Anderson, *We Americans* (Cambridge, Harvard University Press, 1937); Irvin L. Child, *Italian or American* (New Haven, Yale University Press, 1943); Ruth D. Tuck, *Not With The Fist* (New York, Harcourt Brace & Co., 1946). For an analytical survey of the social stratification studies, see the writer's Ph.D. dissertation, *Social Class in Modern American Sociology* (Columbia University, 1950); microfilm publication by University Microfilms, Ann Arbor, Michigan, 1950.

The studies of August B. Hollingshead and Jerome K. Myers at Yale, dealing with the social structure of New Haven, show a clear awareness of the relevance of the combined class-ethnic approach and offer some data to sustain it. See August B. Hollingshead, "Trends In Social Stratification: A Case Study," *American Sociological Review*, Vol. 17, No. 6 (December 1952), pp. 679–86. Hollingshead declares (p. 686): "In short, a major trend in the social structure of the New Haven community during the last half-century has been the development of *parallel class structures* within the limits of race, ethnic origin, and religion."

studies, as far as the combination of a class-ethnic approach is concerned, are those dealing with the Negro group. Here, the historical separation from the white social system has been so apparent that investigators have been able to concentrate structurally on class divisions within the Negro group. Most studies of non-Negro ethnic groups, or those dealing with social class in the white community generally, have been less satisfactory in this respect (the work of Hollingshead and Myers, noted in footnote 7, constitutes a notable exception) largely because of the lack of a theoretical apparatus which could suggest the right questions for research, such as: What is the nature of the class divisions within the ethnic subsystem? To what extent do members of a particular class within an ethnic subsystem (for instance, the Jewish) have clique and institutional contacts with members of the same class but a different ethnic subsystem (for instance, the white Protestant)? To what extent do members of a particular class in a particular ethnic group have social contacts with members of the same ethnic groups but of a lower or a higher class? The need for answers to such queries as these becomes strikingly apparent when, leaving the simpler descriptions of the immigrant colonies, we ask ourselves: What are the social structural and psychological orientations, in the double dimensions of ethnic group and class, of the children of immigrants (and *their* children) who are described so patly and uniformly as "rising in the class structure"? Trying to shake out of the existing literature a focused and even a roughly quantitative answer to this question is a frustrating experience.

The inclusion of the regional and the rural-urban categories in the subcultural construct suggests itself because of the well-known variations in mores which they occasion. Undoubtedly, they are of considerably less importance than the ethnic and the class categories. To round out the outlines of the subcultural social system, however, their inclusion seems justified. A three-way breakdown along the rural-urban continuum is also suggested, as follows: rural—small city—large city. It should be pointed out that spatial separation, in itself, is not an indication of subcultural separation. A lower-middle class white Protestant from Detroit is not to be distinguished subculturally from his counterpart in Chicago. They merely live in different spatial units of the same subculture.

Social structure, psychological orientations, and overt behavior patterns constitute a major segment of interrelated variables. Subcultural analysis provides a theoretical framework for studying different cultural behaviors not simply from the point of view of class differences, or of ethnic group differences, or the regional or rural-urban categories, in artificial isolation from one another, but from the standpoint of their functional integration. After all, no person is *just* an ethnic group member, or *just* a social class member, *just* a Southerner, etc. His social background is a complex, not the solitary category which happens to be the particular enthusiasm of the investigator. Using the subcultural apparatus we can begin to assign behavioral frequencies to the social configurations which provide meaningful comparisons of group cultures within a national society.[8] We can also begin to answer with more cogency such questions as: Which category is more important for predicting specific behavior differences, ethnic group or social class? This is achieved by setting up a comparative causal analysis for ascertaining the relative efficacy of each subcultural component *at different points along each of the other continua.* For instance, behavioral differences in recreation patterns between two ethnic groups may be minimal at the upper-middle-class level, let us say, and considerable at the lower-class level. A statement simply in terms of ethnic group and social class, each unfactored, would cover up these varied relationships. On the other hand, if the differences proved to be minimal at all parts of the class continuum, then such a finding, obtained

[8]For an empirical study which combines the ethnic and class categories in the manner here suggested, see Allison Davis and Robert J. Havighurst, "Social Class and Color Differences In Child Rearing," *American Sociological Review*, Vol. 11 (December 1946), pp. 698–710. From this study we can quantitatively compare behavior frequencies in 4 groups: middle-class white, lower-class white, middle-class Negro, and lower-class Negro. The regional and rural-urban factors were held constant, all respondents being residents of Chicago.

by subcultural analysis, cannot be attacked on the grounds of a skewing occasioned by a hypothetically possible differential class structure in the two ethnic groups.

Adequate theoretical attention to social structure in the terms here suggested would also place many behavioral phenomena in a research setting which gives them more illumination and social meaning. Take, for instance, the already cited phenomenon of ethnic intermarriage. Once the incidence and certain social characteristics of the partners are ascertained, subcultural analysis suggests the third fundamental (and up to now virtually ignored) question of what happens to the intermarried couples and their children with reference to their placement and psychological orientation in the American social structure.[9] Do they identify with one or the other of the ethnic groups of the partners, do they remain marginal, or is some third alternative taking place, such as the gradual building up of an intermediate social structure consisting precisely of "intermarrieds" and other "marginals"? Without such analytical inquiry, intermarriage frequencies actually tell us more, by implication, about those who do not intermarry than about those who do.[10]

[9]A study by Judson T. Landis deals with selected consequences (divorce, religious training of children, and marriage partner change of faith) of Protestant-Catholic marriages which produced children. See "Marriages of Mixed and Non-Mixed Religious Faith," *American Sociological Review*, Vol. 14 (June 1949), pp. 401–07.

[10]Cf. Frazier's statement with regard to Negro-white intermarriage: "What I wish to emphasize is that if studies of intermarriage are to have sociological significance, they must analyze intermarriage within the frame of reference of two social worlds or the social organization of the white and Negro communities. Outside of this frame of reference, the extent and trend of intermarriage as measured by statistics becomes a meaningless abstraction and no extrapolation of statistical trends on intermarriage will provide any key to the future course of this relationship. If intermarriage were studied within the frame of reference of the changing nature of the contacts which are occurring between the social world of the whites and the social world of the Negroes, both the extent and trend of intermarriage would acquire meaning and provide a basis for prediction." "Race Contacts and the Social Structure," pp. 4–5.

See also Milton L. Barron's article "Research on Intermarriage: A Survey of Accomplishments and Prospects," *The American Journal of Sociology*, Vol. LVII (November 1951), pp. 249–55.

The matter of psychological orientations, that is, group identification and patterns of "in-grouping" and "out-grouping," is complicated by the fact that we are dealing here with more than one dimension. Although a person may participate largely in a social field circumscribed by both ethnic group and social class borders, the attribution of ethnic group membership *by itself* is a powerful pattern in our culture—a pattern generated both by pressure from within the ethnic group and from without. Rare is the Negro, or the Jew, for instance, who can fail to respond affectively to events or to evaluative allegations which concern respectively Negroes or Jews as a group. Nevertheless, the participation field and the field of close behavioral similarities are likely to be class-confined, as well as ethnic-confined. Thus we may distinguish two types of psychological constellations corresponding to those respective experience patterns. "I am ultimately bound up with the fate of these people" is the type of constellation attached to the ethnic group as a whole.[11] We may call this *historical identification* since it is a function of the unfolding of past and current historic events. On the other hand, "These are the people I feel at home with and can relax with" is the type of constellation attached to those persons with whom one participates frequently and shares close behavioral similarities. According to the subcultural hypothesis, these persons are likely to be of the same ethnic group *and* social class (and regional and rural-urban categories). This constellation we may call *participational identification*. To sum up: in terms of psychological orientations, the ethnic group is likely to be the group of historical identification, whereas, the subculture will be in the majority of cases, the group of participational identification. It should be pointed out that identification with larger units—that is, American society as a whole, "Western society," "all humanity," are likely to be present at different levels of structuring.

[11]See, in his discussion of the Jewish group, Kurt Lewin's concept of "interdependence of fate" as the major functional criterion of group belongingness: Chapters 10, 11, and 12 of *Resolving Social Conflicts* (New York, Harper, 1948).

Substructural theory is not advanced here as a set of propositions that are completely demonstrated and whose quantitative outlines are completely known. The appropriate vocal motto for large orders of generalization abstracted from evidence of wide divergency and degree of focus is not "How true I am," but "How true *am* I?" The available evidence certainly suggests a high degree of probability that these internal social structures, made up of the combination of social categories specified do exist within American society and that a large proportion of the population participates predominantly within them (respectively), with the afore-mentioned results behaviorally and psychologically. The *degree* to which these propositions are valid is a matter for further empirical inquiry structured by the outlines of the theory itself. A major virtue of the theory is that it can be precisely articulated for such inquiry. Community researches which studied the combined social categories of residents against social participation (home visiting, clique-member-ship, institutional affiliation, courtship, marriage, etc.), eco-logical concentration, behavior patterns, and psychological orientations would give us quantitative and qualitative ex-pression of the degree of validity of the theory. Problems and adjustments of "marginals" would become illuminated by attention to the kinds of structures they are marginal *to*. The important question of to what extent occupational and "interest" groups (for instance, intellectuals) cut across the subcultural categories and form social structures of their own poses itself for analysis by the same criteria which underlie the induction of subcultural existence. The phe-nomenon of social mobility becomes related to the types of structures left and those entered. In this connection we may distinguish between the *subculture of origin*, into which one is born, and the *subculture of achievement*, which one may enter later if he is mobile. Certainly movement from one social class to another involves subcultural change. Changes of ethnic identification or participation, while patently more difficult, call for similar analysis. The oversimplification often attendant on one-category analysis is avoided, and internal outlines of American social structure usually over-looked present themselves for study. To take one such over-looked area: What are the structural relationships of upper-class white Catholics to upper-class white Protestants in the large metropolitan areas where there are at least numerical possibilities for the existence of parallel structures? Do these parallel structures in fact exist? Or does integration take place? Until we ask such a question in these terms, we will not know the answer.

Further use of subcultural theory is indicated in the study of the causes of group prejudice. Granted that some pre-judiced persons will be found in all strata of society, there is the task of allocation of frequencies so that we ultimately may know whether some sub-groups furnish larger proportions of bigots than others and are associated quantitatively with par-ticular kinds of prejudice. "Personality" theories of pre-judice, currently the subject of intensive investigation, should be based on a foundation of subcultural analysis in order that more and more layers of the causational background may be uncovered. Such inquiry would concern itself not only with specifying the subcultures (if any) most significantly related to bigoted attitudes but with discovering the *kinds* of social-structural background which are attached to both the bigot himself and the context of his previous relationships with members of minority groups. Has the bigot been marginal or mobile himself? Has he experienced con-tacts (if any) with minority individuals who are marginal, or have his contacts always taken place in situations where subcultural division was paramount? Have his contacts been across class lines, and, if so, in what direction? Questions such as these are a necessary part of inquiry into the causes of prejudice if a fuller picture is to be secured.

Thus far we have been concerned with the outlines of American social structure as they exist in the present. Subcul-tural analysis is also an indispensable tool for clarifying the whole area of social structural formulations *implicit* in the various end-product attitudinal goals of "better group rela-tions," "the reduction of intergroup tensions," "intergroup harmony," etc. This is a subject (social-structural goals) which, in view of its fundamental importance both to the question of the desirability of alternative termini in themselves, and the strategic considerations respectively attendant upon them, has received far from commensurate attention.[12]

Such discussion of structural goals as may be found is usually placed in the framework of the basic alternatives of assimilation and cultural pluralism. In the typology which this writer proposes, (in addition to assimilation) two types of cultural pluralism are distinguished, an additional integrative type of social structure is delineated, and attention is called to a fifth alternative, combining certain aspects of cultural pluralism and social integration.[13] Certain preliminary remarks, however, are in order. Subcultural analysis points to the need for examining in detail institutional and associational affiliations, the structure of cliques and home-visiting patterns, the kinds of psychological orientations, and other previously mentioned components of cultural-pluralistic living, in order that its functioning and its problems may be delineated. Without such investigation the term "cultural pluralism" is a vague and boneless abstraction. Secondly, adequate analytical theory requires that a distinction be made between structure and behavior in discussions of ethnic group adjustments in American society. It is, for instance, usually assumed that a plurality of groups formed on the ethnic principle assures a corresponding plurality of behaviors. Such need not be the case at all since the persistence of multiple social organization may be the result of psychological pressures continuing to stem from both within

[12]Two of the more cogent discussions are found in Arnold and Caroline Rose, *America Divided* (New York, Knopf, 1948), pp. 166–77; and Robin M. Williams, Jr., *The Reduction of Intergroup Tensions* (New York, Social Science Research Council, 1947), pp. 11–12. It is, perhaps, indicative, however, that the latter monograph, an overall survey of research considerations in the intergroup relations field, devotes only one and one-half pages to this problem of social-structural goals.

[13]Compare with the typologies of the Roses, and of Williams, in the places cited.

and without the group long after major differences in behavior patterns have vanished as a result of common exposure to the mass stimuli of modern industrial society. Third, subcultural focus illuminates the fact that cultural pluralism (in both the structural and behavioral sense) of a certain kind exists regardless of the ethnic factor in modern society in the presence of social class differences. Cultural pluralism in the ethnic sense thus usually adds to—"enriches," if one wishes—the sources of cultural stimuli but is not an exclusive alternative to "a dead level of uniformity," as some of its proponents suggest. On the other hand, the claim of the assimilationists that, except for ethnic divergences, we would have in America a completely unified society with the virtual absence of cultural differences and social divisiveness is thus seen to be specious. And, finally, in this connection, it must be understood that discussions of cultural pluralism in the usual context in terms of its desirability or undesirability deal with the ethnic factor alone; such discussion concerns the desirability or undesirability of the existence of a plurality of *ethnic cultures,* apart from social class, regional, and rural-urban considerations. This procedure is, of course, permissible and even necessary for conceptual focus on the problem at hand as long as one knows what he is holding constant and can bring it back in for consideration when the need arises. It is, then, in the sense of *ethnic cultures* (as distinct from subcultures, which include more than the ethnic factor) that the ensuing typology of alternatives in American social structure with regard to ethnic group relations is offered.[14]

ASSIMILATION

The assimilationist goal calls for the complete acculturation of immigrants, or at least their children and succeeding generations, to "American ways and customs." As a number of

[14]The alternatives distinguished here all fall within the framework of attempts to achieve a nondiscriminatory society. Patterns of segregation involving discrimination and second-class status as, for instance, white-Negro relations in the South, are deliberately excluded.

156

observers have noted, these "ways and customs" on further inspection turn out to be those of the white Protestant Anglo-Saxon middle class.[15] The assimilationist proposal is sometimes phrased in terms of the "melting pot," but whatever the early proponents of the phrase meant by it, it is clear that in the assimilationist process most of the "melting" is to be done by the immigrants and their descendants, who are to melt into the dominant ethnic culture (white Protestant) rather than contribute to a new amalgam composed of equal or proportionate contributions from each group. Viewed from this standpoint, the invitation to assimilate is an invitation not to pool one's ethnic background into a common "American culture" but, rather, to submerge its identity into that of another ethnic group.

Further light on the assimilationist goal is shed by keeping in mind the crucial distinction between behavior and social structure, which may be phrased in this connection as a distinction between *behavioral assimilation* and *structural assimilation*. As far as behavior is concerned, by and large the assimilation process has taken place, regardless of theoretical considerations. With large-scale immigration to the United States curtailed in the middle nineteen twenties, ethnic problems increasingly center around the nativeborn. With few exceptions the descendants of immigrants have enthusiastically adopted "American ways." Indeed, in the vast majority of cases, as a result of their exposure to the larger environment, they have been socialized into them so that these behavior patterns are as indigenous to them as to the children of Anglo-white Protestants. Differences in religious worship still remain, of course, but it is doubtful if these, apart from their social implications, can be considered a major source of

---

[15]Although distribution along the whole class ladder except, perhaps, the very top, is implicitly expected. See, in this connection, Robert K. Merton's stimulating essay which deals, in part, with some of the inconsistences of this position: "The Self-Fulfilling Prophecy," *The Antioch Review*, Vol. 8 (Summer 1948), pp. 193–210; reprinted in Arnold M. Rose, ed., *Race Prejudice and Discrimination* (New York, Knopf, 1951), as "A Social Psychological Factor."

tension.[16] Segmental interest in ancestral folk music, dance, literature, etc., when it exists is hardly a threat to the dominance of American patterns. Minor differences in speech patterns are sometimes apparent, particularly at the lower- and lower-middle-class levels, as a result of inflections received from exposure to the parental language. But even these will probably disappear in successive generations. In short, present conditions, even though characterized by *some* cultural variation, display the essential triumph of behavioral assimilation[17] and the promise of its increasing success. It is in the realm of social structure that the assimilation process has foundered, for reasons that can be analyzed sociologically.

Structural assimilation has not taken place, in the large, for two overall reasons: a sufficient number of members of the majority group have not wanted it; and a sufficient number of members of most of the minority groups have not wanted it. These reasons, to be sure, require further analysis. Either one, by itself, would be sufficient to retard structural assimilation. The combination of the two has been all the more effective. To illustrate the first, consider the Negro. Far from being encouraged to assimilate structurally, the American Negro has been carefully and systematically excluded, with minor exceptions, from white Anglo-Saxon Protestant social structure (cliques, home-visiting patterns, churches, fraternal societies, neighborhoods, etc.). To lesser and varying degrees this exclusion has been leveled at other minorities, falling with least force on Catholics from Northern and Western Europe.

The attitudes of minority group members themselves toward structural assimilation vary both *among* groups and *within* groups. In the mid 1950s there is reason to believe that the Negro group has one of the largest proportions of persons

[16]Compare with R. M. MacIver's statement: "But we do not find sufficient reason to regard religion *by itself* as of crucial importance in provoking the tensions and cleavages manifested in the everyday relationships of American society." *The More Perfect Union* (New York, Macmillan 1948), p. 12.

[17]There are differences of degree, of course, depending particularly on factors of spatial isolation and degree of discrimination. The American Indian on reservations and the poverty-stricken "folk" Negro of the rural South are patently still some distance away from Anglo-Saxon middle-class patterns.

who, at least, theoretically, desire complete structural assimilation.[18] There are logical reasons for this: the vast majority of Negroes are Protestants, and their relationship to an ancestral African heritage is hardly focused enough to interfere with such a goal. The religious minorities, Catholics and Jews, are in a somewhat different position. Religious differences presuppose religious organization and a certain amount of communal life. Thus there are internal pressures to maintain this communal life and particularly to discourage intermarriage. In the case of the Jews, this communal identification and organization was given added impetus by the virulent anti-Semitism (and its consequences) of the Nazis. Nationality background groups have similar although often less powerful, internal stimuli to maintain ethnic identity and communal organization. When seen from the point of view of the alternative of merging not into some neutral overall American social structure but specifically into the social structure of white Anglo-Saxon Protestants, somewhat reluctant themselves to enable the merger, the choice of ethnic identity and social organization becomes more understandable. This is not to say that there is not a considerable number of Catholics and Jews (and white Protestants) who, in all probability, would favor virtually complete structural assimilation even in these terms. But, analyzed in this fashion, the logic of parallel social structures should become clearer.

In short, although there are some community associations and activities which are in their very nature community-wide and not specifically white Anglo-Saxon Protestant (professional organizations, labor unions, and political parties are some of the examples which come to mind), the assimilationist viewpoint has overestimated the degree to which an overall "neutral" American social structure actually exists for minority groups to be assimilated into; it has underestimated the indigenous drive for separate communal organization present in the minority groups them-

[18]See Goodwin Watson, *Action for Unity* (New York and London, Harper, 1947), p. 96. Nevertheless, Watson points out necessary qualifications to the assumption that all elements of the Negro community are so inclined.

selves, and the essential logic of this position, given certain premises; and it has overestimated the willingness of members of the majority group to encourage minority entrance into those aspects of its social structure which imply intimate social intercourse.[19] For these reasons, structural assimilation has not taken place in any quantitatively significant sense, nor does this analysis suggest that it is likely to do so in the near future.

CULTURAL PLURALISM: GENERAL CONSIDERATIONS

The goal of cultural pluralism, broadly speaking, envisages a society where ethnic groups would be encouraged to maintain their own communal social structure and identity, and preserve certain of their values and behavioral patterns which are not in conflict with broader values, patterns, and legal norms common to the entire society. The nature of this social subsystem is seen to be a pattern of intimate social relationships and institutional affiliations which allows for the unfolding of the major aspects of the life-cycle within its borders. Those social class differences and consequent second series of social subsystems which would ordinarily develop would be confined respectively within each of the ethnic systems. Two types of cultural pluralism may be distinguished, hinging on the degree of contact existing across ethnic lines and the nature of the contact—that is, whether *primary*, involving intimate, family or clique-oriented association; or *secondary*, involving relatively impersonal and non-intimate association.

CULTURAL PLURALISM A—THE TOLERANCE LEVEL

At the "tolerance level" of group relations, ethnic groups would maintain such a high degree of social isolation from

---

[19]There are, of course, numerous intimate friendships in American life between persons of different ethnic backgrounds, and some intermarriages. But they are not encouraged by the nature of the dominant outlines of American social structure. They are, so to speak, marginal to it. Limitations of space prevent further development of this point.

each other that virtually all primary contacts would be within the ethnic group and most secondary contacts would be either correspondingly confined or, if across ethnic lines, completely accommodative. The various ethnic groups would be encouraged to have tolerant attitudes toward one another and to maintain such relationships as would be necessary to meet the demands of a common legal system and allegiance to a common government. This type of cultural pluralism is difficult to maintain without considerable spatial separation and is sociologically unsuited to a culture-complex consisting of urban industrial society and democratic norms, which requires considerable interchangeability of individuals and frequent communication and contact. Nevertheless, certain of the social-structural features of this level (as distinct from the psychological) may be seen to characterize Negro-white relationships in the South. The chief value of distinguishing this level here, however, is to throw a clearer focus on the next level of cultural pluralism.

CULTURAL PLURALISM B—THE GOOD GROUP RELATIONS LEVEL

The "good group relations" level envisages a society where ethnic groups maintain their social subsystems, but where the degree of contact across ethnic lines is substantially greater than that existing at the "tolerance level" and where secondary contacts are considerable in number and primary contacts take place in limited frequency. This societal goal implies employment integration, common use of public accommodations, inter-ethnic composition of civic organizations, and frequent symbolic demonstrations of intergroup harmony which emphasize common goals and values. It encourages such degree and frequency of primary relationships as does not threaten the existence of the respective ethnic group's subsystem and identity, support of in-group institutions, and endogamous marriage patterns. Readers will recognize in this description considerable similarity to the outlines of American social structure as it exists, ethnically speaking, at the present time. Attainment of those "secondary" integrative aspects now partially lacking plus the psychological attitudes which will facilitate the harmonious operation of such a social structure emerges as the explicit or implicit goal of many, if not most, agencies and individuals currently working in the "intercultural" field.

THE COMMUNITY INTEGRATION LEVEL

This level is presented as an "ideal type" construct outlining a theoretically attainable goal for those persons who wish to bring people of diverse ethnic backgrounds into a common intimate social structure and who reject assimilation as previously delineated. Precisely in the structural realm it envisages multiple primary contacts across ethnic lines to the point of complete lack of emphasis on ethnic background as a factor in social relationships (except as an "interest" factor). It differs from the "assimilation" goal in that it is not predicated on other ethnic groups merging into the white Protestant Anglo-Saxon, but on common recognition of the fundamental equality of validity of all backgrounds. This requires both appropriate psychological orientations (on this level there are no "hosts" and no "guests") on the part of participating individuals and, in many cases, the refashioning of institutions to proclaim symbolically this equality and the common values which embrace the diversity. It involves no need for renunciation of ethnic background since the common values attest to its co-validity, but allows individuals to make as much of it or as little as they wish. It does, of course, imply emphasis upon the basic value of all-inclusiveness ("the brotherhood of man"), which is probably to be found somewhere in the value-hierarchy of every specific ethnic group in America.

The community integration level may sound strangely similar to what early proponents of the "melting pot" may have had in mind. But it differs from this goal in several respects. First of all, it focuses on social structure rather than on cultural behavior. Its "dynamic" is the bringing of people together in social participation not the amalgamation of cul-

162

tural patterns. Secondly, like cultural pluralism, it emphasizes legitimate and continued pride in ethnic and cultural background and puts positive values on the variety of cultural behaviors, allowing the give and take of current interaction to sort out the patterns of the future. Thirdly, it recognizes the undesirable nature of many aspects of renunciation of ethnic identification, and provides for its retention and positive evaluation, interpreting participation at the community integration level as, in part, a further implementation of specific ethnic values. And finally, it "faces up" to problems of social structure and institutional life implicit in the goal of interethnic social relationships which may be sustained through the life cycle.

A MIXED TYPE:
THE PLURALISTIC-INTEGRATION LEVEL

The rationale of any set of structural goals in interethnic relations must deal with the question of whether these goals are to be achieved by authoritarian pressure or by voluntary choice. Certainly proponents of cultural pluralism have indicated their belief that ethnic groups should be free to develop important features of their special heritage and to maintain respective social structures. As both the Roses [20] and Schermerhorn[21] have noted, by the same principle such choice should also be available to individuals, who should be free to cultivate whatever degree of their ethnic heritage they wish to and to participate socially on the basis of their individual interests. Or, in the words of MacIver, "Only when differences are free to stay apart or to merge or to breed new variations of the community theme can human personality have fulfillment and creative power, drawing its sustenance where it finds its proper nourishment, neither clinging to likeness nor worshiping difference."[22] The assimilationist

[20]*America Divided*, pp. 173–74.
[21]R. A. Schermerhorn, *These Our People* (Boston, D. C. Heath, 1949), p. 443.
[22]*The More Perfect Union*, p. 10.

goal does not meet either of the above criteria. Cultural pluralism by itself meets the criterion of "group choice" but not that of individual choice, since under even the most favorable conditions the "deviating" individual is forced into the position of either some type of ethnic "conversion" or marginality. The community integration goal is similarly authoritarian if made a compulsory norm. The only structural goal which would seem to meet both criteria of democratic choice is one which envisages a "mixed" social structure in which ethnic subsystems would exist alongside a subsystem composed of persons who wished to live at the "community integration" level, and which allowed easy passage from one subsystem to another at the wish of the individual. Such a mixed type of social structure may be called "the pluralistic-integration" level. The implementation of this level requires the conscious effort of those individuals who wish to participate interethnically in significant fashion in providing institutional arrangements which will bring into being the "community integration" social structure as one of the existing array. Such arrangements will include interethnic neighborhoods, cliques, summer resorts, places of worship, fraternal and social organizations, and not least, attitudinal recognition. Since the persons who would be attracted to this task would very likely be persons who are presently on the margins of the existing ethnic structures and/or who are motivated by goals which are not normative in the present society, they might well recruit with the paraphrased call: "Marginals of the world, unite!"

It is not intended to give the impression here that choices in social participation need be definitive or all-embracing. Even in present society persons have the opportunity to select friends from, and to a certain extent participate socially in more than one ethnic subsystem at the same time. Such opportunities would be increased and facilitated at the pluralistic-integration level.

To summarize briefly, this paper has called attention to the need for more than minimal attention to social structure in the group relations area, and has outlined a system of social-structural analysis whose theoretical propositions have partial vertification and are articulated for further research. It has used this system to crystallize and formulate alternative structural goals implicit in the desire for "better group relations." Such analysis may be useful in a field where, as one authority has put it, "our crucial need is not so much for isolated 'new data' as for studies whose significance is mutually reinforced by being placed in a framework of interrelated theory."[23]

---

[23]*The Reduction of Intergroup Tensions,* p. 26.

6

The Nature
of Assimilation

Sociologists and cultural anthropologists have described the processes and results of ethnic "meetings" under such terms as "assimilation" and "acculturation." Sometimes these terms have been used to mean the same thing; in other usages their meanings, rather than being identical, have overlapped. (Sociologists are more likely to use "assimilation"; anthropologists have favored "acculturation" and have given it a narrower but generally consistent meaning.) With regard to the term "assimilation," particularly, there is a certain amount of confusion, and there is further, a compelling need for a rigorous and systematic analysis of the concept of assimilation which would "break it down" into all the possible relevant factors or variables which could conceivably be included under its rubric. Such an analysis will be attempted here. In other words, we propose to isolate and specify the major variables or factors contained in the assimilation process and suggest their characteristic relationships. Illustrations from actual situations will be drawn largely from American life.

Let us, first of all, imagine a hypothetical situation in which a host country, to which we shall give the fictitious name of "Sylvania," is made up of a population all members of which are of the same race, religion, and previous national extraction. Cultural behavior is relatively uniform except for social class divisions. Similarly, the groups and institutions, i.e., the "social structure," of Sylvanian society are divided and differentiated only on a social class basis. Into this country, through immigration, comes a group of people who differ in previous national background and in religion and who thus have different cultural patterns from those of the host society. We shall call them the Mundovians. Let us further imagine that within the span of another generation, this population group of Mundovian national origin (now composed largely of the second generation, born in Sylvania) has taken on completely the cultural patterns of the Sylvanians, has thrown off any sense of peoplehood based on Mundovian nationality, has changed its religion to that of the Sylvanians, has eschewed the formation of any communal organizations made up principally or exclusively of Mundovians, has entered and been hospitably accepted into the social cliques, clubs, and institutions of the Sylvanians at various class levels, has intermarried freely and frequently with the Sylvanians, encounters no prejudice or discrimination (one reason being that they are no longer distinguishable culturally or structurally from the rest of the Sylvanian population), and raises no value conflict issues in Sylvanian public life. Such a situation would represent the ultimate form of assimilation—complete assimilation to the culture and society of the host country. Note that we are making no judgment here of either the sociological desirability, feasibility, or moral rightness of such a goal. We are simply setting it up as a convenient abstraction—an "ideal type"—ideal not in the value sense of being most desirable but in the sense of representing the various elements of the concept and their interrelationships in "pure," or unqualified, fashion (the methodological device of the "ideal type" was developed and named by the German sociologist, Max Weber).

Looking at this example, we may discern that seven major variables are involved in the process discussed—in other words, seven basic subprocesses have taken place in the assimilation of the Mundovians to Sylvanian society. These may be listed in the following manner. We may say that the Mundovians have

1) changed their cultural patterns (including religious belief and observance) to those of the Sylvanians;

2) taken on large-scale primary group relationships with

167

the Sylvanians, i.e., have entered fully into the societal net-work of groups and institutions, or societal structure, of the Sylvanians;

3) have intermarried and interbred fully with the Sylva-nians;

4) have developed a Sylvanian, in place of a Mundovian, sense of peoplehood, or ethnicity;

5) have reached a point where they encounter no dis-criminatory behavior;

6) have reached a point where they encounter no prej-udiced attitudes;

7) do not raise by their demands concerning the nature of Sylvanian public or civic life any issues involving values and power conflict with the original Sylvanians (for example, the issue of birth control).

Each of these steps or subprocesses may be thought of as constituting a particular stage or aspect of the assimilation process. Thus we may, in shorthand fashion, consider them as types of assimilation and characterize them accordingly. We may, then, speak, for instance, of "structural assimilation" to refer to the entrance of Mundovians into primary group rela-tionships with the Sylvanians, or "identificational assimila-tion" to describe the taking on of a sense of Sylvania people-hood. For some of the particular assimilation subprocesses there are existing special terms. For instance, cultural or behavioral assimilation is what has been defined as "accultu-ration." The full list of assimilation subprocesses or variables with their general names, and special names, if any, is given in Table 1.

Not only is the assimilation process mainly a matter of degree, but, obviously, each of the stages or subprocesses distinguished in Table 1 may take place in varying degrees.

In the example just used there has been assimilation in all respects to the society and culture which had exclusively occupied the nation up to the time of the immigrants' arrival. In other instances there may be other subsocieties and subcul-tures already on the scene when the new group arrives but one of these subsocieties and its way of life is dominant by virtue

TABLE 1. The Assimilation Variables

SUBPROCESS OR CONDITION	TYPE OR STAGE OF ASSIMILATION	SPECIAL TERM
Change of cultural patterns to those of host society	Cultural or behavioral assimilation	Acculturation[1]
Large-scale entrance into cliques, clubs, and institutions of host society, on primary group level	Structural assimilation	None
Large-scale intermarriage	Marital assimilation	Amalgamation[2]
Development of sense of peoplehood based exclusively on host society	Identificational assimilation	None
Absence of prejudice	Attitude receptional assimilation	None
Absence of discrimination	Behavior receptional assimilation	None
Absence of value and power conflict	Civic assimilation	None

of original settlement, the preemption of power, or overwhelming predominance in numbers. In both cases we need a term to stand for the dominant subsociety which provides the standard to which other groups adjust or measure their relative degree of adjustment. We have tentatively used the term "host society"; however, a more neutral designation would be desirable. A. B. Hollingshead, in describing the class struc-

[1]The question of reciprocal cultural influence will be considered later.
[2]My use of the term here is not predicated on the diversity in race of the two population groups which are intermarrying and interbreeding. With increasing understanding of the meaning of "race" and its thoroughly relative and arbitrary nature as a scientific term, this criterion becomes progressively less important. We may speak of the "amalgamation" or intermixture of the two "gene pools" which the two populations represent, regardless of how similar or divergent these two gene pools may be.

169

ture of New Haven, has used the term "core group" to refer to the Old Yankee families of colonial, largely Anglo-Saxon ancestry who have traditionally dominated the power and status system of the community, and who provide the "master cultural mould" for the class system of the other groups in the city.[3] Joshua Fishman has referred to the "core society" and the "core culture" in American life, this core being "made up essentially of White Protestant, middle-class clay, to which all other particles are attracted."[4] If there is anything in American life which can be described as an over-all American culture which serves as a reference point for immigrants and their children, it can best be described, it seems to us, as the middle-class cultural patterns of, largely, white Protestant, Anglo-Saxon origins, leaving aside for the moment the question of minor reciprocal influences on this culture exercised by the cultures of later entry into the United States, and ignoring also, for this purpose, the distinction between the upper-middle class and the lower-middle class cultural worlds.

There is a point on which I particularly do not wish to be misunderstood. I am not for one moment implying that the contribution of the non-Anglo-Saxon stock to the nature of

---

[3] See August B. Hollingshead, "Trends in Social Stratification: A Case Study," *American Sociological Review*, Vol. 17, No. 6 (December 1952), p. 686; and August B. Hollingshead and Frederick C. Redlich, *Social Class and Mental Illness*, (New York, Wiley, 1958) chap. 3 and 4. It is not entirely clear to me whether Hollingshead reserves the term "core group" for "old family" Yankees in the upper class and upper-middle class only, or for Yankees throughout the class structure.

[4] Joshua A. Fishman, "Childhood Indoctrination for Minority-Group Membership and the Quest for Minority-Group Biculturism in America," (mimeo); a revised version of this paper was published under the title "Childhood Indoctrination for Minority-Group Membership," in "Ethnic Groups in American Life," *Daedalus: The Journal of the American Academy of Arts and Sciences* (Spring 1961). See also Jurgen Ruesch, "Social Technique, Social Status, and Social Change in Illness," ed. Clyde Kluckhohn and Henry A. Murray *Personality in Nature, Society, and Culture*, (New York, Knopf, 1948), for a use of the term "core culture" to refer to lower-middle class culture in America.

American civilization has been minimal or slight. Quite the contrary. The qualitative record of achievement in industry, business, the professions, and the arts by Americans whose ancestors came from countries and traditions which are not British, or in many cases not even closely similar to British, is an overwhelmingly favorable one, and with reference to many individuals, a thoroughly brilliant one. Taken together with the substantial quantitative impact of these non-Anglo-Saxon groups on American industrial and agricultural development and on the demographic dimensions of the society, this record reveals an America in mid-twentieth century whose greatness rests on the contributions of many races, religions, and national backgrounds.[5] My point, however, is that, with some exceptions, as the immigrants and their children have become Americans, their contributions, as laborers, farmers, doctors, lawyers, scientists, artists, etc., have been made *by way* of cultural patterns that have taken their major impress from the mould of the overwhelmingly English character of the dominant Anglo-Saxon culture or subculture in America, whose dominion dates from colonial times and whose *cultural* domination in the United States has never been seriously threatened. One must make a distinction between influencing the cultural patterns themselves and contributing to the progress and development of the society. It is in the latter area that the influence of the immigrants and their children in the United States has been decisive.

Accordingly, I shall follow Fishman's usage in referring to middle-class white Protestant Americans as constituting the "core society," or in my terms the "core subsociety," and the cultural patterns of this group as the "core culture" or "core subculture." I shall use Hollingshead's term "core group" to refer to the white Protestant element at any social class level.

Let us now, for a moment, return to our fictitious land of Sylvania and imagine an immigration of Mundovians with a

[5]See Oscar and Mary F. Handlin, "The United States," in *The Positive Contribution by Immigrants*, (Paris, Unesco, 1955), chap. 1.

decidedly different outcome. In this case the Sylvanians accept many new behavior patterns and values from the Mundovians, just as the Mundovians change many of their ways in
conformance with Sylvanian customs, this interchange taking place with appropriate modifications and compromises,
and in this process a new cultural system evolves which is
neither exclusively Sylvanian nor Mundovian but a mixture
of both. This is a cultural blend, the result of the "melting
pot," which has melted down the cultures of the two groups
in the same societal container, as it were, and formed a new
cultural product with standard consistency. This process has,
of course, also involved thorough social mixing in primary as
well as secondary groups and a large-scale process of intermarriage. The melting pot has melted the two groups into
one, societally and culturally.

Whether such a process as just described is feasible or
likely of occurrence is beside the point here. It, too, is an
"ideal type," an abstraction against which we can measure
the realities of what actually happens. Our point is that the
seven variables of the assimilation process which we have
isolated can be measured against the "melting pot" goal as
well as against the "adaptation to the core society and culture" goal. That is, assuming the "melting pot" goal, we can
then inquire how much acculturation of both groups has
taken place to form such a blended culture, how much social
structural mixture has taken place, and so on.[6] We now have a
model of assimilation with seven variables which can be used
to analyze the assimilation process with reference to either of
two variant goal-systems: 1) "adaptation to the core society
and culture," and 2) the "melting pot." Theoretically, it
would be possible to apply the analysis model of variables
with reference to carrying out the goal-system of "cultural

[6]I am indebted to Professor Richard D. Lambert of the University of Pennsylvania for pointing out to me that my array of assimilation variables must be
applied with reference to the basic assimilation goal. In my original scheme
of presentation I had implicitly applied it only to the goal-system of "adaptation to the core society and culture."

pluralism" as well. However, this would be rather premature at this point since the concept of cultural pluralism is itself so meagerly understood. In a later chapter, however, we shall investigate the relationship of these seven variables to the cultural pluralism concept. We shall also leave further discussion of the "melting pot" concept till later.

Let us now apply this model of assimilation analysis in tentative fashion to selected "minority" ethnic groups on the American scene. The applied paradigm presented in Table 2 allows us to record and summarize a great deal of information compactly and comparatively. We shall deal here, for illustrative purposes, with four groups: Negroes, Jews, Catholics (excluding Negro and Spanish-speaking Catholics), and Puerto Ricans. The basic goal-referent will be "adaptation to core society and culture." The entries in the table cells may be regarded, at this point, as hypotheses. Qualifying comments will be made in the footnotes to the table. The reader may wish to refer back to page 169 for definitions of each column heading.

One of the tasks of sociological theory is not only to identify the factors or variables present in any given social process or situation, but also to hypothesize how these variables may be related to each other. Let us look at the seven assimilation variables from this point of view. We note that in Table 2, of the four ethnic groups listed, only one, the Puerto Ricans, are designated as being substantially unassimilated culturally (in the early 1960s). The Puerto Ricans are the United States' newest immigrant group of major size. If we now examine the entries for the Negro, one of America's oldest minorities, we find that assimilation has not taken place in most of the other variables, but with allowance for social class factors, *has* taken place culturally. These two facts in juxtaposition should give us a clue to the relation of the cultural assimilation variable to all the others. This relationship may be stated as follows: 1) *cultural assimilation, or acculturation, is likely to be the first of the types of assimilation to occur when a minority group arrives on the scene; and 2) cultural assimilation, or acculturation, of the minority*

173

TABLE 2. Paradigm of Assimilation
Applied to Selected Groups in the United States—
Basic Goal Referent: Adaptation to Core Society and Culture

GROUP	TYPE OF ASSIMILATION						
	CUL-TURAL[7]	STRUC-TURAL	MAR-ITAL	IDEN-TIFICA-TIONAL[9]	ATTI-TUDE RECEP-TIONAL	BE-HAVIOR RECEP-TIONAL	CIVIC
Negroes	Variation by class[8]	No	No	No	No	No	Yes
Jews	Substantially Yes	No	Substantially No	No	No	Partly	Mostly
Catholics (excluding Negro and Spanish-speaking)	Substantially Yes	Partly (variation by area)	Partly	No	Partly	Mostly	Partly[10]
Puerto Ricans	Mostly No	No	No	No	No	No	Partly

[7]Some reciprocal cultural influences have, of course, taken place. American language, diet, recreational patterns, art forms, and economic techniques have been modestly influenced by the cultures of non-Anglo-Saxon resident groups since the first contacts with the American Indians, and the American culture is definitely the richer for these influences. However, the reciprocal influences have not been great. See George R. Stewart, *American Ways of Life*, (New York, Doubleday, 1954). Furthermore, the minority ethnic groups have not given up all their pre-immigration cultural patterns. Particularly, they have preserved their non-Protestant religions. I have thus used the phrase "Substantially Yes" to indicate this degree of adaptation.

[8]Although few, if any, African cultural survivals are to be found among American Negroes, lower-class Negro life with its derivations from slavery, post-Civil War discrimination, both rural and urban poverty, and enforced isolation from the middle-class white world, is still at a considerable distance

174

group may take place even when none of the other types of assimilation occurs simultaneously or later, and this condition of "acculturation only" may continue indefinitely.

If we examine the history of immigration into the United States, both of these propositions are seen to be borne out. After the birth of the republic, as each succeeding wave of immigration, first from Northern and Western Europe, later from Southern and Eastern Europe and the Orient, has spread over America, the first process that has occurred has been the taking on of the English language and American behavior patterns, even while the creation of the immigrant colonies sealed off their members from extensive primary contacts with "core society" Americans and even when prejudice and discrimination against the minority have been at a high point. While this process is only partially completed in the immigrant generation itself, with the second and succeeding generations, exposed to the American public school system and speaking English as their native tongue, the impact of the American acculturation process has been overwhelming; the rest becomes a matter of social class mobility and the kind of acculturation that such mobility demands. On the other hand, the success of the acculturation process has by no means guaranteed entry of each minority into the primary groups and institutions—that is, the subsociety—of the white Protestant group. With the exception of white Protestant immigrant

---

from the American culture norm. Middle and upper-class Negroes, on the other hand, are acculturated to American core culture.

[9]As I pointed out earlier, ethnic identification in a modern complex society may contain several "layers." My point is not that Negroes, Jews, and Catholics in the United States do not think of themselves as Americans. They do. It is that they also have an "inner layer" sense of peoplehood which is Negro, Jewish, or Catholic, as the case may be, and not "white Protestant" or "white, Anglo-Saxon Protestant," which is the corresponding inner layer of ethnic identity of the core society.

[10]Value and power conflict of Catholics with a large portion of the rest of the American population over such issues as birth control, divorce, therapeutic abortion, and church-state relationships constitute the reason for the entry of "Partly" here.

stock from Northern and Western Europe—I am thinking here particularly of the Scandinavians, Dutch, and Germans—by and large such structural mixture on the primary level has not taken place. Nor has such acculturation success eliminated prejudice and discrimination or in many cases led to large-scale intermarriage with the core society.

The only qualifications of my generalizations about the rapidity and success of the acculturation process that the American experience suggests are these: 1) If a minority group is spatially isolated and segregated (whether voluntarily or not) in a rural area, as is the case with the American Indians still on reservations, even the acculturation process will be very slow; and 2) Unusually marked discrimination, such as that which has been faced by the American Negro, if it succeeds in keeping vast numbers of the minority group deprived of educational and occupational opportunities and thus predestined to remain in a lower-class setting, may indefinitely retard the acculturation process for the group. Even in the case of the American Negro, however, from the long view or perspective of American history, this effect of discrimination will be seen to have been a delaying action only; the quantitatively significant emergence of the middle-class Negro is already well on its way.

Before we leave specific examination of the acculturation variable and its relationships, it would be well to distinguish between two types of cultural patterns and traits which may characterize any ethnic group. Some, like its religious beliefs and practices, its ethical values, its musical tastes, folk recreational patterns, literature, historical language, and sense of common past, are essential and vital ingredients of the group's cultural heritage, and derive exactly from that heritage. We shall refer to these as *intrinsic* cultural traits or patterns. Others, such as dress, manner, patterns of emotional expression, and minor oddities in pronouncing and inflecting English, tend to be products of the historical vicissitudes of a group's adjustment to its local environment, including the present one (and also reflect social class experiences and values), and are in a real sense, external to the core of the group's ethnic cultural heritage. These may conveniently be referred to as *extrinsic* cultural traits or patterns.[11] To illustrate, the Catholicism or Judaism of the immigrant from Southern or Eastern Europe represent a difference in *intrinsic culture* from the American core society and its Protestant religious affiliation. However, the greater volatility of emotional expression of the Southern and Eastern European peasant or villager in comparison with the characteristically greater reserve of the upper-middle class American of the core society constitutes a difference in *extrinsic culture*. To take another example, the variant speech pattern, or argot, of the lower-class Negro of recent southern background, which is so widespread both in the South and in northern cities, is a product of external circumstances and is not something vital to Negro culture. It is thus an *extrinsic* cultural trait. Were this argot, which constitutes such a powerful handicap to social mobility and adjustment to the core culture, to disappear, nothing significant for Negro self-regard as a group or the Negro's sense of ethnic history and identity would be violated. While this distinction between intrinsic and extrinsic culture is a tentative one, and cannot be uniformly applied to all cultural traits, it is still a useful one and may help cast further light on the acculturation process, particularly in its relationship to prejudice and discrimination.

As we examine the array of assimilation variables again, several other relationships suggest themselves. One is the indissoluble connection, in the time order indicated, between structural assimilation and marital assimilation. That is, entrance of the minority group into the social cliques, clubs, and institutions of the core society at the primary group level inevitably will lead to a substantial amount of intermarriage. If children of different ethnic backgrounds belong to the same play-group, later the same adolescent cliques, and at college the same fraternities and sororities; if the parents belong to

[11]Compare with the distinction in types of cultural traits made by William E. Vickery and Stewart G. Cole in *Intercultural Education in American Schools* (New York and London, Harper, 1943), pp. 43–44.

177

the same country club and invite each other to their homes for dinner; it is completely unrealistic not to expect these children, now grown, to love and to marry each other, blithely oblivious to previous ethnic extraction. Communal leaders of religious and nationality groups that desire to maintain their ethnic identity are aware of this connection, which is one reason for the proliferation of youth groups, adult clubs, and communal institutions, which tend to confine their members in their primary relationships safely within the ethnic fold.

If marital assimilation, an inevitable by-product of structural assimilation, takes place fully, the minority group loses its ethnic identity in the larger host or core society, and identificational assimilation occurs. Prejudice and discrimination are no longer a problem, since eventually the descendants of the original minority group become indistinguishable, and since primary group relationships tend to build up an "in-group" feeling which encloses all the members of the group. If assimilation has been complete in all intrinsic as well as extrinsic cultural traits, then no value conflicts on civic issues are likely to arise between the now dispersed descendants of the ethnic minority and members of the core society. Thus the remaining types of assimilation have all taken place like a row of tenpins bowled over in rapid succession by a well placed strike. We may state the emergent generalization, then, as follows: *Once structural assimilation has occurred, either simultaneously with or subsequent to acculturation, all of the other types of assimilation will naturally follow.* It need hardly be pointed out that while acculturation, as we have emphasized above, does not necessarily lead to structural assimilation, structural assimilation inevitably produces acculturation. Structural assimilation, then, rather than acculturation, is seen to be the keystone of the arch of assimilation. The price of such assimilation, however, is the disappearance of the ethnic group as a separate entity and the evaporation of its distinctive values.

There are a number of other crucial hypotheses and questions which can be phrased by the manipulation of these variables. One of the most important, of course, is whether "attitude receptional" and "behavior receptional" assimilation—that is, elimination of prejudice and discrimination—may take place when acculturation, *but not structural assimilation,* occurs. This can be shown to be one of the key questions in the application of our analytical model to "cultural pluralism," and thus we shall leave its discussion to a later time. Another interesting question is whether prejudice and discrimination are more closely related to differences between the core group and the ethnic minority in intrinsic culture traits or extrinsic culture traits. I would hypothesize that, at least in our era, differences in extrinsic culture are more crucial in the development of prejudice than those of an intrinsic nature.[12] Differences in religious belief, *per se,* are not the occasion for bitter acrimony in twentieth-century America,[13] particularly when these differences occur in middle-class Americans of native birth whose external appearance, speech patterns, and manner are notably uniform. On the other hand, the gap in extrinsic cultural traits between the zoot-suited side-burned slum juvenile and the conservatively clothed and behaving middle-class American distinctly gives the signal for mutual suspicion and hostility. This is not to say that differences in intrinsic values among ethnic groups in America, particularly as these differences spill over into demands on the shaping of American public life, may not result in power conflict. But one must make a distinction between irrational ethnic prejudice, in what might be called the old-fashioned sense, and the conflict of groups in the civic arena over issues based on opposing value-premises, sincerely held in each case.

We shall forgo additional manipulation of the variables

---

[12]Compare with *Intercultural Education in American Schools,* p. 45.
[13]See R. M. MacIver's statement: "But we do not find sufficient reason to regard religion *by itself* as of crucial importance in provoking the tensions and cleavages manifested in the everyday relationships of American society." *The More Perfect Union* (New York, Macmillan, 1948); p. 12. (Italics as in original.)

in the analytical model at this point[14] since the preceding discussion should have clarified its potential use. We now have an analytical scheme—a set of conceptual categories— which allows us to appreciate the true complexity of the assimilation process, to note the varying directions it may take, and to discern the probable relationships of some of its parts. This set of analytical tools should serve us well as we consider the theories of assimilation and minority group life which have arisen historically in America.

[14]The question, of great contemporary interest to social scientists and others concerned with problems of intergroup relations, of whether the objective behavioral phenomenon of discrimination can be reduced or eliminated prior to the reduction or elimination of the subjective attitudinal phenomenon of prejudice may be considered within this framework; thus, can "behavior receptional" assimilation take place prior to "attitude receptional" assimilation? The Supreme Court ban on racial segregation in the public schools, and state and municipal anti-discrimination legislation constitute, of course, a test of the hypothesis that legal curbs on discrimination may be successful even though prejudice still exists, and that such legal curbs may actually result in the reduction of prejudice. See Robert K. Merton, "Discrimination and the American Creed," *Discrimination and National Welfare,* ed. R. M. MacIver (New York, Harper, 1949); David W. Petegorsky, "On Combating Racism," *Race Prejudice and Discrimination,* ed. Arnold M. Rose (New York, Knopf, 1951); Arnold M. Rose, "The Influence of Legislation on Prejudice," *Race Prejudice and Discrimination;* John P. Roche and Milton M. Gordon, "Can Morality Be Legislated?", *The New York Times Magazine* (May 22, 1955), reprinted in Milton L. Barron, ed., *American Minorities* (New York, Knopf, 1957); and National Community Relations Advisory Council, *The Uses of Law for the Advancement of Community Relations,* A Report of the Special Committee on Reassessment (June 1955).

7

Assimilation in America: Theory & Reality

Three ideologies or conceptual models have competed for attention on the American scene as explanations of the way in which a nation, in the beginning largely white, Anglo-Saxon, and Protestant, has absorbed over 41 million immigrants and their descendants from variegated sources and welded them into the contemporary American people. These ideologies are Anglo-conformity, the melting pot, and cultural pluralism. They have served at various times, and often simultaneously, as explanations of what has happened—descriptive models— and of what should happen—goal models. Not infrequently they have been used in such a fashion that it is difficult to tell which of these two usages the writer has had in mind. In fact, one of the more remarkable omissions in the history of American intellectual thought is the relative lack of close analytical attention given to the theory of immigrant adjust- ment in the United States by its social scientists.

The result has been that this field of discussion—an over- ridingly important one since it has significant implications for the more familiar problems of prejudice, discrimination, and majority-minority group relations generally—has been largely preempted by laymen, representatives of belles lettres, philosophers, and apologists of various persuasions. Even from these sources the amount of attention devoted to ideologies of assimilation is hardly extensive. Consequently,

The materials of this article are based on a larger study of the meaning and implications of minority group assimilation in the United States, which I have carried out with the financial assistance of the Russell Sage Founda- tion.

the work of improving intergroup relations in America is carried out by dedicated professional agencies and individuals who deal as best they can with day-to-day problems of discriminatory behavior, but who for the most part are unable to relate their efforts to an adequate conceptual apparatus. Such an apparatus would, at one and the same time, accurately describe the present structure of American society with respect to its ethnic groups (I shall use the term "ethnic group" to refer to any racial, religious, or national-origins collectivity), and allow for a considered formulation of its assimilation or integration goals for the foreseeable future. One is reminded of Alice's distraught question in her travels in Wonderland: "Would you tell me, please, which way I ought to go from here?" "That depends a good deal," replied the Cat with irrefutable logic, "on where you want to get to."

The story of America's immigration can be quickly told for our present purposes. The white American population at the time of the Revolution was largely English and Protestant in origin, but had already absorbed substantial groups of Germans and Scotch-Irish and smaller contingents of Frenchmen, Dutchmen, Swedes, Swiss, South Irish, Poles, and a handful of migrants from other European nations. Catholics were represented in modest numbers, particularly in the middle colonies, and a small number of Jews were residents of the incipient nation. With the exception of the Quakers and a few missionaries, the colonists had generally treated the Indians and their cultures with contempt and hostility, driving them from the coastal plains and making the western frontier a bloody battleground where eternal vigilance was the price of survival.

Although the Negro at that time made up nearly one-fifth of the total population, his predominantly slave status, together with racial and cultural prejudice, barred him from serious consideration as an assimilable element of the society. And while many groups of European origin started out as determined ethnic enclaves, eventually, most historians believe, considerable ethnic intermixture within the white population took place. "People of different blood" [sic]—write two American historians about the colonial period,

"English, Irish, German, Huguenot, Dutch, Swedish— mingled and intermarried with little thought of any difference."[1] In such a society, its people predominantly English, its white immigrants of other ethnic origins either English-speaking or derived largely from countries of northern and western Europe whose cultural divergences from the English were not great, and its dominant white population excluding by fiat the claims and considerations of welfare of the non-Caucasian minorities, the problem of assimilation understandably did not loom unduly large or complex.

The unfolding events of the next century and a half with increasing momentum dispelled the complacency which rested upon the relative simplicity of colonial and immediate post-Revolutionary conditions. The large-scale immigration to America of the famine-fleeing Irish, the Germans, and later the Scandinavians (along with additional Englishmen and other peoples of northern and western Europe) in the middle of the nineteenth century (the so-called "old immigration"), the emancipation of the Negro slaves and the problems created by post-Civil War reconstruction, the placing of the conquered Indian with his broken culture on government reservations, the arrival of the Oriental, first attracted by the discovery of gold and other opportunities in the West, and finally, beginning in the last quarter of the nineteenth century and continuing to the early 1920s, the swelling to proportions hitherto unimagined of the tide of immigration from the peasantries and "pales" of southern and eastern Europe—the Italians, Jews, and Slavs of the so-called "new immigration," fleeing the persecutions and industrial dislocations of the day—all these events constitute the background against which we may consider the rise of the theories of assimilation mentioned above. After a necessarily foreshortened description of each of these theories and their historical emergence, we shall suggest analytical distinctions designed to aid in clarifying the nature of the assimilation process, and then conclude by focusing on the American scene.

[1] Allan Nevins and Henry Steele Commager, *America: The Story of a Free People* (Boston, Little, Brown, 1942), p. 58.

ANGLO-CONFORMITY

"Anglo-conformity"[2] is a broad term used to cover a variety of viewpoints about assimilation and immigration; they all assume the desirability of maintaining English institutions (as modified by the American Revolution), the English language, and English-oriented cultural patterns as dominant and standard in American life. However, bound up with this assumption are related attitudes. These may range from discredited notions about race and "Nordic" and "Aryan" racial superiority, together with the nativist political programs and exclusionist immigration policies which such notions entail, through an intermediate position of favoring immigration from northern and western Europe on amorphous, unreflective grounds ("They are more like us"), to a lack of opposition to any source of immigration, as long as these immigrants and their descendants duly adopt the standard Anglo-Saxon cultural patterns. There is by no means any necessary equation between Anglo-conformity and racist attitudes.

It is quite likely that "Anglo-conformity" in its more moderate aspects, however explicit its formulation, has been the most prevalent ideology of assimilation goals in America throughout the nation's history. As far back as colonial times, Benjamin Franklin recorded concern about the clannishness of the Germans in Pennsylvania, their slowness in learning English, and the establishment of their own native-language press.[3] Others of the founding fathers had similar reservations about large-scale immigration from Europe. In the context of their times they were unable to foresee the role such immigration was to play in creating the later greatness of the nation. They were not at all men of unthinking prejudices. The disestablishment of religion and the separation of church and state

[2]The phrase is the Coles's. See Stewart G. Cole and Mildred Wiese Cole, *Minorities and the American Promise* (New York, Harper, 1954), chap. 6.
[3]Maurice R. Davie, *World Immigration* (New York, Macmillan, 1936), p. 36, and (cited therein) "Letter of Benjamin Franklin to Peter Collinson, 9th May, 1753, on the condition and character of the Germans in Pennsylvania," in Jared Sparks, *The Works of Benjamin Franklin, with notes and a life of the author*, Vol. 7, (Boston, 1828), pp. 71–73.

(so that no religious group—whether New England Congregationalists, Virginian Anglicans, or even all Protestants combined—could call upon the federal government for special favors or support, and so that man's religious conscience should be free) were cardinal points of the new national policy they fostered. "The Government of the United States," George Washington had written to the Jewish congregation of Newport during his first term as president, "gives to bigotry no sanction, to persecution no assistance."

Political differences with ancestral England had just been written in blood; but there is no reason to suppose that these men looked upon their fledgling country as an impartial melting pot for the merging of the various cultures of Europe, or as a new "nation of nations," or as anything but a society in which, with important political modifications, Anglo-Saxon speech and institutional forms would be standard. Indeed their newly won victory for democracy and republicanism made them especially anxious that these still precarious fruits of revolution should not be threatened by a large influx of European peoples whose life experiences had accustomed them to the bonds of despotic monarchy. Thus, although they explicitly conceived of the new United States of America as a haven for those unfortunates of Europe who were persecuted and oppressed, they had characteristic reservations about the effects of too free a policy. "My opinion, with respect to immigration," Washington wrote to John Adams in 1794, "is that except of useful mechanics and some particular descriptions of men or professions, there is no need of encouragment, while the policy or advantage of its taking place in a body (I mean the settling of them in a body) may be much questioned; for, by so doing, they retain the language, habits and principles (good or bad) which they bring with them."[4] Thomas Jefferson, whose views on race and attitudes towards slavery were notably liberal and advanced for his time, had similar

---

[4]W. C. Ford, ed. and collector, *The Writings of George Washington*, (New York, Putnam's, 1889), vol. 12, p. 489.

doubts concerning the effects of mass immigration on American institutions, while conceding that immigrants, "if they come of themselves . . . are entitled to all the rights of citizenship."[5]

The attitudes of Americans toward foreign immigration in the first three-quarters of the nineteenth century may correctly be described as ambiguous. On the one hand, immigrants were much desired, so as to swell the population and importance of states and territories, to man the farms of expanding prairie settlement, to work the mines, build the railroads and canals, and take their place in expanding industry. This was a period in which no federal legislation of any consequence prevented the entry of aliens, and such state legislation as existed attempted to bar on an individual basis only those who were likely to become a burden on the community, such as convicts and paupers. On the other hand, the arrival in an overwhelmingly Protestant society of large numbers of poverty-stricken Irish Catholics, who settled in groups in the slums of Eastern cities, roused dormant fears of "Popery" and Rome. Another source of anxiety was the substantial influx of Germans, who made their way to the cities and farms of the mid-West and whose different language, separate communal life, and freer ideas on temperance and sabbath observance brought them into conflict with the Anglo-Saxon bearers of the Puritan and Evangelical traditions. Fear of foreign "radicals" and suspicion of the economic demands of the occasionally aroused workingmen added fuel to the nativist fires. In their extreme form these fears resulted in the Native-American movement of the 1830s and 1840s and the "American" or "Know-Nothing" party of the 1850s, with their anti-Catholic campaigns and their demands for restrictive laws on naturalization procedures and for keeping the foreign-born out of political office. While these movements scored local political successes and their turbulences so rent

[5]Thomas Jefferson, "Notes on Virginia, Query 8," *The Writings of Thomas Jefferson*, Vol. 2, ed. A. E. Bergh (Washington, The Thomas Jefferson Memorial Association, 1907), p. 121.

the national social fabric that the patches are not yet entirely invisible, they failed to influence national legislative policy on immigration and immigrants; and their fulminations inevitably provoked the expected reactions from thoughtful observers.

The flood of newcomers to the westward expanding nation grew larger, reaching over one and two-thirds million between 1841 and 1850 and over two and one-half million in the decade before the Civil War. Throughout the entire period, quite apart from the excesses of the Know-Nothings, the predominant (though not exclusive) conception of what the ideal immigrant adjustment should be was probably summed up in a letter written in 1818 by John Quincy Adams, then Secretary of State, in answer to the inquiries of the Baron von Fürstenwaerther. If not the earliest, it is certainly the most elegant version of the sentiment, "If they don't like it here, they can go back where they came from." Adams declared:[6]

> They [immigrants to America] come to a life of independence, but to a life of labor—and, if they cannot accommodate themselves to the character, moral, political and physical, of this country with all its compensating balances of good and evil, the Atlantic is always open to them to return to the land of their nativity and their fathers. To one thing they must make up their minds, or they will be disappointed in every expectation of happiness as Americans. They must cast off the European skin, never to resume it. They must look forward to their posterity rather than backward to their ancestors; they must be sure that whatever their own feelings may be, those of their children will cling to the prejudices of this country.

The events that followed the Civil War created their own ambiguities in attitude toward the immigrant. A nation undergoing wholesale industrial expansion and not yet finished with the march of westward settlement could make good use of the never faltering waves of newcomers. But sporadic bursts of labor unrest, attributed to foreign radicals, the

[6]*Niles' Weekly Register*, Vol. 18, No. 29 (April 1820), pp. 157–58; also, Marcus L. Hansen, *The Atlantic Migration, 1607–1860*, pp. 96–97.

growth of Catholic institutions and the rise of Catholics to municipal political power, and the continuing association of immigrant settlement with urban slums revived familiar fears. The first federal selective law restricting immigration was passed in 1882, and Chinese immigration was cut off in the same year. The most significant development of all, barely recognized at first, was the change in the source of European migrants. Beginning in the 1880s, the countries of southern and eastern Europe began to be represented in substantial numbers for the first time, and in the next decade immigrants from these sources became numerically dominant. Now the notes of a new, or at least hitherto unemphasized, chord from the nativist lyre began to sound—the ugly chord, or discord, of racism. Previously vague and romantic notions of Anglo-Saxon peoplehood, combined with general ethnocentrism, rudimentary wisps of genetics, selected tidbits of evolutionary theory, and naive assumptions from an early and crude imported anthropology produced the doctrine that the English, Germans, and others of the "old immigration" constituted a superior race of tall, blonde, blue-eyed "Nordics" or "Aryans," whereas the peoples of eastern and southern Europe made up the darker Alpines or Mediterraneans—both "inferior" breeds whose presence in America threatened, either by intermixture or supplementation, the traditional American stock and culture. The obvious corollary to this doctrine was to exclude the allegedly inferior breeds; but if the new type of immigrant could not be excluded, then everything must be done to instill Anglo-Saxon virtues in these benighted creatures. Thus, one educator writing in 1909 could state:[7]

> These southern and eastern Europeans are of a very different type from the north Europeans who preceded them. Illiterate, docile, lacking in self-reliance and initiative, and not possessing the Anglo-Teutonic conceptions of law, order, and government, their coming has served to dilute tremendously our

[7]Ellwood P. Cubberly, *Changing Conceptions of Education* (Boston, Houghton Mifflin, 1909), pp. 15–16.

188

national stock, and to corrupt our civic life. . . . Everywhere these people tend to settle in groups or settlements, and to set up here their national manners, customs, and observances. Our task is to break up these groups or settlements, to assimilate and amalgamate these people as a part of our American race, and to implant in their children, so far as can be done, the Anglo-Saxon conception of righteousness, law and order, and popular government, and to awaken in them a reverence for our democratic institutions and for those things in our national life which we as a people hold to be of abiding worth.

Anglo-conformity received its fullest expression in the so-called Americanization movement which gripped the nation during World War I. While "Americanization" in its various stages had more than one emphasis, it was essentially a consciously articulated movement to strip the immigrant of his native culture and attachments and make him over into an American along Anglo-Saxon Lines—all this to be accomplished with great rapidity. To use an image of a later day, it was an attempt at "pressure-cooking assimilation." It had prewar antecedents, but it was during the height of the world conflict that federal agencies, state governments, municipalities, and a host of private organizations joined in the effort to persuade the immigrant to learn English, take out naturalization papers, buy war bonds, forget his former origins and culture, and give himself over to patriotic hysteria.

After the war and the "Red scare" which followed, the excesses of the Americanization movement subsided. In its place, however, came the restriction of immigration through federal law. Foiled at first by presidential vetoes, and later by the failure of the 1917 literacy test to halt the immigrant tide, the proponents of restriction finally put through in the early 1920s a series of acts culminating in the well-known national-origins formula for immigrant quotas which went into effect in 1929. Whatever the merits of a quantitative limit on the number of immigrants to be admitted to the United States, the provisions of the formula, which discriminated sharply against the countries of southern and eastern Europe, in effect institutionalized the assumptions of the rightful dominance of Anglo-Saxon patterns in the land. Reaffirmed with only slight modifications in the McCarran-Walter Act of 1952, these laws, then, stood as a legal monument to the creed of Anglo-conformity and a telling reminder that this ideological system still had numerous and powerful adherents on the American scene.

THE MELTING POT

While Anglo-conformity in various guises has probably been the most prevalent ideology of assimilation in the American historical experience, a competing viewpoint with more generous and idealistic overtones has had its adherents and exponents from the eighteenth century onward. Conditions in the virgin continent, it was clear, were modifying the institutions which the English colonists brought with them from the mother country. Arrivals from non-English homelands such as Germany, Sweden, and France were similarly exposed to this fresh environment. Was it not possible, then, to think of the evolving American society not as a slightly modified England but rather as a totally new blend, culturally and biologically, in which the stocks and folkways of Europe, figuratively speaking, were indiscriminately mixed in the political pot of the emerging nation and fused by the fires of American influence and interaction into a distinctly new type?

Such, at any rate, was the conception of the new society which motivated that eighteenth-century French-born writer and agriculturalist, J. Hector St. John Crèvecoeur, who, after many years of American residence, published his reflections and observations in *Letters from an American Farmer.* [8] Who, he asks, is the American?

> He is either an European, or the descendant of an European, hence that strange mixture of blood, which you will find in no

---

[8] J. Hector St. John Crèvecoeur, *Letters from an American Farmer* (New York, Albert and Charles Boni, 1925, reprinted from the 1st ed., London, 1782), pp. 54–55.

other country. I could point out to you a family whose grand-father was an Englishman, whose wife was Dutch, whose son married a French woman, and whose present four sons have now four wives of different nations. *He* is an American, who leaving behind him all his ancient prejudices and manners, re-ceives new ones from the new mode of life he has embraced, the new government he obeys, and the new rank he holds. He be-comes an American by being received in the broad lap of our great *Alma Mater.* Here individuals of all nations are melted into a new race of men, whose labours and posterity will one day cause great changes in the world.

Some observers have interpreted the open-door policy on immigration of the first three-quarters of the nineteenth cen-tury as reflecting an underlying faith in the effectiveness of the American melting pot, in the belief "that all could be ab-sorbed and that all could contribute to an emerging national character."[9] No doubt many who observed with dismay the nativist agitation of the times felt as did Ralph Waldo Emer-son that such conformity-demanding and immigrant-hating forces represented a perversion of the best American ideals. In 1845, Emerson wrote in his Journal:[10]

I hate the narrowness of the Native American Party. It is the dog in the manger. It is precisely opposite to all the dictates of love and magnanimity; and therefore, of course, opposite to true wisdom. . . . Man is the most composite of all creatures. . . . Well, as in the old burning of the Temple at Corinth, by the melting and intermixture of silver and gold and other metals a new compound more precious than any, called Corinthian brass, was formed; so in this continent,—asylum of all nations,—the energy of Irish, Germans, Swedes, Poles, and Cossacks, and all the European tribes,—of the Africans, and of the Poly-nesians,—will construct a new race, a new religion, a new state, a new literature, which will be as vigorous as the new Europe which came out of the smelting-pot of the Dark Ages, or that which earlier emerged from the Pelasgic and Etruscan bar-barism. *La Nature aime les croisements.*

[9]Oscar Handlin, ed., *Immigration as a Factor in American History* (En-glewood Cliffs, N. J., Prentice-Hall, 1959), p. 146.
[10]Quoted by Stuart P. Sherman in his Introduction to *Essays and Poems of Emerson* (New York, Harcourt Brace, 1921), p. xxxiv.

Eventually, the melting-pot hypothesis found its way into historical scholarship and interpretation. While many American historians of the late nineteenth century, some fresh from graduate study at German universities, tended to adopt the view that American institutions derived in essence from Anglo-Saxon (and ultimately Teutonic) sources, others were not so sure.[11] One of these was Frederick Jackson Turner, a young historian from Wisconsin, not long emerged from his graduate training at Johns Hopkins. Turner presented a paper to the American Historical Association, meeting in Chicago in 1893. Called "The Significance of the Frontier in American History," this paper proved to be one of the most influential essays in the history of American scholarship, and its point of view, supported by Turner's subsequent writings and his teaching, pervaded the field of American historical interpretation for at least a generation. Turner's thesis was that the dominant influence in the shaping of American institutions and American democracy was not this nation's European heritage in any of its forms, nor the forces emanating from the eastern seaboard cities, but rather the experiences created by a moving and variegated western frontier. Among the many effects attributed to the frontier environment and the challenges it presented was that it acted as a solvent for the national heritages and the separatist tendencies of the many nationality groups which had joined the trek westward, including the Germans and Scotch-Irish of the eighteenth century and the Scandinavians and Germans of the nineteenth. "The frontier," asserted Turner, "promoted the formation of a composite nationality for the American people. . . . In the crucible of the frontier the immigrants were Americanized, liberated, and fused into a mixed race, English in neither nationality nor characteristics. The process has gone on from the early days to our own." And later, in an essay on the role of the Mississippi Valley, he refers to "the tide of foreign immigration which has risen so steadily that it

[11]See Edward N. Saveth, *American Historians and European Immigrants, 1875–1925* (New York, Columbia University Press, 1948).

has made a composite American people whose amalgamation is destined to produce a new national stock."[12]

Thus far, the proponents of the melting pot idea had dealt largely with the diversity produced by the sizeable immigration from the countries of northern and western Europe alone—the "old immigration," consisting of peoples with cultures and physical appearance not greatly different from those of the Anglo-Saxon stock. Emerson, it is true, had impartially included Africans, Polynesians, and Cossacks in his conception of the mixture; but it was only in the last two decades of the nineteenth century that a large-scale influx of peoples from the countries of southern and eastern Europe imperatively posed the question of whether these uprooted newcomers who were crowding into the large cities of the nation and the industrial sector of the economy could also be successfully "melted." Would the "urban melting pot" work as well as the "frontier melting pot" of an essentially rural society was alleged to have done?

It remained for an English-Jewish writer with strong social convictions, moved by his observations of the role of the United States as a haven for the poor and oppressed of Europe, to give utterance to the broader view of the American melting pot in a way which attracted public attention. In 1908, Israel Zangwill's drama, *The Melting Pot*, was produced in this country and became a popular success. It is a play dominated by the dream of its protagonist, a young Russian-Jewish immigrant to America, a composer, whose goal is the completion of a vast "American" symphony which will express his deeply felt conception of his adopted country as a divinely appointed crucible in which all the ethnic divisions of mankind will divest themselves of their ancient animosities and differences and become fused into one group, signifying the brotherhood of man. In the process he falls in love with a beautiful and cultured Gentile girl. The play ends with the performance of the symphony and, after numerous vicissitudes and traditional family opposition from both sides,

[12]Frederick Jackson Turner, *The Frontier in American History* (New York, Holt, 1920), pp. 22–23, 190.

with the approaching marriage of David Quixano and his beloved. During the course of these developments, David, in the rhetoric of the time, delivers himself of such sentiments as these:[13]

> America is God's crucible, the great Melting Pot where all the races of Europe are melting and re-forming! Here you stand, good folk, think I, when I see them at Ellis Island, here you stand in your fifty groups, with your fifty languages and histories, and your fifty blood hatreds and rivalries. But you won't be long like that, brothers, for these are the fires of God you've come to— these are the fires of God. A fig for your feuds and vendettas! Germans and Frenchmen, Irishmen and Englishmen, Jews and Russians—into the Crucible with you all! God is making the American.

Here we have a conception of a melting pot which admits of no exceptions or qualifications with regard to the ethnic stocks which will fuse in the great crucible. Englishmen, Germans, Frenchmen, Slavs, Greeks, Syrians, Jews, Gentiles, even the black and yellow races, were specifically mentioned in Zangwill's rhapsodic enumeration. And this pot patently was to boil in the great cities of America.

Thus around the turn of the century the melting-pot idea became embedded in the ideals of the age as one response to the immigrant receiving experience of the nation. Soon to be challenged by a new philosophy of group adjustment (to be discussed below) and always competing with the more pervasive adherence to Anglo-conformity, the melting-pot image, however, continued to draw a portion of the attention consciously directed toward this aspect of the American scene in the first half of the twentieth century. In the mid-1940s a sociologist who had carried out an investigation of intermarriage trends in New Haven, Connecticut, described a revised conception of the melting process in that city and suggested a basic modification of the theory of that process. In New Ha-

---

[13]Israel Zangwill, *The Melting Pot* (New York, Macmillan, 1909), p. 37.

194

ven, Ruby Jo Reeves Kennedy[14] reported from a study of intermarriages from 1870 to 1940 that there was a distinct tendency for the British-Americans, Germans, and Scandinavians to marry among themselves—that is, within a Protestant "pool"; for the Irish, Italians, and Poles to marry among themselves—a Catholic "pool"; and for the Jews to marry other Jews. In other words, intermarriage was taking place across lines of nationality background, but there was a strong tendency for it to stay confined within one or the other of the three major religious groups, Protestants, Catholics, and Jews. Thus, declared Mrs. Kennedy, the picture in New Haven resembled a "triple melting pot" based on religious divisions, rather than a "single melting pot." Her study indicated, she stated, that "while strict endogamy is loosening, religious endogamy is persisting and the future cleavages will be along religious lines rather than along nationality lines as in the past. If this is the case, then the traditional 'single-melting-pot' idea must be abandoned, and a new conception, which we term the 'triple-melting-pot' theory of American assimilation, will take its place as the true expression of what is happening to the various nationality groups in the United States."[15] The triple melting-pot thesis was later taken up by the theologian, Will Herberg, and formed an important sociological frame of reference for his analysis of religious trends in American society, *Protestant-Catholic-Jew.*[16] But the triple-melting-pot hypothesis patently takes us into the realm of a society pluralistically conceived. We turn now to the rise of an ideology which attempts to justify such a conception.

---

[14]Ruby Jo Reeves Kennedy, "Single or Triple Melting-Pot? Intermarriage Trends in New Haven, 1870–1940," *American Journal of Sociology*, Vol. 49 (1944), pp. 331–39. See also her "Single or Triple Melting-Pot? Intermarriage in New Haven, 1870–1950," *American Journal of Sociology*, Vol. 58 (1952), pp. 56–59.

[15]"Single or Triple Melting-Pot? . . . 1870–1940," p. 332, (Author's italics omitted.)

[16]Will Herberg, *Protestant-Catholic-Jew* (Garden City, Doubleday, 1955).

CULTURAL PLURALISM

Probably all the non-English immigrants who came to American shores in any significant numbers from colonial times onward—settling either in the forbidding wilderness, the lonely prairie, or in some accessible urban slum—created ethnic enclaves and looked forward to the preservation of at least some of their native cultural patterns. Such a development, natural as breathing, was supported by the later accretion of friends, relatives, and countrymen seeking out oases of familiarity in a strange land, by the desire of the settlers to rebuild (necessarily in miniature) a society in which they could communicate in the familiar tongue and maintain familiar institutions, and, finally, by the necessity to band together for mutual aid and mutual protection against the uncertainties of a strange and frequently hostile environment. This was as true of the "old" immigrants as of the "new." In fact, some of the liberal intellectuals who fled to America from an inhospitable political climate in Germany in the 1830s, 1840s, and 1850s looked forward to the creation of an all-German state within the union, or, even more hopefully, to the eventual formation of a separate German nation, as soon as the expected dissolution of the union under the impact of the slavery controversy should have taken place.[17] Oscar Handlin, writing of the sons of Erin in mid-nineteenth-century Boston, recent refugees from famine and economic degradation in their homeland, points out: "Unable to participate in the normal associational affairs of the community, the Irish felt obliged to erect a society within a society, to act together in their own way. In every contact therefore the group, acting apart from other sections of the community, became intensely aware of its peculiar and exclusive identity."[18] Thus cultural

[17]Nathan Glazer, "Ethnic Groups in America: From National Culture to Ideology," *Freedom and Control in Modern Society*, eds. Morroe Berger, Theodore Abel, and Charles H. Page (New York, Van Nostrand, 1954), p. 161; Marcus Lee Hansen, *The Immigrant in American History* (Cambridge, Harvard University Press, 1940), pp. 129–40; John A. Hawgood, *The Tragedy of German-America* (New York, Putnam's 1940), *passim*.

[18]Oscar Handlin, *Boston's Immigrants*, rev. ed. (Cambridge, Harvard University Press, 1959), p. 176.

pluralism was a fact in American society before it became a theory—a theory with explicit relevance for the nation as a whole, and articulated and discussed in the English-speaking circles of American intellectual life.

Eventually, the cultural enclaves of the Germans (and the later arriving Scandinavians) were to decline in scope and significance as succeeding generations of their native-born attended public schools, left the farms and villages to strike out as individuals for the Americanizing city, and generally became subject to the influences of a standardizing industrial civilization. The German-American community, too, was struck a powerful blow by the accumulated passions generated by World War I—a blow from which it never fully recovered. The Irish were to be the dominant and pervasive element in the gradual emergence of a pan-Catholic group in America, but these developments would reveal themselves only in the twentieth century. In the meantime, in the last two decades of the nineteenth, the influx of immigrants from southern and eastern Europe had begun. These groups were all the more sociologically visible because the closing of the frontier, the occupational demands of an expanding industrial economy, and their own poverty made it inevitable that they would remain in the urban areas of the nation. In the swirling fires of controversy and the steadier flame of experience created by these new events, the ideology of cultural pluralism as a philosophy for the nation was forged.

The first manifestations of an ideological counterattack against draconic Americanization came not from the beleaguered newcomers (who were, after all, more concerned with survival than with theories of adjustment), but from those idealistic members of the middle class who, in the decade or so before the turn of the century, had followed the example of their English predecessors and "settled" in the slums to "learn to sup sorrow with the poor."[19] Immediately, these workers in the "settlement houses" were forced to come to grips with the realities of immigrant life and adjustment.

[19]From a letter (1883) by Samuel A. Barnett; quoted in Arthur C. Holden, *The Settlement Idea* (New York, Macmillan, 1922), p. 12.

Not all reacted in the same way, but on the whole the settlements developed an approach to the immigrant which was sympathetic to his native cultural heritage and to his newly created ethnic institutions.[20] For one thing, their workers, necessarily in intimate contact with the lives of these often pathetic and bewildered newcomers and their daily problems, could see how unfortunate were the effects of those forces which impelled rapid Americanization in their impact on the immigrants' children, who not infrequently became alienated from their parents and the restraining influence of family authority. Were not their parents ignorant and uneducated "Hunkies," "Sheenies," or "Dagoes," as that limited portion of the American environment in which they moved defined the matter? Ethnic "self-hatred" with its debilitating psychological consequences, family disorganization, and juvenile delinquency, were not unusual results of this state of affairs. Furthermore, the immigrants themselves were adversely affected by the incessant attacks on their culture, their language, their institutions, their very conception of themselves. How were they to maintain their self-respect when all that they knew, felt, and dreamed, beyond their sheer capacity for manual labor—in other words, all that they were—was despised or scoffed at in America? And—unkindest cut of all—their own children had begun to adopt the contemptuous attitude of the "Americans." Jane Addams relates in a moving chapter of her *Twenty Years at Hull House* how, after coming to have some conception of the extent and depth of these problems, she created at the settlement a "Labor Museum," in which the immigrant women of the various nationalities crowded together in the slums of Chicago could illustrate their native methods of spinning and weaving, and in which the relation of these earlier techniques to contemporary factory methods could be graphically shown. For the first time these peasant women were made to feel by some part of their

[20]Jane Addams, *Twenty Years at Hull House* (New York, Macmillan, 1914), pp. 231–58; *The Settlement Idea*, pp. 109–31, 182–89; John Higham, *Strangers in the Land* (New Brunswick, Rutgers University Press, 1955), p. 236.

American environment that they possessed valuable and interesting skills—that they too had something to offer—and for the first time, the daughters of these women who, after a long day's work at their dank "needletrade" sweatshops, came to Hull House to observe, began to appreciate the fact that their mothers, too, had a "culture," that this culture possessed its own merit, and that it was related to their own contemporary lives. How aptly Jane Addams concludes her chapter with the hope that "our American citizenship might be built without disturbing these foundations which were laid of old time."[21]

This appreciative view of the immigrant's cultural heritage and of its distinctive usefulness both to himself and his adopted country received additional sustenance from another source: those intellectual currents of the day which, however overborne by their currently more powerful opposites, emphasized liberalism, internationalism, and tolerance. From time to time, an occasional educator or publicist protested the demands of the "Americanizers," arguing that the immigrant, too, had an ancient and honorable culture, and that this culture had much to offer an America whose character and destiny were still in the process of formation, an America which must serve as an example of the harmonious cooperation of various heritages to a world inflamed by nationalism and war. In 1916 John Dewey, Norman Hapgood, and the young literary critic, Randolph Bourne, published articles or addresses elaborating various aspects of this theme.

The classic statement of the cultural pluralist position, however, had been made over a year before. Early in 1915 there appeared in the pages of *The Nation* two articles under the title "Democracy versus the Melting-Pot." Their author was Horace Kallen, a Harvard-educated philosopher with a concern for the application of philosophy to societal affairs, and, as an American Jew, himself derivative of an ethnic background which was subject to the contemporary pressures for dissolution implicit in the "Americanization," or Anglo-conformity, and the melting-pot theories. In these articles

[21]*Twenty Years at Hull House*, p. 258.

Kallen vigorously rejected the usefulness of these theories as models of what was actually transpiring in American life or as ideals for the future. Rather he was impressed by the way in which the various ethnic groups in America were coincident with particular areas and regions, and with the tendency for each group to preserve its own language, religion, communal institutions, and ancestral culture. All the while, he pointed out, the immigrant has been learning to speak English as the language of general communication, and has participated in the over-all economic and political life of the nation. These developments in which "the United States are in the process of becoming a federal state not merely as a union of geographical and administrative unities, but also as a cooperation of cultural diversities, as a federation or commonwealth of national cultures,"[22] the author argued, far from constituting a violation of historic American political principles, as the "Americanizers" claimed, actually represented the inevitable consequences of democratic ideals, since individuals are implicated in groups, and since democracy for the individual must by extension also mean democracy for his group.

The processes just described, however, as Kallen develops his argument, are far from having been thoroughly realized. They are menaced by "Americanization" programs, assumptions of Anglo-Saxon superiority, and misguided attempts to promote "racial" amalgamation. Thus America stands at a kind of cultural crossroads. It can attempt to impose by force an artificial, Anglo-Saxon oriented uniformity on its peoples, or it can consciously allow and encourage its ethnic groups to develop democratically, each emphasizing its particular cultural heritage. If the latter course is followed, as Kallen puts it at the close of his essay, then,[23]

---

[22]Horace M. Kallen, "Democracy versus the Melting-Pot," The Nation, Vols. 18 and 25 (February 1915); reprinted in his Culture and Democracy in the United States, (New York, Boni and Liveright, 1924); the quotation is on p. 116.

[23]Culture and Democracy . . . , p. 124.

The outlines of a possible great and truly democratic commonwealth become discernible. Its form would be that of the federal
republic; its substance a democracy of nationalities, cooperat-
ing voluntarily and autonomously through common institutions in the enterprise of self-realization through the perfection
of men according to their kind. The common language of the
commonwealth, the language of its great tradition, would be
English, but each nationality would have for its emotional and
involuntary life its own peculiar dialect or speech, its own individual and inevitable esthetic and intellectual forms. The political and economic life of the commonwealth is a single unit
and serves as the foundation and background for the realization
of the distinctive individuality of each *natio* that composes it
and of the pooling of these in a harmony above them all. Thus
"American civilization" may come to mean the perfection of
the cooperative harmonies of "European civilization"—the
waste, the squalor and the distress of Europe being eliminated—a multiplicity in a unity, an orchestration of mankind.

Within the next decade Kallen published more essays
dealing with the theme of American multiple-group life, later
collected in a volume.[24] In the introductory note to this book
he used for the first time the term "cultural pluralism" to refer
to his position. These essays reflected both his increasingly
sharp rejection of the onslaughts on the immigrant and his
culture which the coming of World War I and its attendant
fears, the "Red scare," the projection of themes of racial
superiority, the continued exploitation of the newcomers,
and the rise of the Ku Klux Klan all served to increase in intensity, and also his emphasis on cultural pluralism as the
democratic antidote to these ills. He later published other
essays elaborating or annotating the theme of cultural
pluralism. Thus, for at least forty-five years, most of them
spent teaching at the New School for Social Research, Kallen
has been acknowledged as the originator and leading philosophical exponent of the idea of cultural pluralism.

In the late 1930s and early 1940s, Louis Adamic, the
Yugoslav immigrant who had become an American writer, took up the theme of America's multicultural heritage and

[24]*Culture and Democracy. . . .*

201

the role of these groups in forging the country's national character. Borrowing Walt Whitman's phrase, he described America as "a nation of nations," and while his ultimate goal was closer to the melting-pot idea than to cultural pluralism, he saw the immediate task as that of making America conscious of what it owed to all its ethnic groups, not just to the Anglo-Saxons. The children and grandchildren of immigrants of non-English origins, he was convinced, must be taught to be proud of the cultural heritage of their ancestral ethnic group and of its role in building the American nation; otherwise, they would not lose their sense of ethnic inferiority and the feeling of rootlessness he claimed to find in them.

Thus in the twentieth century, particularly since World War II, "cultural pluralism" has become a concept which has worked its way into the vocabulary and imagery of specialists in intergroup relations and leaders of ethnic communal groups. In view of this new pluralistic emphasis, some writers now prefer to speak of the "integration" of immigrants rather than of their "assimilation."[25] However, with a few exceptions,[26] no close analytical attention has been given either by social scientists or practitioners of intergroup relations to the meaning of cultural pluralism, its nature and relevance for a modern industrialized society, and its implications for problems of prejudice and discrimination—a point to which we referred at the outset of this discussion.

Conclusions

In the remaining pages I can make only a few analytical comments which I shall apply in context to the American scene,

[25]See W. D. Borrie et. al., The Cultural Integration of Immigrants (a survey based on the papers and proceedings of the UNESCO Conference in Havana, April 1956) (Paris, UNESCO, 1959); and William S. Bernard, "The Integration of Immigrants in the United States" (mimeographed), one of the papers for this conference.

[26]See particularly Milton M. Gordon, "Social Structure and Goals in Group Relations,"; and Nathan Glazer, "Ethnic Groups in America; From National Culture to Ideology," both articles in Freedom and Control in Modern Society; S. N. Eisenstadt, The Absorption of Immigrants, (London, Routledge and Kegan Paul. 1954), and The Cultural Integration of Immigrants.

historical and current. My view of the American situation will not be documented here, but may be considered as a series of hypotheses in which I shall attempt to outline the American assimilation process.

First of all, it must be realized that "assimilation" is a blanket term which in reality covers a multitude of sub-processes. The most crucial distinction is one often ignored—the distinction between what I have elsewhere called "behavioral assimilation" and "structural assimilation."[27] The first refers to the absorption of the cultural behavior patterns of the "host" society. (At the same time, there is frequently some modification of the cultural patterns of the immigrant-receiving country, as well.) There is a special term for this process of cultural modification or "behavioral assimilation"—namely, "acculturation." "Structural assimilation," on the other hand, refers to the entrance of the immigrants and their descendants into the social cliques, organizations, institutional activities, and general civic life of the receiving society. If this process takes place on a large enough scale, then a high frequency of intermarriage must result. A further distinction must be made between, on the one hand, those activities of the general civic life which involve earning a living, carrying out political responsibilities, and engaging in the instrumental affairs of the larger community, and, on the other hand, activities which create personal friendship patterns, frequent home intervisiting, communal worship, and communal recreation. The first type usually develops so-called "secondary relationships," which tend to be relatively impersonal and segmental; the latter type leads to "primary relationships," which are warm, intimate, and personal.

With these various distinctions in mind, we may then proceed.

Built on the base of the original immigrant "colony" but frequently extending into the life of successive generations, the characteristic ethnic group experience is this: within the ethnic group there develops a network of organizations and

---

[27]"Social Structure and Goals in Group Relations," p. 151.

informal social relationships which permits and encourages the members of the ethnic group to remain within the confines of the group for all of their primary relationships and some of their secondary relationships throughout all the stages of the life cycle. From the cradle in the sectarian hospital to the child's play group, the social clique in high school, the fraternity and religious center in college, the dating group within which he searches for a spouse, the marriage partner, the neighborhood of his residence, the church affiliation and the church clubs, the men's and the women's social and service organizations, the adult clique of "marrieds," the vacation resort, and then, as the age cycle nears completion, the rest home for the elderly and, finally, the sectarian cemetery—in all these activities and relationships which are close to the core of personality and selfhood—the member of the ethnic group may if he wishes follow a path which never takes him across the boundaries of his ethnic structural network.

The picture is made more complex by the existence of social class divisions which cut across ethnic group lines just as they do those of the white Protestant population in America. As each ethnic group which has been here for the requisite time has developed second, third, or in some cases, succeeding generations, it has produced a college-educated group which composes an upper middle class (and sometimes upper class, as well) segment of the larger groups. Such class divisions tend to restrict primary group relations even further, for although the ethnic-group member feels a general sense of identification with all the bearers of his ethnic heritage, he feels comfortable in intimate social relations only with those who also share his own class background or attainment.

In short, my point is that, while *behavioral assimilation* or acculturation has taken place in America to a considerable degree, *structural assimilation*, with some important exceptions has not been extensive.[28] The exceptions are of two

[28]See Erich Rosenthal, "Acculturation without Assimilation?" *American Journal of Sociology* (1960), Vol. 66, pp. 275–88.

types. The first brings us back to the "triple melting pot" thesis of Ruby Jo Reeves Kennedy and Will Herberg. The "nationality" ethnic groups have tended to merge within each of the three major religious groups. This has been particularly true of the Protestant and Jewish communities. Those descendants of the "old" immigration of the nineteenth century, who were Protestant (many of the Germans and all the Scandinavians), have in considerable part gradually merged into the white Protestant "subsociety." Jews of Sephardic, German, and Eastern-European origins have similarly tended to come together in their communal life. The process of absorbing the various Catholic nationalities, such as the Italians, Poles, and French Canadians, into an American Catholic community hitherto dominated by the Irish has begun, although I do not believe that it is by any means close to completion. Racial and quasi-racial groups such as the Negroes, Indians, Mexican-Americans, and Puerto Ricans still retain their separate sociological structures. The outcome of all this in contemporary American life is thus pluralism—but it is more than "triple" and it is more accurately described as *structural pluralism* than as cultural pluralism, although some of the latter also remains.

My second exception refers to the social structures which implicate intellectuals. There is no space to develop the issue here, but I would argue that there is a social world or subsociety of the intellectuals in America in which true structural intermixture among persons of various ethnic backgrounds, including the religious, has markedly taken place.

My final point deals with the reasons for these developments. If structural assimilation has been retarded in America by religious and racial lines, we must ask why. The answer lies in the attitudes of both the majority and the minority groups and in the way these attitudes have interacted. A saying of the current day is, "It takes two to tango." To apply the analogy, there is no good reason to believe that white Protestant America has ever extended a firm and cordial invitation to its minorities to dance. Furthermore, the attitudes of the minority-group members themselves on the matter have been divided and ambiguous. Particularly for the minority religious groups, there is a certain logic in ethnic communality, since there is a commitment to the perpetuation of the religious ideology and since structural intermixture leads to intermarriage and the possible loss to the group of the intermarried family. Let us then, examine the situation serially for various types of minorities.

With regard to the immigrant, in his characteristic numbers and socioeconomic background, structural assimilation was out of the question. He did not want it, and he had a positive need for the comfort of his own communal institutions. The native American, moreover, whatever the implications of his public pronouncements, had no intention of opening up his primary group life to entrance by these hordes of alien newcomers. The situation was a functionally complementary standoff.

The second generation found a much more complex situation. Many believed they heard the siren call of welcome to the social cliques, clubs, and institutions of white Protestant America. After all, it was simply a matter of learning American ways, was it not? Had they not grown up as Americans, and were they not culturally different from their parents, the "greenhorns?" Or perhaps an especially eager one reasoned (like the Jewish protagonist of Myron Kaufmann's novel, *Remember Me To God*, aspiring to membership in the prestigious club system of Harvard undergraduate social life) "If only I can go the last few steps in Ivy League manners and behavior, they will surely recognize that I am one of them and take me in." But, alas, Brooks Brothers suit notwithstanding, the doors of the fraternity house, the city men's club, and the country club were slammed in the face of the immigrant's offspring. That invitation was not really there in the first place; or, to the extent it was, in Joshua Fishman's phrase, it was a "'look me over but don't touch me' invitation to the American minority group child."[29] And so the rebuffed one

---

[29]Joshua A. Fishman, "Childhood Indoctrination for Minority-Group Membership and the Quest for Minority-Group Biculturism in America," (Mimeo); see, also a revised version of this paper in *Daedalus*, Spring, 1961.

returned to the homelier but dependable comfort of the communal institutions of his ancestral group. There he found his fellows of the same generation who had never stirred from the home fires. Some of these had been too timid to stray; others were ethnic ideologists committed to the group's survival; still others had never really believed in the authenticity of the siren call or were simply too passive to do more than go along the familiar way. All could now join in the task that was well within the realm of the sociologically possible—the build-up of social institutions and organizations within the ethnic enclave, manned increasingly by members of the second generation and suitably separated by social class.

Those who had for a time ventured out gingerly or confidently, as the case might be, had been lured by the vision of an "American" social structure that was somehow larger than all subgroups and was ethnically neutral. Were they, too, not Americans? But they found to their dismay that at the primary group level a neutral American social structure was a mirage. What at a distance seemed to be a quasi-public edifice flying only the all-inclusive flag of American nationality turned out on closer inspection to be the clubhouse of a particular ethnic group—the white Anglo-Saxon Protestants, its operation shot through with the premises and expectations of its parental ethnicity. In these terms, the desirability of whatever invitation was grudgingly extended to those of other ethnic backgrounds could only become a considerably attenuated one.

With the racial minorities, there was not even the pretense of an invitation. Negroes, to take the most salient example, have for the most part been determinedly barred from the cliques, social clubs, and churches of white America. Consequently, with due allowance for internal class differences, they have constructed their own network of organizations and institutions, their own "social world." There are now many vested interests served by the preservation of this separate communal life, and doubtless many Negroes are psychologically comfortable in it, even though at the same time they keenly desire that discrimination in such areas as

207

employment, education, housing, and public accommodations be eliminated. However, the ideological attachment of Negroes to their communal separation is not conspicuous. Their sense of identification with ancestral African national cultures in 1960 is minimal, although Pan-Africanism engages the interest of some intellectuals and although "black nationalist" and "black racist" fringe groups have recently made an appearance at the other end of the communal spectrum. As for their religion, they are either Protestant or Catholic (overwhelmingly the former). Thus, there are no "logical" ideological reasons for their separate communality; dual social structures are created solely by the dynamics of prejudice and discrimination, rather than being reinforced by the ideological commitments of the minority itself.

Structural assimilation, then, has turned out to be the rock on which the ships of Anglo-conformity and the melting pot have foundered. To understand that behavioral assimilation (or acculturation) without massive structural intermingling in primary relationships has been the dominant motif in the American experience of creating and developing a nation out of diverse peoples is to comprehend the most essential sociological fact of that experience. It is against the background of "structural pluralism" that strategies of strengthening intergroup harmony, reducing ethnic discrimination and prejudice, and maintaining the rights of both those who stay within and those who venture beyond their ethnic boundaries must be thoughtfully devised.

part IV

Social
Class

8

Kitty Foyle
& The Concept
of Class as Culture

The traditional approaches to the concept of social class[1] can, on the whole, be placed under one of two categories: (1) economic analysis of income stratification, or the relation of groups to the means of production and (2) class consciousness—that is, concern with the presence or lack of a feeling of class identification. Each has its shortcomings.

Discussion of social class in terms of economic factors alone begs the peculiar function of the social scientist, who should be able to include economic factors in his analysis but not be circumscribed by them, whereas the question of the existence of class consciousness is also a component part of the problem but not an inclusive frame of reference. As Simpson has pointed out:

> Class consciousness is a highly important element in class analysis, but it enters as an objective factor to be studied only after we are aware as to what we mean by class. The presence of classes in a society could not possibly be dependent upon class consciousness, because the degrees of consciousness of individuals vary even among those of identical relative modes of life and we would be forced to accept what men *think* they are as final indication of what they are. Propaganda concerning the equality of all individuals might lead individuals to accept themselves as equal to each other . . . whereas their material equality is nowhere evident.[2]

[1]See, e.g., Page's summary of the work of the "Fathers" of American sociology in social class, Charles H. Page, *Class and American Sociology* (New York, Dial Press, 1940).
[2]George Simpson, "Class Analysis: What Class Is Not," *American Sociological Review*, Vol. IV, No. 6 (1939), p. 829.

The concept of social class can, however, be best approached through the anthropological concept of "culture." In other words, whatever the means by which they have evolved and whatever the degree of psychological awareness of the process on the part of those concerned, social classes in America constitute somewhat separate subgroups in American society, each with its own cultural attributes of behavior, ideas, and life-situations. From the point of view of "class as culture," then, analysis may subsequently be made of the status differentials involved, the historical reasons for the development of classes, the differential rewards obtained from society by the various classes, the avenues and methods of social mobility, and similar problems.

The cultural approach to class is based on two assumptions: (1) that classes are "little worlds" within which a particular individual carries on most of his important social relationships (the point must be made, of course, that there are innumerable spatially separated units of the same class) and (2) that the experience of growing up in a particular class is reflected in one layer, so to speak, of the individual's personality structure. Warner and Lunt have called this aspect of personality structure directly traceable to group experience the "social personality."[3] A review of the research literature on social class published since 1941 reveals that the concept of class as culture is found in the recent important group of studies carried out by Warner, Lunt, Srole, Davis, and the Gardners.[4] It is interesting to note, too, that the director and

[3]W. Lloyd Warner and Paul S. Lunt, *The Social Life of a Modern Community* (Yankee City Series, Vol. I (New Haven, Yale University Press, 1941), pp. 26–27.

[4]*The Social Life of a Modern Community*; W. Lloyd Warner and Paul S. Lunt, *The Status System of a Modern Community*, Yankee City Series, Vol. II (New Haven, Yale University Press, 1942); W. Lloyd Warner and Leo Srole, *The Social Systems of American Ethnic Groups*, Yankee City Series, Vol. III (New Haven, Yale University Press, 1945); Allison Davis, Burleigh B. Gardner, and Mary R. Gardner, *Deep South* (Chicago, University of Chicago Press, 1941); see also W. Lloyd Warner, Robert J. Havighurst, and Martin B. Loeb, *Who Shall Be Educated* (New York and London, Harper, 1944), which contains an analysis of Yankee City materials not previously published.

initiator of these studies, W. Lloyd Warner, was trained in the discipline of cultural anthropology.

The writer is at present making a study of the concept of social class as it has been handled in the American novel of the period between two World Wars, in which the hypothesis that the cultural implications of social class have been perceptively realized and presented by leading American novelists is being investigated. As an example, the novel *Kitty Foyle*,[5] by Christopher Morley, is analyzed from the point of view of its contribution to the "class-as-culture" concept. *Kitty Foyle* is especially interesting to the sociologist of class because it deals largely with the upper class in American life, a group which, for a number of reasons, has not often been the object of sociological investigation.

The locale of *Kitty Foyle* is Philadelphia; the author himself was well acquainted with the upper class Philadelphia background of which he wrote. The plot revolves around the love affair of Kitty, the daughter of a lower-class family of Irish descent living in an industrial section of the city, and Wynnewood Strafford, who lives with his family in Philadelphia's fashionable residential section, the "Main Line." The story takes place during the early 1930s and is told in the first person by Kitty, in retrospect. In a sense, Kitty, in her observations of the mores and behavior patterns of the upper class acts as the anthropological alter ego of Morley, viewing the upper class from the outside. How did Kitty and Wynnewood Strafford meet? As a result of the fact that Kitty's father, now a night watchman, had once been associated in a semiservant capacity with an upperclass institution. He had been groundkeeper at one of the suburban cricket clubs and coach at a private school:

[5]Christopher Morley, *Kitty Foyle* (Philadelphia, Lippincott, 1939), reprinted in an edition by "Penguin Books" (New York, 1944); all page numbers subsequently referred to are from the "Penguin Books" edition.

I suppose Philly is the last place in America where it still matters to be a gentleman. Of course, the old man wasn't, but he was on intimate terms with gentlemen on account of cricket. At the clubs, and at the big private school where he was coach, he knew all the Rittenhouse Square crowd when they were just boys. He was invited to cricket club dinners and used to sing Irish songs for them. There's nobody so snobby about keeping up social hedges as somebody who isn't himself quite the real McCoy. For Pop, men who didn't know about cricket hardly existed. . . .

It was on account of cricket that Wyn first came to the house; he was getting some old scorebooks for that Hundred Years of Philadelphia Cricket they printed. . . . [pp. 14–15].

The association of class position and geographical locale—in other words, some primary group community interaction—is vital to the validity of the class-as-culture concept. This association is repeatedly made in *Kitty Foyle*. The term "Main Line," which refers to the suburban communities strung out along the main westerly tracks of the Pennsylvania Railroad, is used synonymously with "upper class." As a matter of fact, a subtle grading of the class position of various suburbs, including an internal grading of the Main Line itself, is indicated in one passage. Ruminates Kitty:

People who wouldn't live on the Main Line for fear of being high-hatted go out to Oak Lane and Elkins Park. You wouldn't believe how complicated social life can be till you know about the Philadelphia suburbs. It's a riot. Wyn had a theory about how certain kind of people wouldn't dare live further out the Main Line than Merion [p. 131].

Wyn's family is pictured as living far enough out on the Main Line—at St. David's—and as having a town house on Rittenhouse Square, in central Philadelphia, the earlier residential locale of the Philadelphia upper class. Kitty's home, on the other hand, is in a distinctly unfashionable industrial section,

just around the corner from Orthodox Street. That's in Frankford, and a long way from the Main Line, if you know what that means in Philly. It's freight trains and coal yards and factories and the smell of the tanneries down by Frankford Creek. . . . [p. 6].

Kitty's mother had come from a section of Philadelphia of higher social standing than her father: "Mother came from Germantown, which is pretty much top shelf compared to Frankford" (p. 2). But perhaps not from the most fashionable part of Germantown:

> And the old faded photograph of Mother when she was still a young lady in Germantown before she married into Frankford. That's quite a gulf, if you don't know it; though Pop when he got peeved, would say when you get that far down Wissahickon Avenue it's not Germantown but Tioga. Mother said Nonsense, we even had a station in Germantown named for us, Upsal. Who ever heard of a station called Foyle? Then Pop would call her his little chicken from Wissahickon which always tickled her . . . . [pp. 60–61].

Another geographical identification, the association of shopping areas and downtown streets with class, is interestingly made:

> Of course it's no use to think you won't meet people in Philly. All the shopping that amounts to anything socially is along those few blocks on Chestnut and Walnut, and sure enough one day when I went out for lunch I ran into Wyn. There had to be comedy about it, he was standing by the curb scraping one of those beautiful brown shoes on the edge. He said, "Kitty, this is very embarrassing, I walked on some chewing gum, I can't imagine where."
> "What were you doing on Market Street?[6] I asked, and he said, "Kitty, you're adorable" [pp. 215—16].

And in another passage, Kitty, by this time living in New York, discusses class and geography in that city:

> Then I walked up Fifth Avenue all the way to the Plaza and back again, looking in windows and trying to figure out whether

---

[6]Market Street in Philadelphia corresponds roughly to Forty-second Street in New York City: shooting galleries, hamburger stands, cheap movie houses, and inexpensive stores.

women looked different from Philly. I was kind of disappointed. Of course I didn't know then what I do now, you don't see the really smart women on Fifth; they're mostly on Madison and Park Avenue. As a matter of fact Fifth Avenue isn't as smart as the right blocks on Chestnut St. [in Philadelphia]. There's too much of it, and a Public Library and Woolworth's, and clearances of Philippine lingerie certainly drag it down. . . . [p. 162].

If our hypothesis of "class as culture" is valid, class patterns of dress should be discernible. Kitty shows an acute awareness of upper-class patterns of attire: informality and simplicity, expensive material, and, among males, an emphasis on casual tweeds and flannels. In her first meeting with Wyn, when he drops in to talk with her father about cricket, she recalls that he was wearing "old gray pants and the soft shirt, and the cricket club blazer." At first, Kitty's reaction to this deviation from her lowerclass stereotype of upper-class clothes was not favorable:

> I only thought "My God, does he work at a bank in that outfit?"
> . . . Darby Mill, Old St. David's meant nothing to me. How could
> I guess how much swank there is in that intentional shabbiness
> [p. 107].

On another occasion she recalls Wyn's first formal call at the house: "All I can see is an attractive tweed suit in a kind of tobacco brown, and the loveliest deep maroon woolen socks" (p. 19).

As it becomes increasingly clear to her that her affair with Wyn is complicated by the separation of their two worlds, she makes an effort to escape by going to Chicago. Wyn follows her and turns up at her room: "Wyn, west of Paoli! Just the few days I'd been away I'd got used to the way men dress in Chicago,[7] pressed very sharp and neat, and provincial snap-brim hats, and Wyn looked almost foreign" (p. 145).

To celebrate the fact that Wyn came to Chicago to be with Kitty, at the cost of missing the Philadelphia Assembly, the annual upper-class ball, they decide to go dining and dancing in evening clothes:

[7] In contrast to Wyn, "men in Chicago" obviously means "middle-class men."

When I was all equipped he sent me back to Molly's in a taxi and got himself a readymade evening suit. I bet it was the only time Wyn Strafford wore ready mades, and he looked almost too Ritzy. He said he did a few somersaults over the bed to take the shine off [p. 149].

In discussing her Uncle Elmer who lived in the mid-West, Kitty says: "He had genius for choosing the wrong kind of clothes, tweeds that were the color of straw and would have given Wyn apoplexy" (p. 55).

Later in the course of Kitty's life, while she is attempting to break off the affair with Wyn, she goes to New York, and there eventually meets a Jewish doctor named Mark Eisen. Lonely and impressed with Mark's professional competence and intelligence, she begins to go out with him. But the cultural aspects of Jewish middle-class life to which she is introduced bother her. In a paragraph of reminiscing about Wyn, one evening she mentions clothes:

There's a roof of some hotel I can see right from my office desk. The women come out on the terrace and I can see them pause just an instant in the doorway to feel beautiful and sure and to know the dress will float just right as they step off the sill. Their escorts, just like it might be you behind me, following politely right after. You wouldn't be wearing a dentistry coat and a cummerbund, though, and looking like something in café society. Did you make a snob out of me, big boy! I could wring Mark Eisen's neck when I see his clothes, poor sweetheart; and how hard he tries. Always too nifty, always too shiny like cellophane, that's them [pp. 126—27].

Appraising Mark's appearance at a summer gathering, she writes:

Of course Wyn got me so conditioned about men's clothes that I hate to see them overdressed. Mark's striped pants, creased like a knife-edge, would blackball him at any cricket club, and those black and white yachting shoes with perforated breathing holes were definitely Hollywood. What put Big Casino on the outfit was a polo shirt wide open to the fur and a blue tweed coat with a handkerchief made of the same stuff as the shirt. That's pretty terrible, because a man ought to look like he's put together by accident, not added up on purpose. Poor old Mark, you could just see he'd been spending his Saturday afternoons figuring out this cruising kit [pp. 231—32].

He's got the same kind of sureness professionally that the Main Line has socially. He's got respect for intelligence like the Main Line has for flannel pants without any crease in them [pp. 203–4].

About class patterns of women's clothes, Kitty has less to say. On one occasion, however, while demonstrating perfume in a Philadelphia department store, she meets the woman Wyn has eventually married and commenting on her possibilities of attractiveness, says:

She might get that wholesome tweed-skirt, Wayne-Devon and Paoli[8] look.... Her manners were so pleasant it would be hard to know was she really dumb or not; of course all those vintage Main Liners pride themselves to be just lovely with the lower classes as long as they don't go beyond their proper station which would probably be Overbrook [p. 214].

One of the characteristics of Wyn's class (in Warner's terms, it would be the upper-upper class of Philadelphia) is its careful lack of ostentation. Wyn's station wagon (in itself traditionally connected with upper-class status), as he calls at the Foyle house, is described as follows:

I looked out the window and saw a weatherstained old station wagon, and painted on the side of it in small green letters DARBY MILL, OLD ST. DAVID'S.

In line with her early lower-class stereotypes, Kitty evaluates this shabbiness in an amusing mistake:

In the car were some big piles of shingles baled up with wire. Pop had been saying for I don't know how long that we must get new shingles for the backhouse roof, it leaked on him when he was sitting in there. I supposed he ordered some without telling me, and ran downstairs just to see that he wasn't getting cheated.

[8]Stops on the Main Line.

"Is that the man for the backhouse?" I said as I went into the room. Pop cackled with laughter and the visitor rose politely. I could feel my pure and eloquent blood doing its stuff. It was Wyn [p. 106].

Years later, when Kitty has begun to see the status implications of a shabby station wagon, she writes as follows of an unexpected encounter with Wyn's wife.

I get off at 30th Street Station and walk out for a cab, and Jesusgod comes a station wagon pulling up under those pillars marked DARBY MILL. Not a nice old tumble-down station wagon neither but bran shiny new. I bet Ronnie wouldn't understand how much smarter the old one was [p. 208].

And in the scene describing Wyn's call at the Foyle home, when he leaves, Kitty apologizes to her father:

"I thought Mr. Strafford must be in the lumber business," I said.
"Jesusgod," exclaimed the old man. "Don't you ever read your *Ledger*? Strafford, Wynnewood and Company, the oldest private bank in Philly. Darby Mill, that's the name of their country place; there's an old sawmill on the crick out there, where they cut up the logs for Washington at Valley Forge. Honey, those folks are so pedigree they'd be ashamed to press their pants. They hire someone to drive the Rolls for a year before they use it, so it won't look too fresh."
"I think that's just as silly as the opposite." [Kitty notes that she replied.] I think so still [pp. 107—08].

This drive for unostentation goes as far as using circumlocutions to avoid public identification with names connoting prestige:

Wyn said he was getting a lot of work done because he'd taken leave of absence from the bank and his family were all away at their summer cottage in Rhode Island. He had a funny phobia about saying "Newport." I soon got to spot that habit of the Main Line crowd, kind of ashamed to let on how swell they are. Jesusgod they don't even brood on it in secret, they just know [p. 110].

An interesting sidelight on the use of the term "Esquire" among the upper classes is thrown in one paragraph; Wyn for a time engages in an eventually abortive attempt to produce a magazine in Philadelphia patterned after the *New Yorker*, and Kitty becomes his secretary:

> I learned a lot about letters in the office of *Philly* because when I addressed one to Parry I remembered Pop's talk about the high-toned Esq and I wrote it Mr. Parrish Berwyn Esq which Wyn said was wrong. If you're Esq you can't be Mr. at the same time. I think I was rather cute, I said suppose I'd ever write you a letter would it be Wynnewood Strafford Esq VI or Wynnewood Strafford VI Esq? He said at Old St. David's or even at Rittenhouse Square it was his father was really the Esq and he himself was only Wynnewood Strafford VI, but if writing to an office it was better to put Mr. because there you were just the honest trades-man. It seems a man can't properly be Esq away from his inher-ited private property. To put Esq on a business letter is New York phony or the Nouveau Long Island touch, he said [pp. 138–39].

The reason for *Philly's* failure comes from the mouth of Molly, Kitty's shrewd midwestern friend:

> It sounds like fun. . . . But if I get the town from what you've told me I don't think it'll work. The *New Yorker's* grand because it's edited by a lot of boys who are both smart and ambitious. You haven't got 'em like that here. If they're really peppy they clear out. And the *New Yorker's* got a readymade public of all kinds of people who have an awful yen to be In the Know. It's a kind of inferiority. But I don't believe Philadelphia gives a damn about being In the Know. It prefers not to be or it thinks it's there already. The people on top are so damn sure they know it all they don't want to learn anything new; and the people underneath know they haven't got a Chinaman's chance. I think it's rather swell to have one town that simply doesn't give a damn except be comfortable. Why does your friend want to give it the needle? If I were you I'd let Philly be like old Pattyshells. Leave it wag its tail on the porch [pp. 117–18].

Class differences reveal themselves in speech. Morley uses the device of having his lower-class heroine tell the story in racy, slangy prose; but pronounciation and inflection are obviously difficult to present on a printed page without the use of phonetics, and he makes no attempt at it. In one place, however, he has Kitty comment on the speech of Rosey Rittenhouse, one of Wyn's upper-class friends:

> I think of Rosey's voice sometimes, that easy well-bred Philadelphia accent that seems to fit them like a suit of good tweeds. The kind of voice people only get when they've had good meals and good sleep for several generations and horses in the stable [p. 159].

Religious affiliation and class are not dealt with extensively in *Kitty Foyle*, but the close historical association of Quakerism with the upper class in Philadelphia is indicated by the fact that several of Wyn's friends, including Rosey, are specifically mentioned as being members of this sect. A theological discussion is reported:

> We sat by a big fireplace and talked . . . about religion. Wyn said what he liked about Quakerism was the idea of salvation piped direct to the individual, what they called the Inner Light, everybody has it for himself. A kind of neon tubing I guess. Rosey said he wasn't so sure there wasn't something to be said for Indirect Lighting too, like the Catholics. "But don't quote me, I'll be thrown out of Swarthmore Meeting" [p. 159].

What happens when second-generation lower-class Irish tangles with the Main Line? It is to Morley's credit that when Wyn indicates a serious interest in Kitty Foyle to his family,[9] there are no "Go, and never darken my door again," or "You must choose between us" scenes. As a matter of fact, the Straffords' first response to the situation is to invite Kitty to a house party at their country home. Kitty goes reluctantly. As all concerned, with the possible exception of Wyn, had envisaged, Kitty's formal introduction to the Main Line is not a success:

---

[9]Kitty's own mother and father are dead before the affair reaches its climax.

It was a mistake. Of course Wyn had done what any man would, told everybody to be lovely to me and they were so god damn lovely I could have torn their eyes out. I was the only one that wasn't in the union. That crowd, if they stopped to think about it, would reckon that Ben Franklin was still a boy from the wrong side of the tracks, so what could they think about me. Somebody wanted to know if I was one of the Iglehart Foyles from Baltimore or the Saltonstall Foyles from Pride's Crossing. I said no pride ever crossed our family except when the old man carried his bat against Merion C.C. That was Wyn's fault, he tried to ease the situation by making everybody drink too many old fashioneds. But it helped because good old Rosey Rittenhouse turned the talk on cricket and said he wished he could get more girls to show some intelligence about it. . . . I knew either I or the rest of them didn't belong, and the embarrassment went around the dinner table all wrapped up in a napkin like that wine bottle the butlers carried.

Even in a Thanksgiving rainstorm, what a lovely lovely place. When I saw Wyn's old faded station wagon out in a hitching shed I asked him to drive me home. Of course he wouldn't and he couldn't. I was supposed to stay the night and I had to go through with it. "I hope you'll rest well," Mrs. Strafford said, "will you want the maid to undress you?" Jesusgod, I blushed like one of those Cornell chrysanthemums. I wanted to say there's only one person here who's good enough to undress me. Wyn saw me turn red, he kept his eyes on me all evening bless him and came across the room to see what was going wrong.

"You mustn't try to get up in the morning, we'll all sleep late," Mrs. Strafford said.

"I've got to get to the office," I said. "We're closing up and I want to leave everything clean."

"Oh, I'm so glad Wyn is giving up that dreadful magazine," she said. "I don't think Philadelphia enjoys that sort of persiflage."

Either she or I must have been pronouncing that word wrong up to then.

"We know damn well they don't," was what I had a yen to say, but by God K. F. had herself under control.

"I don't know what I would do without Kitty," said Wyn, trying to help. In fact I *won't* do without her. Maybe she'll come and help me at the bank" [pp. 134–35].

It is then that Kitty decides to leave Philadelphia:

"I'm going to Chicago," I said, unexpectedly. I didn't know myself I was going to say it. I'd had a letter from Molly a day or two before. All of a sudden I saw what came next. Wyn was terribly startled, and what a flash of, well, thankfulness, I saw in Mrs. Strafford's eyes. Poor lady, she was only playing on the signals they'd taught her. I could see that down under she had a respect for me, she'd like to have me around if it could have been allowed.

"Really, that's very interesting," she said. "Do you know people in Chicago? We have some very pleasant acquaintances in Lake Forest."

"My best friend has a job at Palmer's, she's in the furnishing department."

"The modern girls are so courageous, I think it's wonderful how enterprising they are."

I looked around at the enterprising modern girls. They were showing a good deal of knee sprawled on the sofas with brandy and sodas and members of the Racquet Club, or they were screeching at ping pong in the game room, or playing some baby chess they called b'gammon. I felt homesick for a good filing case somewhere [pp. 135–36].

Kitty expresses her understanding of the endogamous nature of the Main Line:

The Main Line girls Bill and Parry were accustomed to have to spend so much time on clothes and stuff they don't have a chance to figure out a good line of hidden-ball formations. The Assembly gazelles know they're practically doomed to the clutches of someone in their own set, why waste good energy in broken field running? [p. 133].

The reaction of Wyn's family is obviously not personal hostility toward Kitty. It seems simply to represent a realistic understanding of the separate and distinct nature of the different social worlds from which their son and Kitty come and a feeling of the hopelessness of bringing them together. In a later passage Kitty hints that Wyn's family "were working on him" to discourage the match, and she even indicates her belief that for a time when Wyn's visits are infrequent, he has resolved to "shake" her "out of his system" (p. 151). But this effort fails. Kitty is described as being a most attractive young lady, and their relationship has already reached the stage of sleeping together.

Kitty feels increasingly that the situation cannot be resolved in marriage and makes up her mind to accept an offer of a job in New York. The denouement, however, comes when Wyn's family, believing that Wyn is determined to marry Kitty, take the advice of Mr. Kennet, described as a Quaker banker, and an old friend of the family, and, in despair, propose a cultural renovation for Kitty:

> "Well then I've got to tell you," Wyn said. "Uncle Kennet has a big idea, he wanted to explain it to you himself. He says you're just exactly the girl for me, Kitty, and the girl the family needs, and he wants to send you . . . to college for a year and then maybe go abroad a year and meanwhile I'll try to get some education myself[10] and be ready for you."
>
> Oh Jesusgod I don't know exactly how you said it, Wyn. It was something like that. My poor baby, how could you know what that would do to me the way I was just then. Maybe that nice old man with his *thee* talk could have sold it to me; I don't know. I had a kind of picture of some damned family conference and the Straffords and their advisers trying to figure out how the curse was going to be taken off Kitty Foyle. So that was it, they were going to buy the girl with an education, and polish off her rough Frankford edges, were they, and make her good enough to live with stuffed animals' heads and get advertised in the *Ledger*. I can still see your face, my poor baby, when I turned on you. I felt hot inside my throat and on the rims of my ears.
>
> "You can tell Uncle Ken he's a white slaver. Listen, Wyn Strafford, I'll be your girl whenever I feel like it because I love you from hell to breakfast. But I wouldn't join the little tin family if every old Quaker with an adding machine begged me to. No, not if they all went back to college and got themselves an education. So they tried to sell you the idea they'd trim up Kitty so she could go to the assembly and make Old Philadelphia Family out of her, hey? Cut her out of a copy of *Vogue* and give her a charge account and make a Main Line doll out of her. They

[10]Just what Wyn means by these remarks is not quite clear. He is already described as being a graduate of Princeton.

can't do that to Kitty Foyle. Jesusgod, that's what they are
themselves, a bunch of paper dolls."

Remember you stopped the Buick just before we cut down a
tree with it. Better maybe if we had. You just looked at me, and
tried to light a cigarette and your hand shook pushing in the
dashboard lighter. You were so rattled you threw the lighter
away, you thought it was a match. I loved you specially because
you hadn't shaved. I thought how the old man would rise green
from his grave if he heard a proposition like that. I felt tears
coming like those waves you swam through and I had to hurry
to say it:—

"By God, I'll improve *you* all I want but you can't improve
me" [pp. 174–75].

And so Kitty leaves Philadelphia and becomes a "white-
collar" girl in New York. Although the affair continues on
occasional week ends, both Kitty and Wyn are resigned to the
hopelessness of bringing their worlds together. The meetings
become less frequent, and one day Kitty reads in the society
columns of a New York newspaper of Wyn's engagement to
"Miss Veronica Gladwyn of 'Welshwood' near King of Prus-
sia." The tenuous threads of individual attraction that had
connected the two cultural worlds have at last broken, and
Kitty and Wyn proceed along their separate ways, nursing
their wounds but gradually being reabsorbed into their respective social spheres. In a striking introspective dialogue
with herself, sometime later, Kitty reflects on the affair and
shows an amazingly keen and poignant understanding of the
social issues:

Q. Did you make Wyn happy?

A. I think so. Yes, I know so.

Q. Then why did you leave him?

A. If I had done what he wanted, other people would have
made him unhappier than I could have made him happy.

Q. What do you mean?

A. He was the product of a system. He was at the mercy of
that system.

Q. Is it not your conviction that there are now no systems?
That the whole of society is in flux?

A. Not in—I mean, not where Wyn lives.

225

Q. Was not the way you left him rather cruel?

A. Damn you, I was afraid you'd ask that. Yes, it was. But I *had* to be tough with him, otherwise he'd always have felt he had been unfair to *me*, and it would have made him wretched.

Q. You think, then, he is not unhappy now?

A. Yes. No. Ask that again, please.

Q. You think Wyn is happy now?

A. I think his life is full of delightful routine. He has what the government calls Social Security. Oh, and how. Read the *Public Ledger* on Sundays, or whatever papers they have now.

Q. You think you could have made something more important of him?

A. I could have taught him to do the Wrong Thing sometimes.

Q. What, in Philadelphia?

A. We could have lived somewhere else.

Q. Are you quite fair to Philadelphia?

A. I am thinking of it only as a symbol. Actually I love it dearly.

Q. But are they not the most charming people in the world?

A. Of course. But the enemies of the Future are always the very nicest people.

Q. You think the Future should be encouraged?

A. That's a goofy question, my darling; it's on our necks already. And oh, God, Wyn was so much interested in it when he had a chance. What a man he might have been if everything hadn't been laid in his lap.

Q. Is your mind going to go round and round like this indefinitely?

A. How's about going to bed and try for some sleep [pp. 28–29].

Kitty Foyle, by means of her literary creator, has played the role of the sociologist of the culture of classes.

9

Social Class & American Intellectuals[1]

Thoughtful students of the contemporary social scene must ever be on the alert to perceive new patterns, new groupings which emerge from the endless swirls and eddies of human interaction. Yesterday's sociological concept does not freeze the flesh and blood of today's interpersonal relations, and this is particularly true in an era of intense urbanism, industrialization, and rapid technological change. It was some such shift in focus which led twenty years or so ago to the incipient appearance of fresh perceptions about stratification in the United States and an appreciation of the *social* aspects of social class. Tardy as this perception was, and granted that it could have been presented with more precise analytical and research incisiveness, it was a major contribution; and it is interesting to note that in the great social stratification boom which followed, few of the heavy investors, with the exception of the textbook writers, stopped to thank Mr. Warner for his pioneering pains. As we know, quite the contrary.

Who guards the guardian? Who studies the student? The analysts of American social structure are likely to be academics, many, though certainly not all, of whom fall into the broader category commonly, if imperfectly, known as "the intellectual." Here again I suggest that while the man of ideas and the arts has rarely been studied seriously as a social type by professional students of society, although he has frequently interested the literary essayist and the pam-

[1]Address given at the Twenty-fourth Annual Meeting of the Eastern Sociological Society, in New York City, April 4, 1954.

phleteer, there are signs which point to his increasing relevance as a focus of serious social analysis. I shall not attempt to claim that the status of the intellectual is necessarily the best indicator, by itself, of the health of a civilization. After all, we know that though he functions in ideological chains, the intellectual's status is high in the Soviet Union today. Nevertheless, in combination with other major factors, it is an important index of a culture's situation—its ethos—its total outlook on things. From the point of view of the contemporary student of American social structure, it is important to know where and how the intellectual fits into the social class system, how he relates to the cross cutting forces of ethnicity, and to what extent he is sufficiently aware of and interacting with his fellow-intellectuals to have a group consciousness. In terms of general social theory the problem may be viewed as one of understanding the intricate three-way interplay of common interest factors with social class and ethnic group considerations. Where, in other words, does the intellectual stand, and to what extent does he stand alone?

II

In the face of a dearth of empirical research dealing specifically with the position of intellectuals in American social structure, consideration of the topic must rely at present on general observation, occasional impressionistic essays by sociologists and littèrateurs alike, and inferences made from research on related materials, such as the social class position of occupations in which intellectuals are characteristically found. In a field where insights abound, however, it is a diffident social scientist indeed who will refrain from adding his own. Such a lack of diffidence in the speaker is in no small measure a condition of the presentation of this paper. Let us remember, too, that an insight, at its best, is a statistical operation performed silently by the mind.

Definitions are necessary and primary. I shall not advance seriously the anatomical definition of an intellectual which emerged from the last presidential campaign—namely that he may be identified by the possession of a head which gives the appearance of an egg. Shades of Lombroso! With the caution, however, that social typologies are frequently simply heuristic devices for containing the ceaseless ebb and flow of human phenomena, intellectuals, I think, may be defined as persons who have a serious and relatively informed interest in ideas and the arts. They are people for whom ideas, concepts, literature, music, painting, the dance, have intrinsic meaning—are a part of the social-psychological atmosphere which one breathes. To borrow from Russell Lynes' perceptive description of the subgroup of intellectuals which he calls "the Upper Bohemians,"[2] they are persons who see the general in the particular, who begin with a casual remark about a tomato and end in a discussion of organic gardening, who proceed from a reference to a Buick to an argument about the state of American industrial design. Occupationally, they are characteristically found in the professions—teaching, carrying on research, practicing law, medicine, social work, or architecture, for example; in the arts—writing, painting, dancing, directing; or, if in business, in those areas of buying and selling which deal with communications and the transmission of ideas and art—for instance, advertising or publishing. None of these occupations is made up entirely of intellectuals, and intellectuals will be found, if less frequently, in occupations which I have not mentioned. The age-cycle must also be taken into consideration, and any full examination of the occupational patterns of intellectuals must deal with their occupational origins, their orientation as students, particularly in the colleges, and their progress through the successive stages of occupational achievement.

If we are to inquire about the intellectual's place in the social class system, we must examine and define social classes. I believe that we are emerging from a period of alarms, discursions, confusion, conflict, and frantic partisanship over the meaning of the concept of social class, an emergence

[2]Russell Lynes, "The Upper Bohemians," *Harper's*, Vol. 206, No. 1233 (February 1953), pp. 46–52.

which bespeaks both a maturation of our science and a sharpening of our perceptions. Earlier clashes, among others, between partisans of economic determinism, and thus the economic definition of class, and the defenders of an exclusive and rather undynamic status group approach are giving way to the recognition that social class phenomena are multidimensional in nature. This point of view—briefly adumbrated by Max Weber and developed more systematically by recent writers, including members of this symposium—recognizes that, under the rubric of stratification, an economic dimension, a social status dimension, and a political power dimension may be distinguished, and that other variables, such as cultural way of life, group separation, class consciousness, social mobility, and ethnic group identification, are a part of the total picture. This point of view also recognizes that the essence of wisdom is to study empirically the various relationships of the dimensions and variables, applying the term "social class" as a matter of somewhat arbitrary definition to one of the three major stratification dimensions. If we do this, then we study how economic power affects social status and vice versa, and how both of these variables interact with political power—how social grouping and cultural patterning are associated with social status or economic divisions—and so on, until we have exhausted the interplay of variables.

For reasons which have to do with the immediate stimuli which persuade people to pattern themselves into social groupings, I prefer to assign the term "social class" to the social status groupings of American society, admitting that the empirical evidence with regard to the degree of delineation of the groups is conflicting and that the status dimension itself contains many divisions, the relations among which are at times obscure and problematical. However, both my research and my informal observations lead me to suspect that rough divisions in American society based on a rather generalized concept of social status which derives from income, occupation, and style of life do exist, and that it is helpful to our understanding to refer to them as social classes.

In these terms, I believe that an upper class, a middle class, and a lower class may be distinguished and that these rough social groupings in turn conceivably contain somewhat recognizable subdivisions. I am convinced, certainly, that the division between the upper-middle class and the lower-middle class is an important and functional one and that much of significance is obscured by certain contemporary observers of class, particularly of Marxist intellectual origins, who fail to give this distinction salience in their analysis.

III

If we try to locate the intellectual in the social class, or status group hierarchy, we must also consider, if briefly, his position along the economic continuum and his role in the political struggle. It is also pertinent to ask about the nature of his cultural behavior patterns and the outlines of his relationship to the ethnic group system. Finally, we must seek to ascertain the patterning of his social life with a view to determining the possible presence of a new subcultural group on the American scene.

In examining recently a number of writings which deal, at least in part, with the general status of the intellectual in contemporary American society, I was struck by the existence of two polarized views. One is represented by a new work by Leo Gurko,[3] who decries the picture of the man of ideas and the arts presented in the stereotypes of popular fiction and the movies. The intellectual, according to this view, is regarded by the general American public as something of a boob—an impractical, awkward, socially naive, sexually impotent fellow towards whom the standardized attitude is one of good-natured ridicule. Side by side with this myth of the intellectual, according to Gurko, is one which considers him to be a "city slicker," sly and dangerous, and at the very best unhappy or neurotic because of his high I.Q. Supporting the Gurko thesis, a rather extensive literature on the college

[3]Leo Gurko, *Heroes, Highbrows and the Popular Mind* (New York, Bobbs-Merrill, 1953).

teacher,[4] often a symbol of the intellectual man to the general public, testifies to the complaints about his felt status during the Twentieth century and is strikingly symbolized by the cartoon caricature of the New Deal as a wild-eyed and foolish-looking man of shriveled physical proportions attired in a cap and gown, which was a staple of the conservative press in the 1930s.

The other view, and to my mind the more convincing one, points to recent revolutions in taste, in the impact of scientists, both natural and social, in the availability of music, books, and magazines of fine quality, and in the rôle of academics and other intellectuals in business and governmental operations. It posits a kind of artistic and intellectual renascence in which industrial and communications technology and the complexity of modern living have conspired to give the writer, the artist, the social analyst, and the technical specialist a greater importance than they have ever had before in our culture. Thus Russell Lynes half seriously suggests that the more familiar class system based on wealth or family lineage is gradually being replaced by a status order predicated on intellectual ability and artistic taste in which "highbrows" lord it over "upper-middle and lower-middle brows," and establish an uneasy camaraderie with the noncompeting and slightly suspicious "low-brows."[5] Signs of increased antiintellectualism in the political and ideological realms may well be interpreted as an indication of the increasing importance of the man of ideas rather than the other way around, for do they not contain the implicit admission that ideas *are* powerful preludes and instigators to action? In this connection, I cannot refrain from quoting the cogent comment of David Riesman in a recent article, dealing with intellectual freedom:

[4]For a critical review of this literature, see Richard H. Shryock, "The Academic Profession in the United States," *American Association of University Professors Bulletin*, Vol. 38, No. 1 (Spring 1952). See particularly pp. 50—54.

[5]Russell Lynes, "Highbrow, Lowbrow, Middlebrow," *Harper's*, Vol. 198, No. 1185 (February 1949), pp. 19–28.

In a way, the attention that intellectuals are getting these days, although much of it is venomous and indecent, testifies to the great improvement in our status over that of an earlier day. What might not Henry Adams have given for such signs of recognition! In his day the intellectual was no threat to any-body: whether clergyman or scholar, he had to defer to the "practical" men, the men of business and affairs. It is almost inconceivable today that a father should say, "Where Vander-bilt sits, there is the head of the table. I teach my son to be rich." In the much more fluid and amorphous America of our time, the writer, the artist, the scientist have become figures of glamour, if not of power. It is harder to say where the head of the table is.[6]

And Jacques Barzun, writing on America's new "Passion for Culture," quips: "*Pro Arte* is not just the name of a quartet, it is the motto of the age;" and goes on to add: "In the public eye the man of art and the man of thought have achieved status. We think we are riding a wave of anti-intellectualism because certain such men are attacked; the fact is that they are attacked because they have become important."[7]

As I have indicated, my own informal observations would lead me to support the thesis presented by Lynes, by Riesman, and by Barzun: namely, that the general status of the intellectual is high and that he currently rides the wave of mass distributed culture which sweeps up the beaches of the American middle class.

For ascertaining more specifically the position of the intellectual in the social class structure we may find helpful accumulated research on the general status position of occu-pations. Here all signs point to the great esteem in which the professional man in America (which the intellectual is likely to be) is held. In the nationwide opinion poll on occupations carried out by the National Opinion Research Center in the middle 1940s, as reported by North and Hatt,[8] out of a total

[6]David Riesman, "Some Observations on Intellectual Freedom," *The American Scholar*, Vol. 23, No. 1 (Winter 1953–54), pp. 14–15.
[7]Jacques Barzun, "America's Passion for Culture," *Harper's*, Vol. 208, No. 1246 (March 1954), pp. 40–41.
[8]Cecil C. North and Paul K. Hatt, "Jobs and Occupations: A Popular Evalua-tion ," *Sociological Analysis*, ed. Logan Wilson and William L. Kolb (New York, Harcourt, Brace, 1949) pp. 464–74.

possible score of 100, "College Professor" and "Scientist" scored 89. Highest score was 96, earned by "U. S. Supreme Court Justice." "Physician" scored 93, "Architect" 86, "Artist who paints pictures that are exhibited in galleries" 83, and "Author of novels" 80. All of these scores are in the upper reaches of the scale, as may be seen by a glance at the average for clerical, sales, and kindred workers of 68.2 and for non-farm laborers of 45.8. Business men also rank high on the scale but on the average lower than the professions. ("Sociologist," incidentally, was rated at 82, seven points below "college professor." Apparently we are basking in an unearned glow of incremental status secured by our more polished or our more useful colleagues.) All of the community studies, such as those of Warner and Hollingshead, place professions generally in the middle class or above, and their modal position, dependent, it is true, on type, appears to be the upper middle class rather than the lower middle.

Intellectuals will be found in the lower middle class, to be sure, by economic and occupational circumstance, though doubtless they are uneasy in its cultural patterns, and occasionally intellectuals will appear as deviant workers or tillers of the soil. Nor are they unknown in the stately homes and fashionable town houses of aristocracy. In an interesting study of the interplay of social and occupational prestige in Philadelphia, Digby Baltzell[9] found that 16 percent of the educators in Who's Who for 1940 in that city were also in the Social Register. Notice, however, that 75 percent of all Philadelphia bankers in Who's Who were in the Register. It seems reasonable to assume that the 84 percent of educators not found in the Social Register are somewhere in the upper reaches of the middle class.

When all considerations of status, style of life, and social participation are brought together, the most plausible hypothesis is that the basic social status position from which the

[9]E. Digby Baltzell, " 'Who's Who in America' and 'The Social Register': Elite and Upper Class Indexes in Metropolitan America," Class, Status and Power, ed. Reinhard Bendix and Seymour Martin Lipset (Glencoe, Ill., Free Press, 1953), pp. 172–85.

intellectual looks out on the American scene is that of the upper-middle class. Intellectuals below this level are drawn upward to it by aspiration, intellectuals above it are drawn down by participation.

IV

If the social status of the intellectual is likely to be high, his economic position is likely to be highly variable, covering the range from the low-paid college instructor at the beginning of his career "making do" at $3500 per annum to the public relations or radio network executive with a passion for Proust who banks yearly at $18,000. What strikes me, however, is the question of consumption patterns, or the translation of income into way of life. Time and again one may note with interest the low-paid professional or artist finding an apartment in the gate house or over the garage of a former estate in a plushy neighborhood, with all this means in the way of ground space, general attractiveness, and conveniences, at the same rental that a semi-skilled factory worker with the same salary or more will be paying for a dismal flat or dilapidated row house in a run-down area. Moreover, Mrs. Young Intellectual today, horn-rimmed glasses, horse-tail hair-do, ballet slippers, and all, is not the reckless and extravagant bohemian of yesterday's Greenwich Village, but is likely to be a level-headed girl who makes her own and the baby's lovely clothes out of bargain materials, stitches up the living-room draperies, drives a shrewd bargain with the aid of Consumer Reports, and helps her husband put the finishing touches on the homemade or bought but unpainted furniture. My point is that even the relatively impecunious intellectual usually knows how to get the most for his money and to live in an upper-middle class setting with less. Some day I'd like to see some young sociologist or economist do a doctoral dissertation on the amount of waste and poor value received in the consumption patterns of Mrs. Middle Majority, to use Burleigh Gardner's interesting phrase for the housewife of the

235

lower-middle or upper-lower class, and for that matter the buying patterns of the lady in the class below.

With regard to political power, it seems fair to suggest that on the American scene intellectuals, as a group, have virtually none. In the gigantic politico-economic struggles carried on against each other by Big Business, Big Little Business, Big Labor, and Big Agriculture, to use Clair Wilcox's classification,[10] the intellectual stands on the side-lines, functions as an occasional supporting lobby, or draws his salary and his orders as an individual spokesman for one of the more powerful blocs. Who ever heard of Big Intellectuals? Individually, he may play a key and relatively anonymous rôle in a specific issue as the staff member of a Congressional or executive committee, or, as in the Stevenson candidacy, in a presidential campaign. If he can identify with labor or with Big Business or with any of the other power groups, then he may feel his own interests to be represented by these Goliaths. If he has an independent point of view, however, focused either on his own situation as an intellectual or on the community as a whole, he must feel relatively impotent, as the organizations which represent such views are weak or nonexistent. C. Wright Mills, in his book *White Collar*, has noted the current political impotence and apathy of the intellectual with bitter regret.[11] I wonder if there isn't something about the intellectual's general capacity for thinking abstractly and perhaps at times disinterestedly, that may help to explain his current disillusionment and withdrawal, in so far as they exist. During the 30s the intellectuals, generally, were in one form or another pro-labor, largely out of disinterested motives and emotions—labor was the underdog and the total scheme of things called for a righting of wrongs that existed. In the 1950s, organized labor is big and strong and still fighting—for organized labor, and hang the danger of

[10]Clair Wilcox, "Concentration of Power in the American Economy," *Harvard Business Review*, Vol. 28, No. 6 (November 1950), pp. 54–60.
[11]C. Wright Mills, *White Collar* (New York, Oxford University Press, 1951). See particularly chap. 7.

inflation. The intellectual, I suggest, has some cause for bewilderment as he searches, or gives up the search, for political channels that speak for man, not just some portion thereof. Nevertheless, the intellectual, if he is wise, will develop a political interest and a political action. For, not to speak of the world scene, the current major domestic controversy concerns him greatly. If the reactionary forces which now bluster across the land should ever gain control of the Republican party and eventually the nation, the free intellectual will be one of the first targets of oppresion. The stakes are high.

V

The man of ideas and the arts has an ethnic background. He is a Negro, a Jew, an Irish or Italian Catholic, a white Protestant, or something else. As the culturally assimilating forces of the American social class system exert pressures which bring him into contact with persons of different ethnic but the same social class position, the containing walls of ethnic communality are threatened—but not necessarily broken. The intellectual, because his interests are sharper and rarer, simply faces this conflict in acuter form. On the basis of his resolution of the conflict and the personality style which significantly influences it, I think we may distinguish three "ideal types" of response to the dual pressures of ethnicity and intellectualism. The representatives of these three types may be called "the actively ethnic intellectual," "the passively ethnic intellectual," and "the marginally ethnic intellectual."

The "actively ethnic intellectual" remains within his ethnic group and focuses his intellectual interests precisely on his ethnicity. He is the cultural historian of the group, the theologian, the communal leader, the apologist, the scholar of its art, its music, and its literature. While he maintains a respectable acquaintanceship with the broader ideological currents and events around him, his primary interests and passions are reserved for the racial, religious, or nationality background ethos in which he considers his roots to be firmly placed. His is a confident approach, and he appears to be spared many of the problems of marginality. Incidentally, he may be a white Protestant as well as a member of a minority. White Protestants, after all, are simply our largest ethnic group.

The "passively ethnic intellectual" is a numerous type, though not necessarily the most numerous. Finding it easier, safer, or more in line with his personality style, he remains predominantly within the subcultural boundaries of his ethnic group and social class. If he is a Negro, most of his friends may be intellectuals but they will also be Negroes. If he is a Jew, he confines his friendships primarily to other Jewish intellectuals. While his interests are mostly of the broader, nonethnic variety, he gratifies them within the borders of ethnic communality. Occasionally, he looks wistfully beyond the ethnic boundaries at other intellectuals but he is not moved, or not able, to cross these boundaries in any substantial sense.

The "marginally ethnic intellectual" is, from many points of view, the most interesting and the most significant type. As the appellation indicates, he wears his ethnicity lightly, if not in his own eyes at least in the eyes of the world. Whatever his social psychology, he finds ethnic communality unsatisfactory and takes his friends, and perhaps even his spouse, wherever he finds them, so long as they share his fascination with Kafka and his passion for Heinrich Schuetz. To other, more conventional ethnics he is very occasionally a traitor, sometimes a snob, not infrequently, in Lewin's term, a "leader from the periphery"—mostly they let him alone; if he is successful, they will claim him—and he will be pleased by their claim.

It is the existence of the marginal intellectual and the persistent force of common interest in intellectual pursuits as a pressure against the walls of ethnic communality which leads me to my final point—the possibility of a new subcultural group emerging from the new patterns and the new interests—a subculture of intellectuals. This subculture would contain, ethnically speaking, neither hosts nor guests, would serve as a kind of bridge between ethnic groups, and would be, minimally, a haven for marginals, and at the most, literally a microcosm of a new world to come. A subculture, however, demands social interaction, a reciprocal social psychology of identification and recognition, and communal institutions. In the absence of formal research evidence on the status of any of these items, I can only make on each of them a brief and what I hope is an informed guess. I see considerable social interaction, the beginnings of a social psychology—witness the common cues of FM radio, Hi-Fi, and Panda Prints—and as yet only the faintest stirrings in the realm of social institutions. The eventual outcome of this matter I leave to what should be, at the least, a very interesting future.

10

A System of Social Class Analysis

Social-class analysis represents an attempt to come to grips with the cumulative effect of basic economic factors in stratifying a modern industrial society. Economic factors, however, do not operate in a vacuum. They function within a particular political and community power context which they, in turn, condition. They are associated with particular occupational specializations. They have the effect through time of producing a status order, and this status order in turn plays a role in determining economic rewards in the current society. These economic factors, furthermore, make for different levels of consumption and correspondingly different "ways of life," or cultural attributes. The cumulation of these phenomena produces restrictions on intimate social contacts which lead to "group life" divisions in the society. All of these phenomena, set in motion basically by the operation of the economic system, in turn work back to some extent on the economic mechanism itself and affect its operation. The complex and innumerable interweavings of economic factors with politico-community power, with the status structure, with occupational pre-emption, with cultural attributes, and with group-life divisions constitute what may be called the social-class system.[1]

In the basic conceptual scheme which we favor, we emphasize the necessity for distinguishing among the separate

[1]This theoretical system obviously is based on the multi-dimensional approach to stratification which has its origins in the work of the German sociologist, Max Weber. See his essay "Class, Status, Party," *From Max Weber: Essays in Sociology*, trans. and ed. H. H. Gerth and C. Wright Mills (New York, Oxford University Press, 1946), pp. 180–95.

factors or variables listed above in order that their precise relationships, structural and dynamic, may be empirically discovered. That is, economic power, status-group participation, and politico-community power are closely enmeshed in the actual life of the society. The exact nature of their intercorrelation at any particular point in time we have called their *structural* relationships; the exact nature of their causal effects upon one another through time we have called their *dynamic* relationships. In order to obtain reasonably accurate information on both these types of relationship, the factors themselves must be conceptually distinguished, initially, and a continuum of each must be carefully constructed so that the interplay of the variables can be discovered. For instance, if we wish to study the interrelation of economic power with politico-community power, we must first set up categories to measure economic power, secondly set up adequate categories to measure politico-community power, and then discover by empirical investigation how persons who rank high (or low, etc.) on the first continuum function on the second continuum. Basic neglect of such conceptual distinctions and the consequent focusing of interest on only one dimension have constituted one of the major defects in American research into class. As Kornhauser has pointed out:

> The first requirement is that investigators concern themselves with clearer specification of the class variables and with the relationships among them and between them and the class characteristics stressed by other social students. Nothing useful is gained by pretending that a particular chosen simplification of class is the true account, rather than treating it as one interesting aspect that must be more penetratingly analyzed, coordinated, and integrated with other concepts. The variables are inseparable aspects of a functional social whole. It is fatuous to think that by singling out a favored class characteristic one thereby excludes the other bothersome variables. They are there even if kept tightly locked in the cellar.[2]

Nevertheless, in dealing with the dynamic relationships of class variables, the question must inevitably arise as to

[2]Arthur Kornhauser, "Public Opinion and Social Class," *American Journal of Sociology*, Vol. 55, No. 4 (January 1950), p. 339.

which of the variables are more basic in the causational scheme than others. That is, granted that all the variables interact with and influence each other once the causal mechanism has been set in motion, is there any one factor which stands out above the rest as being more basic or fundamental in its dynamic impact through time? When the problem is posed in this fashion, there can be little doubt that the economic power factor is the one which meets this qualification more successfully than any of the others. In modern capitalist, competitive society, it is quite obviously economic power which provides the means by which through successive generations particular consumption patterns may be enjoyed, occupational positions may be pre-empted, politico-community power may be appropriated, and status differences may be crystallized. There is thus considerable point to the insistence of those investigators who demand that economic factors be kept to the forefront in class analysis. One of the basic defects of those class researches which have focused on other factors such as, for instance, status-group participation, is that the role of economic power in producing position on the status dimension over several generations of social life has been substantially neglected. In the researches of W. Lloyd Warner and associates, for instance, we are given an informative picture of the "upper-upper" status group in Yankee City as of the time of the investigation. But the role of (presumably) high economic position operating through successive generations to produce occupational specialization and cultural differences and eventually the crystallization of highest status position is not systematically delineated. Thus, we do not discover explicitly how, and by means of what factors, the "upper-upper" status group developed.[3]

[3]W. Lloyd Warner and Paul S. Lunt, *The Social Life of a Modern Community*, Yankee City Series, Vol. I (New Haven, Yale University Press, 1941); W. Lloyd Warner and Paul S. Lunt, *The Status System of a Modern Community*, Yankee City Series, Vol. II (New Haven, Yale University Press, 1942); W. Lloyd Warner and Leo Strole, *The Social Systems of American Ethnic Groups*, Yankee City Series, Vol. III (New Haven, Yale University Press, 1945); W. Lloyd Warner and J. O. Low, *The Social System of a Modern Factory*, Yankee City Series, Vol. IV (New Haven, Yale University Press, 1947).

In general, the area of dynamic relationships among class factors is one which needs considerably more research. Such dynamic relationships themselves can be subdivided into two types, depending on the time period under consideration. One type deals with those discernible within the life span of one generation. Here, the basic question is how, in one individual's lifetime, economic position leads to status position, to position in the politico-community power structure, to cultural way of life, and to the restriction of social contacts. And, concomitantly, how does each of the factors other than economic power position further condition economic position in the successive years of the individual's life? For instance, if low status position and lack of culturally provided appropriate motivations and behavior, in themselves, exert an influence in keeping the individual in lower economic circumstances, then these factors, *as well as* the initial economic position must be reckoned with as playing a role in the cumulative set of interacting causes which maintain the individual at a low point on the economic continuum.[4] Or, if mobility in the economic sphere is accomplished, just how is this "converted," to use Benoit-Smullyan's term, into higher status position, or greater political power, etc.? The accumulation of information of this kind about an appropriate number of individuals in the society can then provide some quantitative as well as qualitative expression of the dynamic relationships among the various variables. To obtain information of this kind demands focusing of research on the life-span of a representative sample of given persons in the community. Further information about interrelationships which are demonstrated by incidents or related happenings occuring during the field work of the research would also be valuable. If the owner of the largest factory in the community, by virtue of his position as President of the School Board, succeeds in discharging the local "liberal" high-school civics teacher, or if the bank cuts off credit, without sound financial

[4]See Herbert H. Hyman, "The Value Systems of Different Classes: A Social Psychological Contribution to the Analysis of Stratification," and Genevieve Knupfer, "Portrait of the Underdog," *Class, Status and Power,* ed. Reinhard Bendix and Seymour Martin Lipset (Glencoe, Ill., Free Press, 1953).

243

reason, to the "nonconservative" newspaper, then dynamic interrelationships between economic power position and politico-community power position are being demonstrated.

Furthermore, as Gerhard Lenski and others have pointed out, the intercorrelation or convergence of stratification variables as they affect the social and psychological situation of a given individual or group presents itself as a fruitful area of analysis. Since an individual or group may rank high on one variable—say, economic power—and low on another—for instance, social status—certain strains and pressures towards marginality may come into being. Thus the study of *stratification inconsistency* as a dynamic variable, in itself, hypothetically affecting selected behavior variables, constitutes an important area of social class analysis.

In the second type of dynamic interrelationship among class factors, information over a period of several generations is called for. To what extent, over the span of successive generations, has economic power been hereditarily maintained? How, during this time, has economic power been converted into status position, into occupational appropriation, into political power, etc.? And how have all these factors interacted with each other to crystallize into the respective positions on respective hierarchies for the current generation of families in the community? In the admitted absence of careful historical data with this type of sociological orientation, such questions can be answered only partially, and perhaps fragmentarily. Nevertheless, they must be asked, and some attempt must be made to search for their answers if we are to have an adequate understanding of the dynamic relationships of class variables through time and of possible chronological changes in the nature of these relationships.

Stratification and Associated Variables

In studying the relationships of variables in class analysis to one another both dynamically and structurally, it is important to distinguish between *stratification* variables and *associated* variables. Stratification in a social order is a concept which refers to a vertical arrangement of persons—a hierarchy—a system of higher and lower, greater and lesser, superior and inferior. Basically, in human society, this stratification rests on one or the other of two categories: *power*[5]—a behavioral system in which some persons directly or indirectly manipulate the lives of other persons, or obtain greater rewards from the society by virtue of differential possession of economic goods or institutional authority—and *status*—by which we mean a psychological system of attitudes in which superiority and inferiority are reciprocally ascribed. Although power and status are obviously closely related, it is important to separate them conceptually, not only because they are intrinsically different categories, but because only in this way can the precise nature of their interrelationships be discovered.

The two basic types of community power structure in the contemporary Western World are the *economic* and the *political*, broadly conceived. The economic power structure deals with differences in income, wealth, the control of employment and its conditions, and the control of prices and credit. The political power structure refers to the formal governmental powers which reside in various positions in the local, state, and national governments, to the system of informal controls which may see these governmental powers manipulated by those who hold no formal office, and to the control of opinion-forming agencies in the community and nation such as the newspaper, the television network, the civic association, and the church. Status positions, conceived in terms of both communitywide and nationwide judgments of general status position, make up what may be termed the *social status* structure. Thus, the three fundamental stratification variables are economic power, political power, and social status.

[5]For some valuable theoretical discussions of power, see R. M. MacIver, *The Web of Government* (New York, Macmillan, 1947), especially chap. v; and Robert Bierstedt, "An Analysis of Social Power," *American Sociological Review*, Vol. 15, No. 6 (December 1950), pp. 730–38, and "The Problem of Authority," *Freedom and Control in Modern Society*, ed. Morroe Berger, Theodore Abel, and Charles H. Page (New York, Van Nostrand, 1954), pp. 67–81.

The role of occupational structure, which has so often been used as the basis for stratification, needs a special word here. In the historical development of modern capitalist society there is little doubt that functional occupational categories have been closely associated, indeed inextricably interwoven, with economic power. Nevertheless, empirical evidence is needed to delineate the exact relationships of occupational categories to the power and status hierarchies in American communities as of the present time. This raises questions, of course, as to the nature of each hierarchy. In correlating occupation with economic power, for instance, certainly more than just income averages for each occupational group for a given year must be included. Job security, sickness and retirement benefits, the rise or fall of earning power in middle and old age—all these and many more factors must be considered in the assessment. Once such heuristic assessments have been made, occupation may then be used as an index of the particular stratification hierarchy.

By *associated* variables we mean behavioral categories which are not, in themselves, hierarchical but which are produced by the operation of stratification variables, and which in turn contribute to the dynamics of stratification. The two principal types of associated variables are broad orders of behavior which we have called *group life* and *cultural attributes*. "Group life" refers to the social divisions produced by stratification. Here, the pertinent question is: To what extent are the social relationships, particularly the more intimate ones, of members of a particular section of a stratification continuum confined to other members of the same portion of the continuum? For example, to what extent do persons in the same portion of the economic (or status, etc.) hierarchy confine their clique and associational relationships to each other? This question is of more than structural importance, for to the extent that such confinement exists, the dynamics of economic and political life are presumably affected, and the negatively privileged on the stratification hierarchies are thus additionally handicapped. "Cultural attributes" refers to characteristic behavior, attitudes, and motivations. Here, the question is: To what extent do members of different economic (or status, etc.) aggregates or groups display consistently different behavior, attitudes, and motivations in the various areas of human existence? Again, to the extent that such cultural differences exist, there are important dynamic implications. Differentially privileged environments which inculcate different cultural patterns into their respective members presumably make it that much more difficult for those on the lower end of the stratification hierarchies to rise in the economic, social status, or political scales.

To pose the existence of the three stratification variables of economic power, political power, and social status is not, of course, to solve the problem of their adequate measurement. We turn, then, to a more intensive analysis of the nature of each variable or dimension and the possibility of deriving adequate measures of positions on each one.

Economic Power

Most studies in stratification have, explicitly or implicitly, used income as the decisive factor in indicating economic power. Other factors, however, have also received attention, including steadiness of employment, ownership of various types of property, access to credit, and degree of dominance-subordination in employment relations. Under optimum conditions of obtaining such information, undoubtedly a properly weighted index making use of all such factors would give the most accurate indication of degree of economic power. Several of these factors require particular discussion.

A three- or four- or five-year average of net income is more valuable than a given year return because it will average out fluctuations which may be due to temporarily operative factors. Moreover, age of respondent and the usual trend of income in the particular occupation through the life span must also be taken into account. It is somewhat doubtful whether a $4000 income earned by a young man just out of college and clerking in a securities office while "learning the business' prior to assuming a more responsible and lucrative position in the concern can be equated with a $4000 income for a factory worker who, at age 48, has reached his maximum wage and productivity. Some kind of an empirically derived correction factor should be applied to give a more realistic expression of the different meanings of such numerically equal incomes.

A number of items may be subsumed under the concept of "wealth." These are value of savings, value of insurance, value of ownership, partial or complete, in a business concern or professional practice (as, for instance, a doctor's practice), value of securities, both stocks and bonds, value of real estate, and value of personal property. The total value of all these items would constitute a person's wealth.

A third consideration is access to sources of credit. Information as to frequency of use of banks and personal loan companies for credit purposes, the amounts borrowed, whether loans were for business or personal purposes, and the general "credit risk" reputation of respondents could provide information for rating community residents on a scale indicating the degree of access to sources of credit.

A fourth factor may be called "employment control." This refers to the dominance-subordination factor in occupational relations and to control over the availability of jobs. The scale developed by Centers is useful here.[6] Five categories are distinguished: (a) employer, (b) manager, (c) independent, (d) tenant (as tenant farmer), and (e) employee (nonmanagerial). Employers and managers also differ individually in the degree of their power according to the number of employees and the number of job openings they control. An employer of fifty persons must be rated higher in the power hierarchy than one who employs only five persons. A scale may then be constructed to indicate the relative position of any individual on the "employment control" continuum.

A fifth factor that may be distinguished is the power over determining wages of employees and prices of goods in the

[6]Richard Centers, *The Psychology of Social Classes* (Princeton, N.J., Princeton University Press, 1949), pp. 50–52.

market. Here, the power of employers is augmented, or counterbalanced, by the power of labor unions. Both employers and labor union leaders in unionized industries play a role in determining the wage rates of the worker. Any rise in wage rates may be passed down to the consumer in the form of price increases. Thus both employers and labor union leaders wield "felt" economic power. The power of employers and managers in monopolistic or "oligopolistic" industries to fix prices in the virtual absence of competitive processes[7] is an especially important factor to assess in this dimension. Although such a scale of "wage and price control" would admittedly be difficult to construct, the factor is one which must be dealt with in any complete account of the economic power structure.

With regard to all these factors, economic power may obviously extend beyond a particular community, and in some cases will have regional or even national extension. Such extension increases the degree of economic power correspondingly.

These five factors of (a) income, (b) wealth, (c) credit access, (d) employment control, and (e) wage and price control have been distinguished as constituting the basic dimensions of economic power. In a heuristic attempt to combine these dimensions into an over-all rating of economic power, an eight- or ten- or twelve- (or any other number, depending on the degree of discrimination desired) point scale could be constructed for each dimension. Since income and wealth constitute the immediate personal crystallization of economic power, possibly these two dimensions should be given double weight. The total of scores, then, weighted and unweighted, on all the scales would give the person's total "economic power" score.

[7]See the *Temporary National Economic Committee Investigation of Concentration of Economic Power Final Report and Recommendations* (Washington, United States Government Printing Office, 1941). For a summary and analysis of the TNEC reports and findings, see David Lynch, *The Concentration of Economic Power* (New York, Columbia University Press, 1946).

Such a scale could be used in studies having either a local community or national "mass society" framework. The institutional and associational structures (for instance, corporations, employers' associations, and labor unions) through which such control was maintained and exercised would also constitute a focus of research in this area.

Political Power

Political power has been broadly conceived here as power to manipulate people through either the formal governing process or the control of opinion-forming agencies of the community and nation. Three dimensions may be distinguished: (a) the formal structure of government, (b) the system of informal controls and influences bearing on political offices and officers, and (c) the controls and influences affecting opinion-forming agencies such as newspapers, radio and television stations, schools, churches, and civic associations.

For the measurement of power in the formal governing structure, municipal offices may be divided (as was Warner's procedure in the Yankee City research) into "high control," "medium control," and "low control" positions, or into further refinements of power and control, if desired. Persons who hold state or national offices may be similarly categorized according to the relative degree of importance of their positions.

Measurement of the degree of power in the "system of informal controls" over political offices and political functioning would admittedly be difficult to make. In many communities, however, it is well known that certain private citizens, either as "political bosses" or as more remote but powerful controlling figures, manipulate the filling of many political offices and their functioning. Intensive investigation in a particular community should provide data for rating of such individuals in the scale of political power, along with those who possess lesser degrees of such power, or none at all. Special consideration given by the police force, the courts, the school boards, licensing boards, and other municipal agencies to persons of particular economic or status positions provides bases for rating such persons in terms of their indirect influence over the governmental structure. On the state and national level, the study of lobbyists and lobbying groups should prove fruitful in this connection.

Measurement of degree of control and influence over opinion-forming agencies in the community, region, or nation raises further difficulties, yet deserves attempt. Actual incidents occurring during the period of research or verified incidents occurring prior to the research demonstrating the power of individuals from particular parts of the economic and status hierarchies over schools, press, church, and civic associations, and influencing the viewpoint of these agencies on economic and political issues would provide bases for ratings.[8] The structural interrelationships of the economic and status hierarchies with these institutions could provide evidence of at least the possibilities of such control. For instance, if the wealthy department store owner is also the largest advertiser in the community's only newspaper, such structural relationships should at least be noted and investigation made of the editorial views of the newspaper in relation to the views of the advertiser. The economic and status positions of newspaper and radio and television station owners, school and college board members, and officers of civic associations such as chambers of commerce, "service" clubs, labor unions, etc., also demand attention as factors making influence and control possible. From the welter of such evidence, a rough scale may be devised on which degree of "public opinion control" could be indicated. Of course, the "possibility" of control does not necessarily indicate that such control is actually exercised. Nevertheless, if the structural relationships making such control possible exist, and if

[8]For a study of power relationships in a large American city of half a million population which relies heavily on interviews with a selected group of community leaders themselves, and which includes considerable anecdotal material to illustrate the exercise of community power, see Floyd Hunter, *Community Power Structure* (Chapel Hill, N.C., University of North Carolina Press, 1953).

decisions and pronouncements of the agencies specified are consistently phrased in the direction of the economic interests of those in control, the presumption that such control, direct or indirect, is being exercised may be high. Thus, the study of such decisions and pronouncements in relation to the range of opinion in the community and to the opinion of those in positions of control must constitute an important part of the investigation.

Sociometric techniques by which community members rated and chose each other with regard to hypothetical situations which called for the exercise of power and leadership constitute another possible method.[9]

The combination of the ratings of a person in each of the dimensions of political power—i.e., direct governmental control, indirect governmental control, and public-opinion control—would give the over-all rating of his place in the hierarchy of "political power." And, again, the study must include a delineation of the institutional and associational network which helps to make this control possible and which provides the setting for its exercise.

Social Status

The term "social status" refers to a psychological system of attitudes in which superiority and inferiority are reciprocally ascribed. Here we shall summarize briefly and present certain basic distinctions and hypotheses which appear justified by the available evidence and discussion.

In the realm of types of status judgments, a fourfold analytical distinction is minimally necessary: (a) As Kingsley Davis points out, a given person may be evaluated with regard to some specific "postion" which he holds in a social structure—for instance, assistant manager of the First National Bank, president of the community Parent-Teachers Association, or professor. We may call this type of received

---

[9]See *Community Power Structure.*

evaluation *specific status*.[10] (b) He may be evaluated with respect to the way in which he carries out the duties of this position, that is, performs his role. This is what Davis refers to as *esteem*. (c) He may be evaluated in terms of certain personal qualities apart from any particular role performance; he may be generally regarded, for example, as a reliable, industrious man who does not drink and goes to church regularly, or he may have a charismatic personality, or be regarded as highly personable and pleasant in social relationships. We may refer to this as his *repute*. All of these are, in Goldhamer and Shils's term, "segmental status judgments." There is considerable reason to believe that all of these are combined into a "total status judgment" (Goldhamer and Shils's phrase) which constitutes a person's *general social status*.[11] Thus, a person's "general social status" is made up of a combination of all his "specific statuses," all his "esteems," and all his "reputes." It is probable that the specific statuses bulk larger in the total evaluation than the other categories, and that among these specific statuses those pertaining to the occupational-economic complex are given greatest weight.

We may also distinguish between *locally transferable status*, which is the form of general social status existing on the local community level and transferable from one community to another, and *national status*, which attaches to figures of national reputation and renown.

In modern Western societies which have no institutionally defined caste or estate lines it is theoretically conceivable, though not probable, that the standards of status attribution would be so diverse and uncorrelated that no consistent

[10]We prefer this term to Davis's term "prestige," which is too closely identified in the literature with status as a general concept.

[11]In these distinctions we have relied heavily on the work of Kingsley Davis and Herbert Goldhamer and Edward Shils. See Kingsley Davis, "A Conceptual Analysis of Stratification," *American Sociological Review*, Vol. 7, No. 3 (June 1942), pp. 309–21; and Herbert Goldhamer and Edward A. Shils, "Types of Power and Status," *American Journal of Sociology*, Vol. 45, No. 2 (September 1939), pp. 171–82. The concept of "repute," however, is our own and appears necessary for identification of a type of status judgment which overlaps "esteem" but is not coincidental with it.

hierarchical structure would be discernible. Thus a situation of *status conflict* could emerge where no social status claims were consistently honored. This is a polar concept in contrast to its opposite, a system of complete and consistent *status hierarchy*, where all status claims were made and evaluated according to a value-system well understood and uniformly accepted by everyone in the society. Such evidence as is available does not indicate that contemporary American society represents either polar type completely but that, while some status conflict exists, the society is closer to the status-hierarchy type—that general social status distinctions, while informally rather than officially maintained, and often obliquely rather than directly expressed, are based on a complex of evaluations which, though varying in detail from person to person and group to group, has a certain rough similarity over the nation and social structure as a whole. Much further research is needed, however, in the area of evocation of the status judgments of residents of American communities, and the research instruments need considerable sharpening in order to break through the barriers of ego-defense and cultural expectation and to separate oblique status attribution from the culturally permissive hostility which may frequently accompany it.

The status dimension, even if hierarchical, may be conceptualized on the one hand, as a *continuum* along which there are no "breaks" which set off status groups, but only individual status positions. MacIver's term *competitive class feeling* is appropriate for the psychological attitudes which would accompany such a status order. At the other conceptual extreme is a status arrangement where groups are sharply delineated on the status dimension, and where these groups face each other with a maximum of group identification and, in some cases, clearly articulated hostility and predisposition to conflict. MacIver has called this type of status attitude *corporate class consciousness*. In an intermediate type, groups on the status dimension exist in only semi-crystallized form with somewhat indistinct and highly permeable boundaries, feelings of status-group identification are general and diffuse, hostility is low, and vocalized articulations or admissions of the status order and one's position in it are oblique and somewhat reluctantly offered. We have called the characteristic type of status feeling here *generalized class awareness*.

There is little evidence to support the hypothesis that corporate class consciousness exists in any significant degree on the American scene. The evidence on the question of the relevance of the status continuum theory versus the hypothesis that semi-crystallized groupings and generalized class awareness characterize American society is conflicting. However, it seems unlikely, in view of the generally known human tendency to categorize large arrays of ordered data, that some categorization of the status order is not performed by most Americans. If, as we have hypothesized, this categorization is based on value standards which have some rough similarity throughout the culture, then the hypothesis of generalized class awareness would give a closer fit to the American status order than the concept of an undivided status continuum. Such categorization would not preclude the existence of a further internal status rating within these broad categories on the part of some community residents—a distinction which needs to be faced in community status research.

In general, it would appear that research information on the American status order and the status feelings of residents of American communities is at present of a highly preliminary and tentative nature. We are convinced that it will remain so until there is adequate recognition of the fact that the subject of social status, because of the strong feelings of ego-involvement evoked in such invidious distinctions and the presence of cultural expectations which predispose to offering verbalizations which minimize status distinctions, is one in which routine answers given to strangers in routine interviewing situations cannot be unhesitatingly accepted at face value. As we have indicated earlier, it is not patent that there is any immediately foreseeable, practicable, and complete solution to this problem. It may be not only graceful but scientifically appropriate for sociologists to concede that there may be some information which respondents could conceivably communicate to them if they were willing, but which, on a statistically valid basis, they will not. However, before such a counsel of despair is taken seriously in this instance, it would be wise to attempt a more intensive and sophisticated attack on the question of the status attitudes of the American population with the aid of depth interviews, open-ended questions with considerable probing, suitably designed projective tests, greater rapport conditions, and a general wariness of possible discrepancies between what is said and what is actually felt.

SOCIAL CLASSES

We have now outlined the nature of the three basic stratification variables—economic power, political power, and social status—the need for studying both the structural and dynamic interrelationships of these variables with each other, and the need for studying the structural and dynamic relationships of each of these variables with two associated variables which we have called group life and cultural attributes. So far we have been concerned with the nature of the analytical and research task. From the expository point of view, there remains the question of how to apply the term "social class," over which there has been such lack of consensus. As we have seen, for the sake of conceptual clarity the term must be applied precisely to one of the stratification variables. In terms of the overwhelming dynamic importance of the economic power factor, the term could with considerable cogency be applied to groups formed along the economic power continuum at arbitrarily selected points. Nevertheless, there seems to be at least equal and, in some ways, greater value in applying the term to the social-status levels of a society, and this, in fact, is our proposal. This equation of the social-status structure with "social classes" rests, conceptually, on the nature of the term "social" itself, which is concerned with affective human relationships, on the peculiar focus of the sociologist, and on a hypothesis as to which stratification dimension is most closely related to the repulsions and attractions which divide and integrate social relationships—that is, the factor of "group life." In the words of MacIver and Page, "Sociology alone studies social relationships themselves, society itself . . . As sociologists we are interested . . . in social relationships not because they are economic or political or religious but because they are at the same time *social*."[12]

Our hypothesis, based on the incomplete and by no means entirely consistent evidence available thus far is that, of the three basic stratification dimensions, it is the social status structure rather than the economic or political power dimensions which plays the largest immediate role in producing those social divisions, shifting and amorphous as they may be, of American communities which center around intimate friendships, clique life, association membership and participation, and intermarriage.

It should be noted that this has not been demonstrated in rigorous experimental fashion, which would necessitate correlation of each stratification hierarchy separately with social separation. Nevertheless, in the substantial demonstrated correlations of the social-status structure with social separation, in the qualitative remarks of community informants, and in case history material, there is a suggestive accumulation of evidence to support the hypothesis that it is the social-status structure which would most effectively divide the community into social layers. In any sense in which social integration is a desired component of "social class," it would appear that the term is most aptly applied to the social status levels of the community. However, the role of economic power factors operating through time in conjunction with the other factors to produce the crystallizing of the status structure should be kept to the fore at all times.

---

[12]R. M. MacIver and Charles H. Page, *Society: An Introductory Analysis* (New York, Rinehart, 1949), p. v.

For the purpose of achieving a consistent terminology, then, we propose that the term *social classes* be applied to the major status divisions which stratify a community, the term *economic classes* be used to designate segments of the economic power continuum (however divided), the term *political classes* be used to designate segments of the politico-community power continuum, and the term *occupational classes* be applied to groups in an occupational classification where the classification has been validated against a specified stratification variable.

It is clear from the available evidence that, structurally speaking, the social status, or social class structure, of American communities is closely associated with the economic-power structure and the political-power structure. The relationship is a positive and substantial one, although the correlation is by no means perfect and must be discovered empirically in each community or national sample studied. On the whole, however, the higher the level of social status, the more economic power will be found and the greater power to manipulate community affairs through direct or indirect political control, or dominance of the community's institutional functioning and the channels of communication. Occupational complexes also tend to be associated with particular social classes, with the proprietors and executives of the larger businesses, certain of the wealthier professionals, and large landowners being characteristic of the highest classes, and semiskilled and unskilled laborers characteristic of the lower classes. The intermediate range, however, shows considerable occupational variation, and the correlation is in no sense a perfect one. In the dynamic interplay of all the stratification variables, the economic and occupational factors undoubtedly play the most significant role. A tendency toward the restriction of "group life" to one's own portion of the status hierarchy and the association of status levels with numerous differential cultural attributes (with some overlapping in both cases) have also been substantially demonstrated.

Limited procedure for smaller studies. Basic stratification procedures for any one of the three stratification variables constitute an extensive task, requiring a considerable amount of field work. In many types of stratification researches which do not purport to be full-scale community studies, the goal will be simply to correlate position in a stratified sample of persons or families with some specific attitude or behavior pattern (as, for instance, political attitudes or birth rates). For this type of study, where "basic" stratification of the community is impossible from the point of view of time and resources, *limited* items in the particular stratification hierarchy must be used for stratifying the sample. Income, or rent, or home valuation, for instance, may be used as a limited indicator of position in the economic-power hierarchy (with the necessary limitations specified). An occupational scale, previously validated against one of the stratification hierarchies, lends itself to use in such studies. Or a multi-factor index of social status, properly constructed and validated against some actual "basic" social-status stratification procedure, may be used. In all such cases, the particular stratification hierarchy of which the instrument is an index should be rigorously specified, and the necessary imperfections of the stratification procedure admitted.

THE RELATIONSHIP OF ETHNIC TO CLASS STRATIFICATION

The relationship of ethnic group stratification to social class stratification is a difficult problem for both conceptualization and empirical study. American society is criss-crossed by two sets of stratification structures, one based on social status, economic power, and political power differences, regardless of ethnic background, the other a set of status and power relationships based precisely on division of the population by racial, nationality background, and religious categories into "Old Americans," Negroes, Jews, Catholics, Japanese-Americans, Italians, French-Canadians, etc. The two systems must be kept conceptually separate, for otherwise the nature of their interrelationships cannot be discovered. Operationally, the problem has been handled in class research, thus far, largely by analyzing the class system of the Negro group separately, and including members of other ethnic groups in the general American class system. Actually, however, the nature of the relationship of Negroes to the American class system differs only in degree, rather than in kind, from the relation of other ethnic groups to this system. From the point of view of economic power, political power, and occupational classification, there is no special analytical problem since these are objective manifestations which can be measured without regard to the ethnic factor. However, from the point of view of social classes as status levels with tendencies toward social closure and differential cultural attributes, there are three important questions:

1. In the reciprocal status attitudes of members of American communities, how are the status factor and the ethnic factor operationally related? That is, how does A, member of the Old American group and the "upper-lower" class, articulate his status attitude toward B, a member of the Jewish (or Italian or French-Canadian, etc.) ethnic group who has "upper-middle" class status? In the social class configuration of status and power A is outranked by B, but in terms of majority community attitudes he outranks the latter in ethnic group position. Reciprocally, the question reads: How does B articulate his status feelings toward A? Does one set of status feelings (either ethnic or class) dominate the other? Are they mutually maintained without tension?[13] In a specific behavior situation, would deference behavior follow the class or the ethnic status structure? Research evidence on this set of questions is largely nonexistent, with the exception of some data on Negro-white relations in the South, where the "caste etiquette" enforced by the power system introduced a complicating factor for many years.

2. To what extent is the intimate group life of members of the same social class or status level divided by the ethnic

[13]See Everett Cherrington Hughes, "Dilemmas and Contradictions of Status," *American Journal of Sociology*, Vol. 50, No. 5 (March 1945), pp. 353–59, for a theoretical discussion of this question.

factor? Although the evidence suggests that family, clique, associational, and general intimate social relationships tend to be confined to members of one's own or closely adjoining class, does the ethnic factor further subdivide the social class into subgroups which maintain their own clique and associational relations, and confine marriage to the ethnic subgroup? How do social class and ethnic factors affect the structure of relationships across ethnic and class lines? Do upper-middle-class Jews, for instance, have more intimate social contacts with upper-middle-class Gentiles or with lower-middle-class Jews? Do upper-class Catholics have more intimate social contacts with middle-class Catholics or with upper-class Protestants? Again, the most conclusive evidence on questions of this nature has been gathered in research into the social life of American Negroes. Certainly in the South, and to a substantial extent in the North, the intimate social contacts of Negroes are confined to the Negro group, so that the class structure of the Negro community is a social order of its own (with somewhat differently placed dividing lines from the white class structure) within the Negro social system. Only to the extent that interracial contacts of a social nature increase will this picture be changed. With regard to other ethnic groups, the few studies that touch on this point indicate that the ethnic factor plays a large role in restricting intimate social relationships not only to members of one's own status level or social class, but to members of one's own ethnic group.[14] Only further research can determine the quantitative extent of this restrictive influence, and its variation for different ethnic groups. Pending such further research, it may be hypothetically advanced that a given social class or status

[14]See August B. Hollingshead, "Trends in Social Stratification: A Case Study," *American Sociological Review*, Vol. 17, No. 6 (December 1952), pp. 679–86; E. Digby Baltzell, *Philadelphia Gentlemen: The Making of a National Upper Class* (Glencoe, Ill., Free Press, 1958); Elin L. Anderson, *We Americans* (Cambridge, Harvard University Press, 1938); and Mhyra S. Minnis, "Cleavage in Women's Organizations: A Reflection of the Social Structure of A City," *American Sociological Review*, Vol. 18, No. 1 (February 1953), pp. 47–53.

level, considered with a view to its internal structure of social relationships, is subdivided into a series of subgroups determined by the ethnic factor.

3. To what extent does the ethnic factor modify the tendency towards a similarity of cultural attributes in members of the same social class? Presumptively, the effect of the social transmission of areas of behavior related to the particular segregation and discrimination experiences and the nationality background and religious heritage of the ethnic group will modify the relative cultural homogeneity of social classes. Actually, such research evidence as exists indicates that the behavioral similarities of social class are more pronounced than those of ethnic group.[15] Nevertheless, this is a problem of quantitative expression and requires much further research.

The Concept of the Subculture

To the extent that ethnic factors in combination with social-class factors tend to delimit the area of intimate social contact in the adult world, and concomitantly provide the particular setting for the socialization of the child, it may be usefully hypothesized that American society consists of a series of informally and unrigorously bounded smaller societal units with varying degrees of interrelationship, each with its own variation and version of the American culture pattern. It is suggested that in this perception lies a conceptual tool which constitutes a useful dimension of sociological analysis.[16] The division of American society into ethnic group systems has been variously recognized in sociological writings; the division into social-class systems has been suggested in many of the researches in class considered in this survey. If one adds the "area" divisional factors of urban or rural residence and

[15]See, particularly, Allison Davis and Robert J. Havighurst, "Social Class and Color Differences in Child Rearing," *American Sociological Review*, Vol. 11, (December 1946), pp. 698–710.

[16]Compare with August B. Hollingshead, "Trends in Social Stratification: A Case Study."

regional residence (Northeastern United States, South, Midwest, etc.), one has the four major factors or life-conditions (the latter two, perhaps, of less operational significance) which determine, *in combination*, the sociological setting in which the child is socialized, and either remains in or leaves in later life. To the social world made up of the combination of these four factors, this writer has applied the term *subculture*.[17] The concept of the subculture is offered here to refer to a subdivision of a national culture composed of a combination of the four social situations of class status, ethnic background, rural or urban residence, and regional residence, *each analytically distinguishable but forming in their combination a functioning unity which has an integrated impact on the participating individual*. It is a social system which contains the sex divisions and allows for the unfolding of the lifecycle of the individual within its own social borders.[18] Those individuals who change their class status, attempt to change ethnic affiliation, or make decisive moves from one type of residential situation to another, are, in terms of this theory, marginal until they have consolidated their position in the new subculture. This conceptual scheme has implications for personality theory as well, since, in addition to internalizing those aspects of behavior common to the national culture, presumably the individual internalizes the

[17]Milton M. Gordon, "Social Structure and Goals in Group Relations," *Freedom and Control in Modern Society*, pp. 141–57, and "The Concept of the Sub-Culture and Its Application," *Social Forces*, Vol. 26, No. 1 (October 1947), pp. 40–42. The term is used elliptically, here, to refer to both the subgroup of the national society and the particular cultural patterns which it carries. For stricter conceptional clarity one might refer to the "subsociety" and its "subculture."

[18]The term "subculture" has had increasing use in the sociological literature to refer to the cultural patterns of any subgroup or type of subgroup which has some persistence through time, such as a gang, a neighborhood, a factory, an age-group, etc. For an excellent study based on this use of the term, see Albert K. Cohen, *Delinquent Boys* (Glencoe, Ill., Free Press, 1955). We prefer to reserve its use, however, for the patterns of a subsociety which parallels the main society in that it extends through the entire life-cycle of the individual.

behavior patterns characteristic of the particular subculture in which he was socialized.[19] While this is not the place for a full development of the concept of the subculture, it may be pointed out that attention has been called in two widely different subfields of sociology, race relations and social pathology, to the need for analysis of these phenomena within the framework of the actual outlines and divisions of American social structure.[20] In the meeting of this need, the concept of the "subculture," which has received partial verification in some of the class materials surveyed earlier, may prove of value.

We have attempted here to analyze, classify, and systematize research and theory in social stratification in the modern period of American sociology. The cutting edge of our analysis has been the principle that social status, economic power, and politico-community power structures must be seen as conceptually distinct entities, whose dynamic and structural interrelationships must be studied empirically. Specific analysis has been made of the nature of each hierarchy or structure. On the basis of research evidence bearing on its existence and nature, and certain theoretical considerations, the social-status structure has been selected as the logical bearer of the term "social classes." Economic and occupational factors operating through time have been adduced as the primary causal determinants of the status order. The empirically determined relationships of these social-status levels, or social classes, to the other stratification structures of economic power and politico-community power, to occupational categories, to group life, to cultural attributes, and to the structure of ethnic group relations constitute

[19]See Mirra Komarovsky and S. Stansfeld Sargent, "Research into Subcultural Influences upon Personality," Culture and Personality, ed. S. Stansfeld Sargent and Marian W. Smith (New York, Viking Fund, 1949).
[20]E. Franklin Frazier, "Race Contacts and the Social Structure," American Sociological Review, Vol. 14, No. 1 (February 1949), pp. 1–11; and C. Wright Mills, "The Professional Ideology of Social Pathologists," American Journal of Sociology, Vol. 49, No. 2 (September 1943), pp. 165–80. See also, Milton M. Gordon, "Social Structure and Goals in Group Relations."

the full outlines of the social class system. An accumulated body of research has begun to provide some of the details of these relationships. Considerable further research is needed in this area. Conceptual clarification, however, is a necessary prerequisite to the production and systematic advance of knowledge in any field of social investigation. It is hoped that this essay will aid in this task of clarification and will constitute a contribution to the formulation of systematically related researches which will provide increasing understanding of the structure and dynamics of American social life.

Marginality part V

11

A Qualification of the Marginal Man Theory

This paper suggests a qualification of the theory of the "marginal man" as conceived by Park[1] and elaborated by Stonequist.[2] The concept around which this qualification is oriented is that of the "marginal culture." Anthropologists have sometimes used this term to refer to a distant or border culture, but it will be used in this discussion as a nongeographical equivalent of the anthropological concept of "marginal area." The "marginal area" is conceived as a region where two cultures overlap and where the occupying group partakes of the traits of both cultures. The essence of our qualification is contained in the following statement by Goldenweiser: "Psychologically, the marginal area is but a type of culture area, for its cultural content is as much of a unit and has the same value to its human carriers as the content of a full-fledged culture area."[3] Stonequist, in considering this statement, disposes of it all too briefly with the remark that "Such marginal areas may or may not involve cultural conflict. When they do, we may also expect to find marginal men."[4] His only other reference to the concept is an indirect one to the effect that "Again, the intermediate group—say of

---

[1]R. E. Park, "Human Migration and the Marginal Man," *American Journal of Sociology* (May 1928), pp. 881–93.
[2]Everett V. Stonequist, "The Problem of the Marginal Man," *American Journal of Sociology* (July 1935), pp. 1–12. *The Marginal Man* (New York, Scribners, 1937).
[3]A. Goldenweiser, "Cultural Anthropology," in *History and Prospects of the Social Sciences*, ed. H. E. Barnes (New York, Knopf, 1925), p. 245.
[4]*The Marginal Man*, p. 213.

mixed-bloods—may be large enough to afford a moderately satisfying life."[5]

Here we may review briefly the Park and Stonequist exposition of the theory of the marginal man. When an individual shaped and moulded by one culture is brought by migration, education, marriage, or other influence into permanent contact with a culture of a different content, or when an individual from birth is initiated into two or more historic traditions, languages, political loyalties, moral codes, or religions, then he is likely to find himself on the margin of each culture, but a member of neither. Thus Park speaks of

> ... a cultural hybrid, a man living and sharing intimately in the cultural life and traditions of two distinct peoples; never quite willing to break, even if he were permitted to do so, with his past and his traditions, and not quite accepted, because of racial prejudice, in the new society in which he now sought to find a place. He was a man on the margin of two cultures and two societies which never completely interpenetrated and fused.[6]

And Stonequist defines the marginal man as one who is

> ... poised in psychological uncertainty between two (or more) social worlds; reflecting in his soul the discords and harmonies, repulsions and attractions of these worlds, one of which is often "dominant" over the other; within which membership is implicitly if not explicitly based upon birth or ancestry (race or nationality); and where exclusion removes the individual from a system of group relations.[7]

The marginal man, it is pointed out, may be a racial (and cultural) hybrid, i.e., he may be a person of mixed racial ancestry, or he may be racially pure (relatively speaking) and yet participant in two cultures. In either case he is a "marginal" individual possessed of characteristic feelings and attitudes of insecurity, ambivalence, excessive self-consciousness, and chronic nervous strain.

---

[5]"The Problem of the Marginal Man," p. 11.
[6]"Human Migration and the Marginal Man," p. 892.
[7]*The Marginal Man*, p. 8.

The qualification of this theory here suggested may be stated as follows. If (1) the so-called "marginal" individual is conditioned to his existence on the borders of two cultures from birth, if (2) he shares this existence and conditioning process with a large number of individuals in his primary groups, if (3) his years of early growth, maturation, and even adulthood find him participating in institutional activities manned largely by other "marginal" individuals like himself, and finally, if (4) his marginal position results in no major blockages or frustrations of his learned expectations and desires, then he is not a true "marginal" individual in the defined sense, but a participant member of a *marginal culture*, every bit as real and complete to him as is the nonmarginal culture to the nonmarginal man. This transposes Goldenweiser's remarks about the "unity" and "value" of the marginal culture *area* to a nongeographically based situation, for, beyond the family and the early play group, the concept of the marginal culture does not depend on geographical but rather on institutional and associational proximity.

The presentation of the first three conditions postulated as prerequisite for the realization of the revised marginal man concept is based on a functional analysis of culture. The function of a culture is to provide the individual with norms, standardized behavior patterns, or in Thomas' phraseology, definitions of his situation. Although the marginal individual, then, may be aware of the immediate existence of one or more cultures other than his own to which he will be forced to react, if his own reaction patterns to these cultures are provided or defined by his own group, if he is not forced to *define the situation by himself*, and moreover, if these definitions have been instilled in him from birth onward so that he knows no others, then he is likely to be a stable and normal person participating in an integrated manner in the activities of a unitary culture. A point somewhat of this nature was made by Kurt Lewin, in an article dealing with the subject of the imposition of culture patterns on Jewish children:

> In judging the importance of experiences related to our belonging to, or our status in, a social group, or related to any other

constituents of the ground on which we stand, one should not give much weight to the frequency or the unpleasantness of those experiences themselves. Instead, one should consider the meaning of those experiences in terms of how much the structure of the life-space of the individual is changed. . . . It is of first importance that a stable social ground be laid very early. . . . The variety of social structures to which a growing child can adapt himself in a relatively stable way is astonishingly great. It seems, however, extremely difficult to establish a new stable social ground after one has broken down.[8]

It is evident then that the concept of the marginal culture does not apply very well to the typical immigrant, even when he proceeds immediately to a ghetto and there finds solace and comfort among his compatriots. For the norms and behavior patterns which he has absorbed and made a part of himself over a long period of years are inadequate to meet the new situation, and although the ghetto group hastily devises new definitions, these are impositions on a mature personality and can never erase the old perspective, and thus the immigrant usually remains for the rest of his life a marginal man.

The fourth prerequisite, namely, that of nonfrustration of acquired expectations and desires, is based on observation of the fact that a subordinate or marginal culture may give the individual definitions of his situation which are inadequate—inadequate in the sense that they conflict or are in contrast with definitions provided him by the other culture or cultures in which he is participating. Thus the northern reasonably well-educated Negro was traditionally conditioned by his own Negro culture to a realization of his position as a member of a subordinate caste, but formally in the schools, and informally in the wider white culture around him, he was taught to value highly the concepts of human equality, democracy, and freedom. Thus, the definitions of his situation made by the primary Negro culture were rejected, although the wishes generated by his contact with the

[8]Kurt Lewin, "Bringing up the Child," *The Menorah Journal* (January-March 1940), pp. 35–36.

dominant culture remained unsatisfied, and thus, in many instances, he became insecure and emotionally unstable, a typical marginal man.

One of the best illustrations of a true marginal culture—a situation which meets all the conditions referred to above—is the second or third generation Jewish immigrants residing in the United States, the sons, or grandsons of Jews who have come to America from European lands. The author of this paper, as a result of observation of the activities of members of this group and participation in them, is convinced that, although Stonequist's statement that "The Jew is likely to be a marginal man," and his reference to the Jew as "the classic illustration of this problem [of the marginal man]" may be historically valid, a valuable sociological focus on the situation of the Jew in America will be ignored if an analysis is not made in terms of the marginal culture concept. Stonequist makes use of many case-histories of Jews in illustrating his theory of the marginal man, but most of these are case-histories of a selected nonmodal group, fairly high on the distribution curves of intelligence and sensitivity. Moreover, it is not necessary to prove that the marginal culture concept is applicable to all second-generation Jews in the United States, or even to a majority (a real possibility, however) in order to substantiate our thesis; it is sufficient to show that it is valid with regard to a definitely significant portion of the Jewish population.

The marginal culture of the second-generation Jew is a mixture of the cultural elements of immigrant Judaism provided by his family situation and of the elements contained in the wider Gentile culture in which he must function. A paragraph by Konrad Bercovici in the *Nation* some years ago describes certain aspects of the situation in New York City. His statement although perhaps not an objective or fair one, at least shows a keen awareness of the phenomenon:

> There is now a generation of Bronx Jews, quite distinct from the East Side Jew. It's the second-generation Jew with all the outward characteristics minus beard and mustache, playing

baseball, great fight fans, commercial travelers, clean-shirted, white-collared, derby-hatted, creased-trousered. The women are stylish and stout, white-skinned, long-nosed, bediamoned; social workers, actresses, stumpspeakers, jazz dancers, with none of the color and the virtues of their erstwhile bearded, bewigged parents, and a few vices of their own acquisition. But they bathe frequently.[9]

The validity of the marginal culture concept is, of course, most obvious with regard to the Jewish populations of the large metropolises such as New York, Chicago, and Boston. Moreover, within the metropolitan situation, because of the large numbers involved and the wide range of statuses to be found, it is even possible to distinguish the existence of sub-cultures within the greater marginal culture (but not "sub-marginal cultures," please!), based on social and economic position. However, it may be pointed out that in spite of the heavy urban concentration of the Jewish population, all Jews do not live in metropolitan areas. This is quite true and we must therefore take account of the situation as it exists in the medium-sized city. The author, from observing and participating in Jewish activities in three medium-sized New England cities, will now outline briefly the life history of a modal native-born Jew residing in such a community.

X was born in Urbana, population 100,000. His parents (or possibly merely his grandparents who reside with the family) came to the United States some years ago from a country in Eastern Europe. His father now owns a clothing store in the city's business section and has a moderate but comfortable income. There are possibly 1200 Jewish families in Urbana.

X's family lives in one of the better residential sections of Urbana. It is not a predominantly Jewish section (there are no *predominantly* Jewish residential areas in Urbana), but there are many Jewish neighbors interspersed among the Gentiles. His early play group probably contains a few Gentile children, but also many native-born Jewish children like himself. In his home, he rarely encounters a Gentile except for a brief moment

[9]Konrad Bercovici, "The Greatest Jewish City in the World," *Nation* (September 12, 1923), p. 261.

on a symbiotic level (the insurance man, the ice-man, the grocer's delivery boy, etc.). When he begins school he finds himself in the company of a large number of Gentile children, but other institutional activities will now begin to make his more intimate playgroup a closed affair. He will probably begin the study of Hebrew at a local Hebrew school and will go there after the public school session is over in the company of other Jewish children. His parents may also urge and encourage his association with members of his own "race." At this time, any former Gentile companions whom he might have had will begin to feel slightly uncomfortable when they follow him into the Jewish group, and, in complementary fashion, he will find himself ill at ease when alone in the Gentile group. Thus, by a gradual and unconscious process of mutual consent, the two groups are defined and from this time on X functions as a member of a Jewish playgroup.

As he grows older, X will play pingpong and basketball at the Urbana Young Men's Hebrew Association building or at the Jewish Community Center. If there are none of these in Urbana, there will be a Jewish club for young adolescents with club-rooms and gymnasium facilities. His regular attendance at the Synagogue will also begin now. At this time, he may be conscious of the existence of two cultures in his life-situation, the Jewish immigrant culture of his home and the Gentile culture of the outside world. He may even be somewhat ashamed of certain aspects of the former culture, as, for instance, the fact that his mother speaks broken English, but this feeling of shame arises only when he sees it brought to the attention of a Gentile. His Jewish friends, he knows, are more or less in the same situation, and they may freely observe the functioning of non-Gentile behavior patterns in his home without causing him any embarrassment. Vaguely, he realizes that his is not a purely personal problem but one that he shares with other members of his group.

In the high school, X may find a Jewish fraternity or club which he will join, or he may simply advance to the young men's branch of the Y.M.H.A., or Center, activities. Any of these organizations will now direct his newly awakened interest in the opposite sex along lines considered appropriate by the Jewish community. This means dating with Jewish girls[10] only.

[10]The growth and maturation of the Jewish girl follows the same general pattern.

Most of the girls he already knows, and together with the other members of his male group, he readily follows along the indicated path. If he ever dates a Gentile girl, later on in his school days, he does so usually alone, and may find it an unsatisfactory experience for it never becomes integrated into his group activity; he finds that he cannot share the experience with other members of the group except possibly as he relates it as an exploit. This is not to say that he has no contact with Gentiles, male and female, in school. Obviously he does, and he may even become prominent in, or participate in, the broad activities of the school, athletic or otherwise, thus mingling freely with the members of the non-Jewish group. These relationships, although usually friendly, are never intimate ones, and at all times his integrated group background is recognized by the Gentiles, and he, in turn, views his broader activities with his group focus.

If X goes to college, he finds the high school patterns present merely in more rigid form. He will join a Jewish fraternity, and either date only Jewish co-eds or invite to the college dances Jewish girls from Urbana. He will by this time have encountered aspects of anti-Semitic behavior, but his secure position in an integrated group, the other members of which he knows have encountered the same phenomenon, prevent him from viewing the matter as a peculiarly personal problem. Moreover, he will have participated in various discussions and bull-sessions with his Jewish intimates on the problem of anti-Semitism and thus has a general conception of the group definition of the situation and the accepted methods of response. Also, it must be remembered that anti-Semitism has as yet caused him little inconvenience. His major needs have found readily available institutional mechanisms for fulfillment, and even his desire for extragroup response is reasonably well met since his Jewish group has, both in high school and in college, been accorded full recognition and has been allowed to participate in all the activities of the school. Thus, although the definitions handed down to him by his Jewish group do not square precisely with the definitions provided him by the broader Gentile culture (the ideals of equality, democracy, etc.), the difference is not so great that X will not be able to make a satisfactory adjustment. Of course, if he encounters severe difficulty in entering a professional school or in securing a job because of the fact that he is a Jew, then he may begin to question the Jewish definitions, but even should he meet with such an experience, he still may be able to make an adjustment by securing work in a Jewish firm or through Jewish connections.

Upon graduation, then, X marries a Jewish girl and comes back to take up a business career, or practice a profession, and make his home in Urbana. There he is now recognized as an adult member of the Jewish community and continues to function as a member of the group. He will join the adult section of the Center and contribute to its upkeep. His wife will become a member of the Ladies Auxiliary to the Center and will help in selling tickets for the annual bazaar. If she has any dramatic ability, she may coach the Jewish Community Center Theater Group in putting on a play by Clifford Odets. There will be a Winter formal and a Spring dinner party at Urbana's leading hotel at which all Urbana Jewry, including X and his wife, will turn out. All the intimate friends of the young couple will be other Jews of their own age and status. The pattern is now fixed. For the rest of his life, X, as he always has been, will be a member of a geographically dispersed, but thoroughly integrated group which is well equipped to take care of his major social needs.

This theoretical case history prepared by the author is believed to be a fairly typical one. Meeting the four requirements suggested earlier, i.e., early indoctrination and habituation as to status, intimate sharing of status with members of primary groups, participation in major institutional activities provided, ordered, and arranged by individuals of like status, and reasonable satisfaction of learned wishes and desires, it indicates the existence of a complete and unitary culture poised between two other cultures, and for that reason described as marginal. For the individual concerned, however, we must remember that it is not marginal but normal. He knows nothing else. It defines his relationship with the older immigrant group and with the wider Gentile culture. Within the confines of his own group, the native-born Jew is completely at home and at ease and it is here that he carries on the major part of his activities.

The sociological significance of the marginal culture, with special reference to the Jew, may be stated as follows. On the one hand, it allows him a normal form of participation in group activities, an opportunity for the expression of his own cultural interests, and, finally, a sense of security which the marginal individual who calls no culture his own ever has. On the other hand, in so far as the Jewish marginal culture produces a "type" individual definitely distinguishable from the members of the dominant Gentile culture by appearance (not necessarily physiological), mannerisms, and inflection of speech, it is a contributing cause of anti-Semitism. For, in the words of Park, ". . . race prejudice is a function of visibility. The races of high visibility, to speak in naval parlance, are the natural and inevitable objects of race prejudice."[11] This latter point the author believes to be particularly valid in a situation where the "visible" group (in this case the native-born Jews) operates on a competitive rather than on an accommodative basis in the total culture. The problem of the marginal culture, then, as long as its existence is conceived as necessary or desirable, would seem to be one of fulfilling its major goals of providing its members security, adequate facilities for participation in group life, and the opportunity to express their own cultural interests, without at the same time making them in appearance and behavior distinguishable from the members of the dominant culture.

[11]R. E. Park, "Behind Our Masks," *Survey Graphic*, (May 1926), p. 136. Quoted in Louis Wirth, *The Ghetto* (Chicago, The University of Chicago Press, 1928).

12

Marginality
&
the Jewish Intellectual

Ever since the Jews in Western Civilization began to emerge from the ghettoes of Europe and to confront the values and the social life of the Enlightenment era, they have been faced by choices and have variously executed decisions which have earned them the sociological title of classic "marginal men." The marginal man, so the conceptualization goes,[1] is a person poised on the edge or dividing line of two cultures, fully at home in neither, and therefore on the margins of both. His marginality may be produced by the situation of being the offspring of an interracial marriage when, usually, the two races have different subcultures and subsocieties,[2] or, more applicable to the case at hand, it may stem from new cultural contacts engendered by immigration or social change. While

---

[1]See Robert E. Park, "Human Migration and the Marginal Man," *American Journal of Sociology*, Vol. 33, No. 6 (May 1928), pp. 881–93; and Everett V. Stonequist, "The Problem of the Marginal Man," *American Journal of Sociology*, Vol. 41, No. 1 (July 1935), pp. 1–12; and *The Marginal Man* (New York, Scribner's, 1937). Later discussions include Arnold W. Green, "A Reexamination of the Marginal Man Concept," *Social Forces*, Vol. 26, No. 2 (December 1947), pp. 167–71; Everett C. Hughes, "Social Change and Status Protest: An Essay on the Marginal Man," *Phylon*, Vol. 10, No. 1 (First Quarter 1949), pp. 58–65; David Riesman, *Individualism Reconsidered* (New York, Free Press, 1954), pp. 153–78; David I. Golovensky, "The Marginal Man Concept: An Analysis and Critique," *Social Forces*, Vol. 30, No. 3 (March 1952), pp. 333–39, and Aaron Antonovsky, "Toward a Refinement of the 'Marginal Man' Concept," *Social Forces*, Vol. 35, No. 1 (October 1956), pp. 57–62.

[2]For a discussion of these concepts, see Milton M. Gordon, *Assimilation in American Life* (New York, Oxford University Press, 1964), pp. 19–59.

psychological correlates of marginality have been hypothesized as insecurity feelings, nervousness, and hypersensitivity, such hypotheses have never been decisively proven, and some observers have pointed to possible positive traits attendant on marginality such as objectivity, creativity, insight, and self-understanding.[3]

At any rate, the sociological "position" of marginality may be clearly discerned, whatever its psychological consequences. And since the Jew in America has lived, since his initial arrival in colonial times, in a society predominantly Christian and non-Jewish, and under conditions of democratic choice and freedom from official persecution or enforced segregation, much of his adjustment history in the United States has been discussed in terms of the classical kinds of choices which confront the situation of the "marginal man." A large part of this discussion, however, has been rendered less efficacious by a failure to distinguish between the marginality of a man—a single individual—and the marginality of a group. Individual marginality has already been defined. Group marginality may be said to exist in an assimilative process where all or most members of a minority group *together* face the problem of adjusting the values, behavior patterns, and social relationships into which they have been socialized (or which in the case of the native born second generation exist as parental models), to the values, norms, and social system of the host society. This is a rather different sort of situation from individual marginality, and although in the case of group marginality individuals do face problems of choice, they face them more or less in concert, so to speak, with other individuals who are in the same situation and who, collectively, make up a subsociety that provides a sociological home and source of comfort for the members of the group. In our subsequent discussion, therefore, we shall need to

[3]See Georg Simmel's discussion of "The Stranger," in *The Sociology of Georg Simmel*, trans. and ed. Kurt H. Wolf (Glencoe, Ill., Free Press, 1950), pp. 402–08; and David Riesman, *Individualism Reconsidered* (New York, Free Press, 1954), pp. 153–78.

distinguish from time to time these two kinds of marginality, and specify which is more applicable to the subject under discussion.

Group marginality, since it is, virtually by definition, a characteristic to some degree of the minority group undergoing cultural contact, has been present throughout the whole of American Jewish history, although perhaps less so in the present than at any other time because of the massive success of the acculturation process in the United States,[4] and the increasing acceptance of Judaism as one of the three major faiths in America.[5] Instances of individual marginality must be sought in situations of low density, either ecologically, for instance, the case of a few Jewish families living in a small town, or in social space, as when a member of a minority moves up in social class position and finds that none or only a few members of his ethnic group have moved with him. Thus, for instance, W. Lloyd Warner, out of the research done by himself and his associates on ethnic groups in "Yankee City" and "Jonesville," concludes that when members of ethnic minorities move into the upper middle class or higher, they are drawn out of their ethnic group into a position initially of marginality and eventually of incorporation into the class system of the dominant group.[6] This conclusion may well be true for small communities (although, even here it may fail to do justice to the tendency for minority members in a particular small town to band together with families of similar ethnic background in nearby communities, or to attach themselves in part to the organized ethnic communal life in the nearest large city), but it ignores the point that in large cities and metropolitan areas enough other ethnics are also going up the class scale for a "parallel class structure," to use A. B. Hol-

[4]See *Assimilation in American Life*, passim.
[5]See Will Herberg, *Protestant-Catholic-Jew* (New York, Doubleday, 1955).
[6]W. Lloyd Warner and Leo Srole, *The Social Systems of American Ethnic Groups* (New Haven, Yale University Press, 1945); W. Lloyd Warner and Associates, *Democracy in Jonesville* (New York, Harper, 1949), pp. 168–92.

lingshead's phrase, to develop *within* the ethnic group.[7] Thus, Digby Baltzell's study of the general (or Protestant) upper class in Philadelphia in 1940 includes a section on the Jewish upper class that has developed in the City of Brotherly Love, with its own areas of residence, its own synagogues, its own fashionable men's city clubs, and its own country clubs.[8] And Kramer and Leventman, in their later study of Jewish communal life in "North City," a large city in the American Midwest, point to separation in life styles and communal living between the upper portion ("the clubniks") and the lower portion ("the lodgniks") of the class structure within the Jewish community.[9]

Marginality may be factored not only into group and individual subtypes but also by whether the conflicting choices lie in the area of cultural behavior or social structure.[10] If one views modern pluralistic societies as composed of smaller subsocieties, each one made up by the intersection of ethnic group and social class, so that what emerges is a series of "ethclasses"[11] such as "upper lower class white Protestant," lower middle class white Catholics," or "upper middle class Jews," etc., then the "marginal man" is marginal in social structure to two or more of these subsocieties—that is, he does not confine his primary group relationships and organizational affiliations (if any) to one subsociety but spreads them over at least two, or perhaps neither. He is thus marginal structurally. At the same time, he may be faced with choices in behavior patterns which reflect different values in the ethclass of origin (the minority group) and the ethclass of

---

[7]See August B. Hollingshead, "Trends in Social Stratification: A Case Study," *American Sociological Review*, Vol. 17, No. 6 (December 1952), pp. 685–86.

[8]E. Digby Baltzell, *Philadelphia Gentlemen* (New York, Free Press, 1958), pp. 273–91.

[9]Judith R. Kramer and Seymour Leventman, *Children of the Gilded Ghetto* (New Haven and London, Yale University Press, 1961).

[10]This parallels my distinction between cultural assimilation and structural assimilation in the model of "assimilation variables" presented in *Assimilation in American Life*. See particularly pp. 70–71.

[11]See *Assimilation in American Life*, pp. 51–59.

aspiration (the majority group). This would constitute cultural marginality. While these two processes of marginality and choice probably frequently go together, they may at times exist independently of each other and thus should be conceptually distinguished. The full model may be economically depicted as follows:

Types of Marginality

	Structural	Cultural
Individual		
Group		

With these conceptual tools in hand, we may now begin to examine the American Jewish experience in relation to marginality more closely. Out of this examination the position of the American Jewish intellectual will gradually emerge.

All three migratory streams of Jews who came to America, the trickle of Sephardim and Ashkenazim who came to the colonies and set up institutions under Sephardic dominance, the larger number of Germans who spread westward in the mid-nineteenth century, and the great tide of Eastern Europeans who poured into the United States in the last two decades of the nineteenth century and the first quarter of the twentieth and whose descendants constitute the vast bulk of the Jewish population today—created communities and the institutions of communal life where they settled.[12] Thus while all Jews faced problems of cultural choice, the great majority confronted these problems from the security of a communal structure of their own. This has been true, as we now can see, not only for the immigrant generation, but for

---

[12]Oscar Handlin, *Adventure in Freedom* (New York, Mc Graw-Hill, 1954); *Philadelphia Gentlemen*, pp. 273–91; Nathan Glazer, *American Judaism* (Chicago, University of Chicago Press, 1957).

succeeding generations as well. Thus we may say that problems of *group marginality* and *cultural marginality* (for the first, and to a considerably lesser extent the second generation) have been the characteristic kinds of marginality faced by the Americn Jew. To be sure, from the very beginning we hear of individual cases of intermarriage, conversion, and disappearance from Jewish communal rolls, and these phenomena have accompanied the whole history of Jewish life in America. In such instances we know that individual marginality, both of a structural and a cultural nature, has been involved. These have not, however, constituted the dominant process.

Culturally speaking, American values of basically Anglo-Saxon origin, operating through the public school system and mass communications media, have interacted with values stemming from European Jewish life and have largely transmuted the latter into their own image. Thus, not even to mention the triumph of the English language and American clothing styles, Reform Judaism, brought in by some of the German Jewish migrants, and Conservative Judaism, developed by socially mobile Eastern European Jews, greatly modified the Orthodox *shul* of *shtetl* origin in the direction of conformity to American ideals of propriety and decorum in religious worship, and wrought similar changes in the realms of ideology and pious observances.[13] In turn, the United States of America, itself, at first more or less self-consciously a Protestant nation, gradually took on the image of itself as a nation of the three major faiths—Protestant, Catholic, and Jewish.

Degrees in the phenomenon of group marginality of a cultural nature, however, can probably be distinguished between generations. The second generation of Jews faced the problem of reconciling the fact of Yiddish speaking immigrant parents and immigrant cultural values in the home with their English speaking and American oriented way of life

[13]*American Judaism*; Marshall Sklare, *Conservative Judaism* (New York, Free Press, 1955).

284

eagerly absorbed in the public schools and in the larger society. This was a larger and more tension-producing problem than that more recently and currently faced by the native-born of native parents, even when, in the latter case, social class mobility produced by exposure to a college education, is in the offing.

The role of the Jewish intellectual, then, in relation to the phenomenon of marginality, whether of a cultural or a structural nature, must be seen against the background of general American social structure—which we have already described in terms of an interlocking series of ethclasses, with primary group relationships more or less confined to one's own ethclass, and some secondary group relationships established across class and ethnic lines—and the fact that Jewish communal life has, at least in the larger cities, always been present as a sociological "home" for the vast majority of Jews of whatever generation. Thus those Jews who may have ventured "out" structurally in a tentative sense, attracted by the social institutions of the white Protestant American community, could always retreat to safer, more comfortable sociological territory upon meeting the usual rebuffs. It seems likely that most Jews up until recently never really ventured out in a structural manner to any appreciable extent. Thus was built the American Jewish community with a full array of social institutions, some differentiated from each other by social class, some serving the entire spectrum of social classes. Nor was this process, by any means, simply a Jewish phenomenon. Similar social structures were erected among ethnic groups of Catholic origin, and eventually a pan-Catholic subsociety began to take shape; Negroes and other racial groups developed indigenous institutions under the pressures of discrimination and rigid barriers; and the white Protestants, while assuming that they were simply the Americans, put their own stamp of race and religion on the institutions which they controlled.

It should be remembered, however, that Jews who intermarried with gentiles put themselves in a situation of structural marginality and henceforth faced three basic choices: (1)

to identify as a family with the Jewish group; (2) to identify as a family with the white Protestant or white Catholic group; (3) to remain structurally marginal. In the absence of any substantial body of research focussed on this question we do not know how many made which choices or what the respective outcomes were, although in one recent study of the Jews of Washington, D.C., it was found that in 66 percent of the intermarried families who had children living at home, the children were being raised as gentiles.[14] Even in those cases where the family identifies as a unit with one or the other of the three major religious communities through the process of formal religious conversion of one of the partners, the converted partner may obviously still face personal problems of marginality of a psychological nature.

It is against this general background that we must view the situation of the Jewish intellectual.

If the question Who is a Jew? is a difficult one, as many observers have agreed, the question Who is an Intellectual? is difficulty many times compounded. "Few modern terms," writes Lewis Coser in his valuable socio-historical account of the rise of the institutions fostering intellectual life in the modern period, "are as imprecise as the term 'intellectual.' Its very mention is likely to provoke debate about both meaning and evaluation. To many, it stands for qualities deeply distrusted and despised; to others, it connotes excellence aspired to though not often achieved. To some, intellectuals are impractical dreamers who interfere with the serious business of life; to others, they are the 'antennae of the race.' "[15] While Coser in his formal definition reserves the term for those "men of ideas" who take a critical stance toward their society and its values, I prefer to cast the definitional net more widely[16] to

[14]Stanley K. Bigman, The Jewish Population of Greater Washington in 1956 (Washington, D.C., The Jewish Community Council of Greater Washington, May 1957); cited in Albert I. Gordon, Intermarriage (Boston, Beacon, 1964), p. 206

[15]Lewis Coser, Men of Ideas (New York, Free Press, 1965), p. vii.

[16]There is, I believe, good reason for doing so. Not all people who have the intellect that gives them a serious interest in ideas and the arts and who participate in the intellectual milieu are "critical" of society in Coser's sense.

include all "people for whom ideas, concepts, literature, music, painting, the dance have intrinsic meaning—are a part of the social-psychological atmosphere which one breathes."[17] As I have put it elsewhere:

> Occupationally, they are characteristically found in the professions, particularly college teaching, research, and the upper reaches of journalism (to a lesser degree, law and medicine), and in the arts, either as creators or performers. If they are engaged in business, they are likely to be in communications or publishing. Not all persons in each of these occupational categories are intellectuals, and intellectuals will at times be found in other occupations. The academic world of teaching and research, supplemented now by the world of the Foundation, which either carries out or commissions research, is the most salient concentration point of the intellectual life, and this becomes increasingly so as writers, artists, and musicians begin to take on the role of faculty members and "artists in residence," alongside professors of the humanities and the natural and social sciences.[18]

The above occupational discussion, however, implicitly assumes a developmental history—a history of incipient institutions fostering not simply the isolated intellectual but a structured intellectual milieu in which intellectuals could interact with each other and begin to take on the characteristics of a sociological group. The delineation of this history has been Professor Coser's accomplishment in the aforementioned book[19] in which he traces the emergence of institutions fostering the intellectual life from the coffeehouse of eighteenth century London, the French salon, the scientific society, the nineteenth century expansion of the book and periodical market, the rise of the political sect, the appearance

[17]Milton M. Gordon, "Social Class and American Intellectuals," *American Association of University Professors Bulletin*, Vol. 40, No. 4 (Winter 1954–55), pp. 518–19.

[18]*Assimilation in American Life*, pp. 224–25.

[19]*Men of Ideas*. From a somewhat different point of view the historian Christopher Lasch has also dealt with the rise of "the intellectual as a social type," the subtitle of his *The New Radicalism in America, 1889–1963* (New York, Knopf, 1965).

of Bohemias and "little magazines" in the early twentieth century, and the more recent explosive growth of the university, the bureaucratically maintained scientific research laboratory, and the foundation.

Before this institutional development has matured, however, the ethnic group member who finds that the possession of intellectual interests constitutes a basic part of his personality structure has three basic choices of sociological response that are represented by the following "ideal types"; the passively ethnic intellectual; the actively ethnic intellectual; and the marginally ethnic intellectual. The first type remains within the ethnic group and gratifies his intellectual interests by finding, if he can, other persons of the same ethnic identity who share his concerns. The second type also remains within his ethnic group and "focuses his intellectual interests precisely on his ethnicity. He is the cultural historian of the group, the theologian, the communal leader, the apologist, the scholar of its art, its music and its literature."[20] The third type ignores ethnicity and its boundaries and simply looks for companionship where his ideologies, his politics, his tastes in literature, music and the other arts may lead him. Historically he has been, as his appellation indicates, without question a marginal man.

In the American Jewish experience all three types of intellectual have been present. The passive type is destined to be unsung, but an Abraham Cahan, editor of the *Jewish Daily Forward* and a leading figure in Yiddish journalism until his death in 1951, and a Horace Kallen, Harvard trained social philosopher and principal exponent of the ideology of cultural pluralism, stand in different ways as exemplars of the actively ethnic type. On the other hand, the career of the internationally famous art critic Bernard Berenson, also educated at Harvard around the turn of the century and later to become both expatriate and apostate, illustrates in rather extreme fashion, one type of response to individual structural and cultural marginality.

[20]*Assimilation in American Life*, p. 228. See also, "Social Class and American Intellectuals," p. 526.

The basic point is that, with regard to the choices before the marginally ethnic intellectual, for approximately the first forty or fifty years of the twentieth century, intellectual life in America was only minimally structured, and what institutional structure did exist was dominated by white Anglo-Saxon Protestants from the upper portion of the social class hierarchy. College teaching, for example, in consonance with trends carried over from the nineteenth century, was traditionally the province of the white Protestant gentleman, of at least upper middle class origins or orientation. Jewish intellectuals were present in such a setting, but in small numbers and, as it were, on sufferance. Under such conditions, it is the fate of the marginal man when he alights in the institutional setting of his aspiration to be the perennial guest and not really an integrated member of the establishment.

After World War II, however, certain demographic and scientific trends that had been building up prior to that time exploded with great sociological force. These include the great boom in higher education, a phenomenon that meant not only a greatly increased college student body, but a vastly expanded faculty as well; the rise in importance of the professionally trained scientific expert in business and government settings; the development of new industries requiring many employees with advanced degrees in chemistry, physics, and mathematics; the invention of the LP record, thus stimulating the dissemination of classical music on a numerically broad basis; the coming to America of the foreign art film displayed in metropolitan and university centers; the expansion of the market for serious books and periodicals; and many others of an allied nature. Their cumulative effect was to expand greatly the number of people intellectually trained and oriented, and to stimulate the development of institutions that began to give intellectual life in America a sociological format and setting of its own. In other words, there began to be created an intellectual subsociety,[21] the main bastion of which was the world of the academy, but which also included enclaves of people in the various performing arts.

[21]See *Assimilation in American Life*, pp. 224–32.

Within this larger subsociety of intellectuals the various smaller groups may have particular concerns, but they tend to share the same communications media and reference groups. *The New York Times*, daily, and even more particularly, the Sunday edition, is the national newspaper of the intellectuals. "More than half the college presidents in the U.S. read the *Times*, and it circulates to virtually every university and college library," writes Roger Kahn in a recent article on that venerable journalistic phenomenon.

> The *Times* is The Paper of The Arts and The Intellectual Community. [sic] It staffs a distinct Cultural Affairs Department, with 40 men and women, and it considers Isaac Stern's purchase of a new Guarnerius as news worth two-thirds of a column on a busy day. Most of its critics are scorned, disliked, patronized, cursed and sometimes faintly cheered. Nonetheless, they are critics of the *Times*. No one else can so powerfully influence the life and death of a play, the reputation of a conductor, the success of a prodigy's debut.[22]

Magazines in the homes of intellectuals, apart from professional journals, tend to be selected from such as *Harper's*, *The Atlantic Monthly*, *The New Yorker*, *The Reporter*, *Commentary*, *The Saturday Review*, *Daedalus*, *Consumer Reports*, *The Nation*, *The New Republic*, *Partisan Review*, and a few others. Thus, while intellectuals in their status and the ordinary amenities of life-style tend to be upper middle class, they have a particular orientation that is peculiar to them as intellectuals and separates them from other upper middle class members in way of life and social interaction.

In the world or subsociety of the intellectual, ethnicity is not a very relevant issue either in structural or cultural terms.[23] It is in these circles, I would maintain, that considerable primary group interaction takes place across ethnic lines,

[22] Roger Kahn, "The House of Adolph Ochs," *Saturday Evening Post* (October 9, 1965), p. 33.
[23] See Charles H. Anderson, *The Intellectual Subsociety: An Empirical Test*, Ph.D. Dissertation, University of Massachusetts, 1966, carried out under the direction of this writer.

interfaith marriage is common, and the real melting pot in American life emerges. While it is not uncommon for such intellectuals to take a nostalgic interest in their particular ethnic background, considerations of religion, national origin, or even race are not the main criteria for choices in dining companions, inter-home visiting, social cliquing, or (race excepted) courtship. Moreover, there is reason to believe that many intellectuals have an awareness of themselves as a distinct group—a group even somewhat alienated from the larger society. Thus Jan Hajda's analysis of survey data on over 2,000 native-born graduate students in twenty-five American universities found that 47 percent defined themselves as intellectuals. This proportion was as high as 53 percent of students in the humanities. About two-thirds of the entire student group gave evidence of a feeling of alienation from the larger society, and Hajda further found that:

> alienation, coupled with intellectual orientation, is generally characteristic of those who expect to stay in the academic world after graduation. . . . The alienated intellectuals among graduate students are persons committed more or less exclusively to the academic community. They are most prone to regard the larger society as anti-intellectual; to have no religious affiliation, or merely formal church membership; to have less intense attachment to their parental families than other students; to have few if any friends from high school days. Their personal career is marked by dissent from religious traditions in which they were reared and by a history of conflict with parental authority. The only non-academic organization that sometimes commands their loyalty is a liberal political movement.[24]

In this newly emerging subsociety of the intellectual, the Jew is no longer a guest. He is, quite to the contrary, a prominent and well-recognized element in its leadership structure and a significantly large and well integrated segment of its rank and file. Creative writers such as Norman Mailer, Saul Bellow,

---

[24] Jan Hajda, "Alienation and Integration of Student Intellectuals," *American Sociological Review*, Vol. 26, No. 5 (October 1961), pp. 758–77. The quotations are from pages 772 and 775 respectively.

Bernard Malamud, and Philip Roth are at the very crest of the wave of American fiction that surfaced after World War II; literary critics such as Alfred Kazin, Norman Podhoretz, and Theodore Solatoroff assess the world of letters from positions of well-recognized eminence; and social commentators such as David Riesman, Daniel Bell, Lewis Coser, and Max Lerner are household names in those households where serious ideas are seriously discussed. All these men, to my knowledge, are Jews. In fact, the salience (I consciously avoid the word "dominance" here, since it contains connotations that are distinctly not in order) of Jews in American intellectual life occasioned from the writer of a recent semi-serious essay in *The New York Times Magazine* entitled, "Notes on Cult; or, How to Join the Intellectual Establishment," the wry remark, "Rumors to the contrary notwithstanding, you don't have to be Jewish to be an intellectual."[25] And at lesser levels of popular eminence the interlocking worlds of academic life, scientific research, and the creative and performing arts now have such widespread Jewish participation as to make such participation routine and unnoteworthy.

By the foregoing I do not mean to imply that the subsociety of the intellectual is fully developed in all its potential lineaments. Many age-graded organizations and institutional structures present in the standard subsocieties of America are not yet present in the social world of the intellectual, and perhaps many of them, for reasons peculiar to the nature of the intellectual's makeup, never will be. Furthermore, full subsocietal development signifies a degree of self-recognition *as such* (that is, as a subsociety) and recognition by members of other subsocieties that has not yet been achieved, although the dichotomous terms "town and gown" and the separation of social life that the phrase implies carry overtones of such recognition. It is possible that the rudimentary nature of this identificational aspect poses more problems for the children of intellectuals than for their parents, particularly for those

[25] Victor S. Navasky, "Notes on Cult; or, How to Join the Intellectual Establishment," *The New York Times Magazine* (March 27, 1966), p. 29.

families without formal religious affiliation. When little Johnnie, in such a family, comes home and queries, "Daddy, Freddie says he's a Protestant, Susie says she's a Catholic, and Michael says he's a Jew; what am I? it is unlikely that Daddy can or will settle the matter meaningfully for his son by replying, "Why, Johnnie, you're an intellectual!"

One of the results of the rise of the intellectual subsociety in America is that many intellectuals—perhaps a large majority— become alienated from their ethnic subsocieties of origin. This is not, it should be noted, the same thing as saying that they have become detached from the ongoing functional concerns and processes of American society as a whole. Quite the contrary is the case. There has probably never been a time when American intellectuals have taken such an active part in major party politics, in consultant and high and middle level executive roles in government, and even in the operation of large business concerns, which increasingly draw upon the research skills of highly trained professionals both in production and marketing. But the everyday concerns of the ethnic community and the bustling organizational life that provide the institutional setting for the community's activities function without the participation of those intellectuals who have now found a comfortable milieu elsewhere and for whom the issues and life of ethnic communality are extremely peripheral.[26] For no major ethnic group in America is this problem greater than for the Jews, whose percentage of young people who go on to college and graduate school (and thus become exposed to the existence and attractions of the intellectual subsociety) is extraordinarily high. "One of the first things I discovered," writes Marion K. Sanders in a recent article in *Harper's* reporting on her informal study of Jewish communal life across the nation, "is that Jewish activists worry mightily about the flight of the intellectuals." And her

[26]To be sure, the "actively ethnic intellectual" participates in ethnic communality and often in leadership roles. However, it is at least a plausible hypothesis that their number is diminishing and that the pull of the intellectual subsociety becomes increasingly strong for those individuals with intellectual interests and inclinations.

own reception by Jewish communal leaders indicates that this flight is viewed by them more with puzzled hurt than with anger. "I was not prepared," she relates, "to be everywhere welcomed as a prodigal daughter, as a member of the 'Jewish intelligentsia' who had 'come home.'"[27]

The flight of the Jewish intellectual in America from Jewish communal participation and specifically Jewish concerns (I purposefully do not say "flight from Jewish identity"—at least in its minimal from—since I know very few academic Jews who deny that they are Jewish) is by no means complete. *Commentary's* famous symposium on "Jewishness and The Younger Intellectuals," just a few years ago, which overwhelmingly revealed an estrangement on the part of its participants from Jewish communal life and its characteristic issues and idologies,[28] was followed, perhaps pointedly, in the same year by a symposium in the quarterly journal *Judaism* (published by the American Jewish Congress) in which a group of Jewish intellectuals, drawn largely but not exclusively from the academic world, expressed a constellation of views much closer in feeling and content to the spirit of the symposium title: "My Jewish Affirmation."[29] Moreover, in one town with which I am familiar, a number of Jewish academics drawn largely from the university situated there have together with their families formed a local Jewish community organization that meets periodically to discuss intellectual topics of Jewish and general concern and sponsors an occasional Jewish holiday party that includes the children. Thus it is clear that there are some Jewish academicians who wish to retain some sense of group identity as Jews and some relationship to specific Jewish values either for the benefit of themselves or their children, or both.

The general picture, then, appears to be one in which increasingly large numbers of Jewish intellectuals find them-

[27]Marion K. Sanders, "The Several Worlds of American Jews," *Harper's* (April 1966), p. 54.
[28]"Jewishness and The Younger Intellectuals: A Symposium," *Commentary*, Vol 31, No. 4 (April 1961), pp. 306–59.
[29]"Symposium: My Jewish Affirmation," *Judaism: A Quarterly Journal of Jewish Life and Thought*, Vol. 10, No. 4 (1961), pp. 291–352.

selves drawn by common intellectual and aesthetic interests and by professional activities and concerns into the buildup of the new, intellectual subsociety in America. They seem to find themselves sociologically and psychologically reasonably comfortable there, while a smaller number (which participates in the intellectual subsociety also) has, or searches for, more explicit ties to Jewish communal life and Jewish culture. In either case the problems of marginality for the Jewish intellectual have clearly been considerably reduced. The eventual outcome in communal and identificational terms for later generations of Jewish intellectuals cannot now be forseen and, in part, depends on the general outcome in the development of the total intellectual subsociety. That outcome itself, however, will be shaped in part by whatever efforts, or lack of such, the ethnic subsocieties themselves make to institute an effective dialogue with and contribute to the intellectual subsociety and more especially to their own ethnic members. To date such efforts on the part of the Jewish ethnic community in relation to Jewish intellectuals do not appear to have been either substantial or particularly effective. When a firstrate writer such as Philip Roth is taken to task by some members of the organized Jewish community for his portrayal of Jewish characters in his fiction—a portrayal that many intellectuals, at least, would regard as varied, thoughtful, and conforming to the highest standards of artistic integrity—and when Roth himself rephrases the charge with rueful and elegant irony as, "I had told the Gentiles what apparently it would otherwise have been possible to keep secret from them: that the perils of human nature afflict the members of our minority,"[30] then the gap in basic assumptions and basic thought processes that exists between some parts of ethnic communal life and the intellectual is revealed as clearly and poignantly as it could be by any learned study. It is this gap that needs to be bridged if the no-longer marginal Jewish intellectual is to be able to draw current sustenance from Jewish communal life and culture and, in turn, contribute to the continuing development of his ancestral tradition.

[30]Philip Roth, "Writing About Jews," *Commentary*, Vol. 36, No. 6 (December 1963), p. 450.

Index

297

Index